Rules of the Road™
A Plaintiff Lawyer's Guide to Proving Liability

Second Edition
Revised and Expanded

ALSO BY RICK FRIEDMAN

Polarizing the Case: Exposing and Defeating the Malingering Myth (Trial Guides, 2007)

Rick Friedman on Becoming a Trial Lawyer (Trial Guides, 2008)

ALSO BY PATRICK MALONE

The Life You Save: Nine Steps to Finding the Best Medical Care— and Avoiding the Worst (Da Capo Lifelong, 2009)

Rules of the Road™
A Plaintiff Lawyer's Guide to Proving Liability

Second Edition
Revised and Expanded

By
Rick Friedman
and
Patrick Malone

Trial Guides, LLC

Trial Guides, LLC, Portland, OR 97205

Rules of the Road: A Plaintiff Lawyer's Guide to Proving Liability
Second Edition—Revised and Expanded

© 2010 by Rick Friedman and Patrick Malone

All rights reserved.

Printed in the United States of America.

ISBN: 978-1-934833-17-9

Library of Congress Control Number: 2010927680

These materials, or any parts or portions thereof, may not be reproduced in any form, written or mechanical, or be programmed into any electronic storage or retrieval system without the express written permission of Trial Guides, LLC unless such copying is expressly permitted by federal copyright law. Please direct inquiries to:

Reproduction permission:

Trial Guides, LLC
2400 SW Park Place
Portland, OR 97205
(800) 309-6845
www.trialguides.com

RULES OF THE ROAD is a trademark of Trial Guides, LLC.

Jacket design by Theodore Marshall

Interior design by Laura Lind Design

This book is printed on acid-free paper.

Acknowledgments and Dedications

I am indebted to many people who generously contributed their time to help with this book: Kim Dvorak, Jeff Feldman, Gary Fye, Katie Kalahar, Jeff Rubin, Paul Scoptur, Jackie Shepherd, Trina Tinglum. It is as good as it is because of their help. It undoubtedly would be better if I had accepted more of their suggestions.

I must also thank Janet Crook, who is always watching my back, above and beyond the call of duty.

Finally, this book would not have been written but for my wife, Kirsten, who kept insisting I had something to say that someone would want to read.

I dedicate this book to the best trial partners anyone could ever want: Jeff Rubin and Dee Taylor.

—Rick Friedman

So many friends and colleagues in the plaintiff's bar have generously helped me to grow in this profession that I cannot count all of them, let alone list them here. I feel blessed and thank them all. Some nonlawyer special people (you know who you are) also have helped me a lot. My wife, Vicki, deserves the rest of the credit.

Dedication goes to our sons: Ian, Chris, and Brendan.
May 2010

—Patrick Malone

Publisher's Note

This book is intended for practicing attorneys. It does not offer legal advice or take the place of consultation with an attorney who has appropriate expertise and experience.

Attorneys are strongly cautioned to evaluate the information, ideas, and opinions set forth in this book in light of their own research, experience, and judgment. Readers should also consult applicable rules, regulations, procedures, cases, and statutes (including those issued after the publication date of this book), and make independent decisions about whether and how to apply such information, ideas, and opinions to a particular case.

Quotations from cases, pleadings, discovery, and other sources are for illustrative purposes only and may not be suitable for use in litigation in any particular case.

Names of some defendants and witnesses have been fictionalized.

The publisher disclaims any liability or responsibility for loss or damage resulting from the use of this book or the information, ideas, and opinions contained in this book.

Table of Contents

Preface to the Second Edition xv

Introduction 1

1. Defining the Problem 7
   Disability Case 9
   Uninsured-Motorist Case 9
   Property Case 10

2. Solving the Problem 15

3. Identifying the Rules of the Road 21
   Attributes of Rules of the Road 22

4. Developing a Working List of Rules 31
   Sources for Rules 31
   Jury Instructions as Rules Sources 32
   Incorporate Jury Instructions into Your Rules 35
   Administrative Regulations as Rules Sources 40
   Avoid the Implied Cause of Action 41
   Other Sources of Rules 44
   Admissions in the Answer to the Complaint 46

5. Why Rules and Principles Need to Be
   Kept Distinct 49
   Why Our Cases Need Rules and Not Just Principles . . 52

6. The Plaintiff's Experts 59

7. The *Daubert*-Proofed Expert 63
   Rule 1: Find a Methodology Appropriate for the
      Expert's Field, and Make Sure the Expert Follows It . . 64
   Rule 2: Find Literature Support for the Expert's
      Theory 67
   Rule 3: Make the Expert Read the Relevant Literature . . 68
   Rule 4: Go to the Top in Your Search for Experts 69

Rule 5: Avoid Experts Who Won't Explain the
  Basis for Their Opinions........................69
Rule 6: Enlist Help from the Other Side's Experts....69
Rule 7: Attack the Other Side's Experts............70

8. DISCOVERY..71
   Requests for Production of Documents...........71
   Interrogatories and Requests for Admission.........73
   Depositions....................................74
   Planning and Conducting the Deposition..........82
   Handling Deposition Objections..................95
   Don't Forget to Ask "Why?".....................100
   Questions for the End of a Deposition..........101
   Conclusion.....................................102

9. TROUBLESHOOTING YOUR RULES......................103
   Make Your Rules Specific.......................104
   Don't Quibble..................................107
   The Causation Defense..........................108
   Other Common Mistakes..........................109
   Improving Your Rules...........................110

10. FITTING THE RULES INTO YOUR CASE STORY..........115

11. A SPECIAL PROBLEM: RULES OF THE ROAD IN
    AUTOMOBILE CASES...............................121
    Excessive Complication........................122
    Loss of Perspective...........................122
    Beating a Dead Horse..........................122
    Emphasize the Differences.....................124
    Polarize the Case.............................124
    Breach of Contract............................125

12. MOTIONS AND THE RULES OF THE ROAD..............127
    Spoon-Feeding the Judge.......................129

13. FINALIZING THE RULES OF THE ROAD...............137
    Guideline the Authors Disagree On.............140
    Guidelines the Authors Agree On...............142
    Coordinating the Evidence with Your Rules.....144

14. Motions *In Limine* About the Rules 145
15. *Voir Dire* 147
16. Opening Statement 151
    Handling Objections to Opening 153
    Concluding Thoughts on Opening Statement 156
17. Direct Examination of Your Expert 157
    Explaining Reasons for the Rule. 158
    Explaining That the Rule Is Well Recognized. 159
    Setting Up Evidence from Learned Treatises. 160
    Testimony About Sources of Rules. 161
    Rules Violations and Plaintiff's Experts 161
18. Cross-Examination 163
    Intellectually Honest Witnesses 164
    Intellectually Dishonest Witnesses 168
    Handling "Learned Treatises" at Trial. 168
    The "Blocking Interrogatory" Technique 172
19. Closing Argument 175
    Jury Instructions: the Judge's Rules 175
    Boilerplate Instructions to Enforce Rules 177
    Damages Instructions and Rules of the Road 180
    Your Own Rules in Closing Argument. 181
20. Final Thoughts 185
    Using the Rules in Midstream 185
    Using the Rules with Co-counsel 186
    Using the Rules with Other Advocacy Advice 187

Appendix A: Annotated Rules of the Road:
    A Master List 191

Appendix B: Sample Insurance Bad Faith Rules
    of the Road 201
    Commercial Property Claim 201
    Disability Case 1 202
    Disability Case 2 203

APPENDIX C: BUS STOP SAFETY PRINCIPLES 205

APPENDIX D: BUS STOP SAFETY PRINCIPLES ANNOTATED . . .207

APPENDIX E: PROPOSED JURY INSTRUCTIONS IN A
    DISABILITY BAD FAITH CASE. 211

APPENDIX F: DIRECT EXAMINATION OF PLAINTIFF'S
    INSURANCE EXPERT IN A BAD FAITH CASE. 227
    Direct Examination Continued by Mr. Friedman . . .227

APPENDIX G: DIRECT EXAMINATION OF PLAINTIFF'S
    BUS STOP EXPERT. 237
    Direct Examination Continued 237
    Direct Examination Continued by Mr. Friedman . . .245

APPENDIX H: DISCOVERY REQUESTS. 257
    Expert Interrogatory 257
    Document Request 258

APPENDIX I: BAD FAITH CASE OPENING STATEMENT. 261
    Comments by Rick Friedman 261
    Opening Statement by Mr. Friedman 262

APPENDIX J: BUS STOP CASE OPENING STATEMENT. 267
    Opening Statement by Mr. Friedman 267

APPENDIX K: CROSS-EXAMINATION OF SCHOOL BUS
    COMPANY MANAGER. 273
    Cross-Examination by Mr. Friedman. 273
    Direct Examination Continued by Mr. Friedman . . .283
    Redirect Examination by Mr. Friedman. 284

APPENDIX L: RESPONSE TO MOTION *IN LIMINE* 287
    Summary. 287
    Background 288
    Argument 290

APPENDIX M: SAMPLES OF RULES IN DIFFERENT TYPES
    OF CASES 303
    Rules for an Unnecessary Surgery Case 304
    Travel Insurance Failure to Disclose Benefits 306

    Medical Malpractice: Poor Handoff from
        Generalist to Specialist 307
    Landowner's Duty for His Animals 308
    Jet Ski/Personal Watercraft Products Case 308
    Rules and Principles for High School Football. 311

APPENDIX N: RULES IN A SURGICAL MALPRACTICE CASE. . . .313
    Direct Examination by Mr. Malone (excerpt) 314

INDEX. 323

Preface to the Second Edition

We've learned a lot in the five years since the first edition of this book was published. We've continued to try cases using the Rules of the Road, of course, and those experiences inform this edition. We've also taught seminars on Rules of the Road, which have allowed us to see where problems arise for lawyers using these methods for the first time.

More important, we've been the beneficiaries of hundreds of comments and suggestions from lawyers around the country, generously sharing their experiences with us, for which we are grateful. Many of their ideas show up in this edition.

Like those of countless other plaintiff's lawyers, our ideas have been picked up, polished, and refined by one of the great legal tacticians of our age, David Ball. Ball picked up an early copy of *Rules of the Road* and ran so fast we often lost sight of him. He immediately understood the power of this approach and brought his own energy and creativity to improving it. He saw things we did not and knew how to teach things we had trouble articulating.

In chapter 3, we have clarified the definition of an effective "Rule of the Road," and have explained the key distinction between Rules and principles. We also have new chapters:

- Chapter 5, "Why Rules and Principles Need to Be Kept Distinct" expands this discussion of why rules and principles need to be kept separate.

- Chapter 9, "Troubleshooting Your Rules" is intended to help both beginners and advanced students of the Rules system hone their case rules down to the most powerful set.

- Chapter 10, "Fitting the Rules into Your Case Story" talks about the interplay between case themes and rules, and how an effective set of rules can enhance a case theme.

- Chapter 11, "A Special Problem: Rules of the Road in Automobile Cases" explains the role of Rules in automobile cases, where the use of the Rules system can backfire if not used adroitly.

- Chapter 14, "Motions *In Limine* About the Rules" and appendix L, "Response to Motion *In Limine*" discuss motions *in limine* about the rules themselves.

- Chapter 15, "*Voir Dire*" discusses using the rules in *voir dire*.

- Appendix M, "Samples of Rules in Different Types of Cases" will hopefully stimulate the creative process in our readers.

Throughout the book, we offer new examples that we hope will make points clearer and show the varieties of settings where our approach can be used.

We continue to believe what we said in the first edition: If properly executed—and if you have a meritorious case—there is no defense to the Rules of the Road approach. We hope this second edition helps you win the cases that deserve to be won.

Introduction

Has this ever happened to you? You are an attorney for the underdog, representing someone hurt by the indifference, carelessness, or greed of a large institution. You are on the right side of the case. Morally and legally, you deserve to win. You believe you are scoring points with the judge and jury. The other side's arguments are weak and disorganized.

And then you lose.

How did that happen?

We think we have some answers, and some ways to keep it from happening again.

The defense wields three weapons to defeat plaintiffs' cases that should be won:

- Complexity
- Confusion
- Ambiguity

Complexity, confusion, and ambiguity are insidious enemies. They creep up when you are not looking. They rarely attack head-on. They are particularly abundant and pernicious in complex cases such as insurance bad faith or medical malpractice. This is because both the facts and the jury instructions in these cases are often complex, confusing, and ambiguous. But these enemies appear in simple cases too.

Sometimes, complexity, confusion, and ambiguity are inherent in the case; other times, they proliferate due to a conscious defense strategy of confounding the jury and judge with endless, immaterial detail. In either event, you must defeat complexity, confusion, and ambiguity, or they will defeat you.

In this book, we set out a technique to neutralize these three defense allies and bring clarity and focus to any case. It has helped us win worthy cases that otherwise might have been lost.

We wrote this book for our fellow attorneys who represent consumers, patients, and other real people in lawsuits brought to redress injustice and injury. Between us, we have more than four decades of experience preparing and trying cases. We have tasted the ashes of unfair defeat. We have also enjoyed great successes. We love our profession, and we chafe at the untruths peddled regularly these days by the rich and the powerful who don't like it when we hold them accountable in a court of law. Every time our side loses, the other side harrumphs that another frivolous lawsuit has flamed out. Most of the time, we think the opposite is true: frivolous defenses have triumphed because of complexity, confusion, and ambiguity.

Here is a road map for this book.

- Chapter 1, "Defining the Problem," defines the problem of complexity, confusion, and ambiguity in some detail. The core problem stems from ambiguous liability standards that permeate jury instructions. Remember the "reasonable person"? What does it mean?

- Chapter 2, "Solving the Problem," introduces our solution: the Rules of the Road. These are the specific, concrete liability standards that you must discover—and then articulate—from the first interview with a prospective client through to the posttrial motions and appeal.

- Chapter 3, "Identifying the Rules of the Road," focuses on finding and defining the Rules of the Road for any case.

The hunt for good Rules of the Road must range far and wide: from the defendant's files to the public library to statute books and regulatory pamphlets.

- Chapters 4–13 show how to develop the Rules. We cover the initial case investigation, writing the complaint, and working with experts; then we move through discovery, pretrial motions, and the trial. Along the way, we cover expert preparation, depositions of corporate spokespersons, and the construction of an opening statement. You will find nuggets on the killer interrogatory, how to cross-examine an opposing expert with a learned treatise, and the best preventative to jury nullification.

- Chapters 14–19 show how to apply the Rules from *voir dire* and opening statement, through direct and cross-examinations and closing arguments. We add some final thoughts in chapter 20, which includes a list of other essential reading for plaintiff's lawyers.

Ultimately, this book is about how to breathe life into ambiguous legal standards and create an indisputable standard for everyone—judges, juries, and defendants—to see. The standard must be as clear as a double yellow line on a highway.

The Rules of the Road techniques can help you focus your own thoughts and efforts and thus focus the reasoning and decision making of the judge and jury. It can *help* you work more productively and effectively—but you still have to do the hard work.

A few disclaimers and explanations are in order:

- Our examples come from actual briefs, depositions, and trial transcripts. The examples illustrate how a Rule or principle works, leaving you to adapt the concept for your own cases.

- Because most of the examples are from actual litigation materials, we elected to present them unvarnished and uncorrected, as they appear in the official court records. The impression some trial educators give—that everything must be executed with perfection in the courtroom—is not only misleading, but inhibiting and harmful. This is a messy business we are in. If we think we must be perfect, we may be unwilling to take the risk of looking messy—a risk we must often take if we want to win. So you will see bad grammar, awkward questions, and a fair amount of fumbling.

- This book presumes you either know the basics of trial practice or are learning the basics from other sources.

- Names of defendants and witnesses have been changed to let the publisher sleep better at night.

- We have tried to communicate what we think you need to know about the Rules of the Road as directly and efficiently as possible—with a minimum of anecdotes.

However one war story is worth repeating, because it really started this book. Rick Friedman tells it now:

> It was 1996. I was trying an insurance bad faith case. It was going well. Our expert witness explained to the jury how and why the claims handling was improper. In cross-examination, the claims handlers were evasive.
>
> But I was uneasy. I had tried many cases by this point in my career, but this was only my second bad faith case. I had been uncomfortable in the first one too. In both, I felt like I was punching a paper bag or trying to climb a smooth greased pole. Did the jury understand what we were proving, how bad this conduct was? It didn't seem to.
>
> Before closing argument, I had a three-day weekend to think about this problem. I was frustrated. I thought and thought and thought. What was different about bad faith cases that made me so uncomfortable? And then it came to me.
>
> When trying other types of cases, I had always been able to hold the facts up alongside a standard and show the jury that the standard was or was not

violated. In criminal cases, the standards are clear: "criminal intent" is defined; "deadly weapon" is defined. In employment cases the standard is found in specific contract or statutory provisions. In traffic cases the negligence standard is vague—what a reasonable person would do—but everyone knows —or thinks he knows—what a reasonable person would or would not do while driving a car. In bad faith cases, the standard is also vague—was there a reasonable basis for the company's actions? Jurors (and most judges) lack much knowledge of what a reasonable company would do in adjusting a claim. I was faced with the three horsemen of defeat: complexity, confusion, and ambiguity.

The answer I supplied to the jurors was what they understood and brought with them into the courtroom in any traffic case—the Rules of the Road. I defined "reasonable basis" for the jury in a way that the defense could not dispute or avoid.

When judges and juries learn the Rules of the Road of insurance claims handling, there is no ambiguity or confusion about the wrongfulness of the defendant's conduct.

That weekend, I took the uncontested statements of my expert and the admissions of the defendant's experts and claims adjusters and constructed my first Rules of the Road chart for the jury.[1] The result was a substantial verdict for the plaintiff,[2] and the beginning, for me, of a new approach to trying cases.

A final word: some have asked why write a book and possibly reveal these secrets to the defense bar. We believe there is no effective defense to this technique. It cuts through subterfuge and evasion; that means it will always help plaintiffs with worthy cases and can never be used to hurt them.

---

1. See appendix B, "Sample Insurance Bad Faith Rules of the Road."
2. *Ace v. Aetna*, 139 F.3d 1241 (9th Cir. 1998).

1

DEFINING THE PROBLEM

The word "reasonable" turns up so often in civil jury instructions on liability that it can become invisible to the plaintiff's lawyer. This is where the problem takes root.

Consider the following:

- In medical malpractice cases, the key instruction asks the jury to measure the defendant's conduct in comparison to what a "reasonably prudent" or "reasonably competent practitioner" in the same field would have done.

- In product liability cases, the jury is asked to determine if the product was "unreasonably dangerous" or if the manufacturer failed to act in a "reasonably prudent" way.

- In most states, the first-party insurance bad faith jury instruction will be similar to Arizona's pattern instruction as follows:[1]

---

[1]. Arizona bad faith law is among the most supportive in enforcing policyholder rights. The problems illustrated by the Arizona bad faith instructions are even worse in many other states.

There is an implied duty of good faith and fair dealing in every insurance policy. The plaintiff claims that the defendant breached this duty.

To prove that the defendant breached the duty of good faith and fair dealing, the plaintiff must prove:

1. The defendant intentionally [denied the claim] [failed to pay the claim] [delayed payment of the claim] *without a reasonable basis* for such action; and

2. The defendant knew that it acted *without a reasonable basis,* or the defendant failed to perform an investigation or evaluation adequate to determine whether its action was supported by a *reasonable basis.*[2]

So what does it mean, "reasonable"? Look it up in the dictionary,[3] and you will find a wide range of meanings:

- Showing sound judgment
- Rational
- Moderate (as in a "reasonably priced house")
- Conforming with established standards or rules[4]

There's the one we want: "conforming with established standards or rules."

So we have two imperatives that require us to focus carefully on this ubiquitous word "reasonable." First, we need to show the jury that in the legal context, reasonable refers to "established

---

2. RAJI (Civil) 3d Bad Faith 1, emphasis added.
3. By the way, we've all heard about juries who used, or at least asked for, a dictionary in their deliberations. How often does this happen because the lawyers have left the jury at sea without good definitions of the critical words they are asked to apply?
4. This one can be found in a list of thesaurus equivalents for "reasonable" at http://www.thefreedictionary.com.

standards or rules." Second, we need to pour content into those rules. If we fail to meet both imperatives, the complexity, confusion, and ambiguity of the case threaten to overwhelm us.

Let's see how this can happen in insurance bad faith cases. The reasonable-basis instructions allow defense arguments like these.

DISABILITY CASE

It is true that both of the plaintiff's treating doctors sent letters stating she was disabled. But the question for you to decide is not whether or not we made the right decision; the question is whether we acted in bad faith. The judge will tell you in his instructions that we are only guilty of bad faith if we acted with *no reasonable basis.*

It is true there are 1,000 pages of medical records, spanning four years that support the proposition that the plaintiff was disabled, but remember Dr. Smith's 9/25/04 note: "Unclear why she hasn't improved by now." That gave us a *reasonable basis* to [delay payment and investigate further] [ask for an IME] [deny the claim]. Maybe, with 20/20 hindsight, you can say we were wrong, maybe the claims people here—who are human beings, like you and me—used *bad judgment,* but we are not guilty of acting without a *reasonable basis.*

UNINSURED-MOTORIST CASE

The plaintiff claims that her injuries were caused by the accident. But in none of these thousand pages of medical records is there a single entry that says this accident caused her herniated disc. It was *reasonable* for us to question this.

Property Case

When the plaintiff signed her proof-of-loss form under oath and stated that her couch, which we know was worth only $900, was worth $1,000, we were on notice that this might not be an honest claim. We had a *reasonable basis* to be skeptical. We had a *reasonable basis* to request more supporting documentation on her claim. We had a *reasonable basis* to take seven years to adjust a $10,000 claim.

In a third-party bad faith case, the Arizona jury instruction has a "prudent insurer" standard. This is even worse than "reasonable basis." Can't you hear the defense arguments? "We can't be throwing our money away. We were just being prudent."

You get the idea. Even the slowest defense lawyer can recognize that these concepts of "reasonable basis" and "prudent insurer" provide safe harbors for egregious insurance-company conduct. Why? Because "reasonable basis" and "prudent insurer" are *ambiguous* standards. So are the concepts of a "reasonably prudent" doctor or an "unreasonably dangerous" product.

Two things can happen when the jury is asked to apply an ambiguous standard. First, the jury may be confused. Faced with a confusing situation, most of us prefer not to act—to wait. Jurors are no different. To render a verdict for the plaintiff, the jury needs to be confident, willing to act. A confused jury is rarely a plaintiff's jury.

Second, the jurors are free to invent their own definition for the standard—in this instance, reasonable basis. There may have been a time—before corporate America bombarded us with antiplaintiff propaganda—when jurors were inclined to define an ambiguous standard in a way favorable to plaintiffs. Those times are gone and are unlikely to return in our lifetime. Now an ambiguous standard is like a magnet, attracting antiplaintiff slogans, beliefs, and stereotypes. Even those jurors who would like to rule in your favor will have a hard time resisting reasonable basis arguments like those illustrated above.

As already noted, this same problem often arises in personal injury cases. Most jury instructions in negligence cases say something like: "Negligence is the failure to do something a reasonable person would do under the circumstances, or doing something a reasonable person would not do under the circumstances." Again, we are back to the problem of reasonableness.

This may not be a problem in automobile accident cases because most jurors think they know what a reasonable driver would do in specific circumstances. (This is why the Rules approach can be problematic in automobile cases; see chapter 11.) But you don't have to stray very far from typical auto cases to have the concept of reasonableness create ambiguity problems.

Here's an example from a case Rick handled a few years ago. This fact pattern will be used as an example throughout the book to illustrate various points.[5]

An eight-year-old girl lived with her family on a rural two-lane road in Alaska. The speed limit was 50 mph. To get to school, she would leave her house (A), walk down her driveway, and cross the road to the designated school bus stop (B). She had been instructed by the bus driver to be on the (B) side of the road before the bus arrived.

In this area of Alaska, it is dark until nine or ten o'clock in the morning for many months of the year. The roads are often icy.

One dark winter morning, while crossing the road, she was struck by a car (C) traveling approximately 55 mph. The school bus was nowhere in sight.

The claim against the school bus company focused on its placement of the school bus stop across the road from the girl's house and its requirement that she had to cross the road to get to her stop, *before the bus arrived.* The plaintiff argued that the stop, or student waiting area, should have been on the house side of the road, in the vicinity of (D). The bus driver should then have either picked her up on that side, while driving west, or alternatively, if driving east, should have stopped, displayed the stop sign, put on the flashing lights, and waved her across to the (B) side.

---

5. Refer to Figure 1-1 as you read the description of the case.

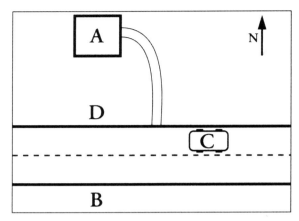

Figure 1-1

The bus company claimed it was reasonable to put the stop at (B) because there was a wider shoulder there, making it a safer waiting and stopping area. It was also reasonable to put the stop there, they claimed, because that was the most efficient place for it. The bus needed to travel east on the road to get to the school. To travel west first, so that students would not have to cross the road, would result in longer bus rides for the children and more expense for the school district. In addition, with the stop at (B) and the student already across the road, the bus could simply travel down the road, picking up students on the (B) side of the road, reducing traffic delays that would come from having to wave students across.

This is a difficult liability case against the bus company in almost any part of the country. The typical reasonableness negligence instruction makes it particularly hard. It might have been better to put the stop on the other side of the road, but can we really say the bus company's decision was *unreasonable*?

The defense will argue the bus company could have done several things. Each had positive and negative aspects. Each carried a cost and a possibility of injury. The company simply did its best to choose from among reasonable alternatives.

Here's another example from a medical malpractice case. A fifty-three-year-old man who had just eaten a heavy meal of spicy food went to the emergency room with chest pain. He hoped it was just indigestion. The harried emergency room doctor looked him over quickly and agreed. The man dropped dead a few hours later of an undiagnosed heart attack. The "diagnosis" of indigestion was certainly reasonable for the victim to have entertained. Why not for the doctor too?

So there you have the problem: ambiguous or ill-defined liability standards strongly favor the defense—and many of our most difficult cases involve ambiguous or ill-defined liability standards. The more complicated or confusing the facts, the more difficult the problem.

2

SOLVING THE PROBLEM

For the jury, we need to define "reasonably prudent doctor" and "reasonable basis" and "prudent insurance company"— and all the other "reasonables" and "prudents" too. We cannot let jurors make up their own definitions, and we certainly cannot allow the defense to define these terms. We may get some help from the judge, in the form of jury instructions,[1] but for the most part we need to provide the definitions ourselves.

In a bad faith case, we might say in the opening statement:

> At the end of this case, the judge is going to ask you to decide whether Acme Insurance had a reasonable basis for denying this claim.
>
> If the judge were to ask you if a driver employed by Acme drove from San Diego to Phoenix in a reasonable manner, you would all know how to judge that. You would know what it means to cross a double-yellow line. You would know what it means to go fifty miles an hour in a school zone. You would know what it means to be applying makeup

---

1. This is discussed more fully in chapter 4, "Developing a Working List of Rules."

or reading the paper while doing sixty-five on the expressway.

Well, there are principles and standards for handling insurance claims that are just as basic and commonly understood as the rules of the road for driving a car. To understand this case, and to understand how to make the right decision in this case, you need to understand these principles and standards.

We can then show the jury an enlargement of eight to twelve principles or standards. The following is an example from a commercial property insurance bad faith trial.

Claim Handling Principles and Standards

1. Company must treat its policyholders' interests with equal regard as it does its own interests. This is not an adversarial process.

2. Company should assist the policyholder with the claim.

3. Company must disclose to its insured all benefits, coverages, and time limits that may apply to the claim.

4. Company must conduct a full, fair, and prompt investigation of the claim at its own expense.

5. Company must fully, fairly, and promptly evaluate and adjust the claim.

6. Company must pay all amounts not in dispute within thirty days.

7. Company may not deny a claim or any part of a claim based upon insufficient information, speculation, or biased information.

8. If full or partial denial, Company must give written explanation, pointing to facts and policy provisions.

9. Company must not misrepresent facts or policy provisions.

10. Company may not make unreasonably low settlement offers.

11. Company must give claimant written update on status of claim every thirty days, including a description of what is needed to finalize the claim.

We can go on to say:

> You will hear during this trial that these principles are not controversial. Every reputable insurance company understands, agrees with, and follows these principles. In fact, Acme's own claims handlers and executives will tell you they agree that a claim should be handled in accordance with these principles.
>
> And if you look at these principles and think about them, you will see that they are fair and make sense.

We then walk the jury through the principles, describing what they mean and why they make sense. When that is done, we can say:

> Over the next two weeks we will prove to you that every one of these principles was violated by Acme when it handled John's claim.

Later chapters will discuss in greater detail how to formulate Rules of the Road and how to use them at various stages of litigation and trial. The purpose here is to simply introduce the concept of how we solve the "reasonable" problem.

If everyone agrees with these standards, and if we can prove these standards were violated, it will be very hard for the defense to convince the jury there was a reasonable basis for its actions. Stated another way, these principles define "reasonableness" for the jury. We no longer have a single ambiguous, amorphous standard; we have a number of specific concrete standards—ones we know we can prove were violated.

Let's go back to the "failure to diagnose" malpractice case for another example of how we pour content into the empty word "reasonable."

"Failure to diagnose" cases are the bread and butter of plaintiff's lawyers' malpractice work. We've handled cases involving failure to diagnose cancer (lung, colon, breast, cervix, and others), failure to diagnose heart attack, and even failure to diagnose rare conditions like lupus nephritis (an autoimmune disease that attacks the kidneys) and cardiac myxoma (a benign tumor inside the heart). All these cases have widely diverse facts but share a common core.

Every "failure to diagnose" case can be lost if the Rules of the Road are not carefully defined up front for the jury. The mere fact that a doctor's diagnosis turns out to be wrong, in hindsight, doesn't mean that he or she was unreasonable in the original diagnosis—particularly if the eventual diagnosis points to a rare disease. The medical record always contains some facts that show why the diagnosis tilted the way it did. Every good defense lawyer will hammer one *reasonableness* rule: it's not fair and reasonable to judge someone's conduct today on what can't be known until tomorrow. If people were judged for failing to predict the future, we'd all get a flunking grade. Hindsight is 20/20. Nobody has a crystal ball.

Hold it right there, you say. The issue is "knew *or* should have known." True enough. But that's lawyer talk. We're looking for the germ of an idea or standard, a Rule of the Road, that doctors will agree governs their conduct. Here it is:

> A doctor who is diagnosing a patient's symptoms has a duty to rule out the most dangerous, treatable potential diseases first.

There's a term for that in medicine. It's *differential diagnosis*. It is taught in every medical school. Examples can be found in virtually every medical chart. Differential diagnosis is the method the medical profession uses to deal with uncertainty and doubt, the way it handles the fact that medical diagnoses are rarely 100 percent certain. When there's uncertainty about what is wrong with a patient, differential diagnosis says the reasonable physician must first rule out the worst possibilities.

So for our patient who goes to the emergency room with chest pain after a heavy, spicy meal, it's not enough to make a good guess that he has a mere case of indigestion. The doctor should rule out the big gorilla—heart attack—before sending the patient home. After all, why did the patient come to an emergency room anyway? To see if he has an emergency! Given the differential-diagnosis Rule we just stated, it is *unreasonable* for the doctor to send the patient home without ruling out a heart attack.

Most every adult who comes to an emergency room with nontraumatic chest pain will get an electrocardiogram (EKG) test. But the EKG comes back normal about 50 percent of the time in patients in the early stages of an acute myocardial infarction (heart attack). This statistic means that a reasonable physician cannot send that patient home on the strength of a negative EKG alone. Why? Because the doctor has not yet satisfied the Rule of the Road requiring that dangerous, treatable conditions be ruled out.

See how this simple Rule of the Road makes murky situations clear? If, on the other hand, we leave the *reasonable physician* term undefined, then any doctor who puts in "the old college try" might get a passing grade.

Here is the basic paradigm for a "failure to diagnose" case:

1. The defendant admits there is a requirement (Rule) to perform a differential diagnosis.
2. The defendant admits the condition ultimately diagnosed was part of the differential diagnosis of the signs and symptoms with which the patient presented.

3. The defendant admits there is a priority in the differential diagnosis; conditions in need of urgent attention, which might be catastrophic if not attended to, must be ruled out first.

4. The condition ultimately diagnosed was not ruled out in this instance.

5. Medicine has a general principle: the earlier the diagnosis, the better the chances are for cure and the more you can do for the patient. Conversely, later diagnosis generally reduces the chances for improvement.

The benefits of the Rules of the Road extend beyond defining "reasonableness." Remember the other enemies of a plaintiff's case: complexity and confusion? The Rules of the Road give the jury (and you) an effective tool for cutting through complexity and confusion.

Suppose we are dealing with a condominium association's claim that its buildings were damaged in an earthquake and the insurance company handled the repairs in bad faith. Lengthy correspondence went back and forth between the insurance company and the association's agents, addressing complex insurance, engineering, and construction issues. The insurance company also has produced a three-foot-thick file stuffed with self-serving internal documents covering the claim. Making sense of these documents is difficult for the jury (or anyone).

But suppose we look at these documents through the lens of the Claim Handling Principles and Standards. Do they show the company was treating the policyholder's interests with equal regard to its own interests? Did the company assist the policyholder with the claim? Did the company pay all amounts not in dispute within thirty days? Chances are, the answer to all these questions is no.

The jury may never understand the fine points of the engineering and construction issues addressed in the documents, but it will easily understand whether these principles were honored. Complexity and confusion are replaced by clarity. And if you are on the right side of a case, clarity can only help you.

Identifying the Rules of the Road

As lawyers, we venture into complex fields of human endeavor—medicine, engineering, insurance—and ask the jury to follow us there. Each field has innumerable standards, customs, principles, rules, and regulations. Most lawyers like nothing better than to immerse themselves in this material. That's our job. But many lawyers fail to appreciate that only a small portion of this material is actually *relevant* to the dispute the jury must resolve; even less is actually *material* or significant to that dispute; and still less is *actually helpful* to having the dispute resolved in the plaintiff's favor. The failure of the plaintiff's lawyer to recognize these distinctions is responsible for many meritorious cases being lost.

At its most basic level, the purpose of the Rules of the Road technique is to educate, first the plaintiff's lawyer, then the judge and the jury, about the basic principles in the field that *require* the dispute be resolved in the plaintiff's favor.

Are there principles that require the dispute be resolved in the plaintiff's favor? Absolutely, if you have properly screened the case. Does that mean the Rules of the Road technique can guarantee victory? No. But properly articulated Rules of the Road can make you more successful at every stage of litigation—from screening the case to its appeal.

The next chapter discusses how to find source material for Rules of the Road and how to fashion that material into usable Rules. In general, the process starts by looking at the material you'd refer to while litigating any case, such as statutes and regulations, case law, contracts between the defendant and another party, professional literature, training manuals, expert testimony, ethical codes, and commonsense imperatives.

You review this material to see if it contains principles that could help you formulate Rules of the Road.

Attributes of Rules of the Road

There are five basic attributes of every good Rule of the Road, and you must work hard to make sure your Rules meet each of these attributes.

A Rule of the Road should be:

1. A requirement that the defendant do, or not do, something.

2. Easy for the jury to understand.

3. A requirement the defense cannot credibly dispute.

4. A requirement the defendant has violated.

5. Important enough in the context of the case that proof of its violation will significantly increase the chance of a plaintiff's verdict.

Let's discuss these attributes in order.

Attribute 1: Must Prescribe Conduct

A Rule of the Road, first of all, is a statement of conduct that the defendant should (or should not) do. It must be prescriptive, not merely descriptive, and it must be aimed squarely at the defendant. It has this basic structure:

A [type of defendant] should (or should not, depending on the case and the Rule) do _____ [fill in relevant conduct sought to be enforced by plaintiff].

This initial attribute of a Rule of the Road was left out of the first edition of this book, and its omission has caused many lawyers to stumble. Simply stated, there is a difference between a principle and a Rule (a difference that we will observe from this point forward in this book). This distinction is so important that chapter 5 is devoted to clarifying it.[1]

For now it is enough to note that a Rule must require conduct and must identify who is to exercise that conduct. "A patient can get injured if the surgeon does not carefully identify what he is supposed to be cutting" is a good *description* of what can happen without appropriate conduct, but it is not a Rule, because it does not say in a straightforward way what the prescribed conduct should be. In a case where the surgeon admits he did not know what he was cutting, the Rule, based on this principle, might be: "A surgeon should not cut human tissue unless he knows what he is cutting."

Attribute 2: Easy to Understand

As we will discuss in chapter 4, "Developing a Working List of Rules," potential Rules come from a variety of sources. But many, such as those from textbooks or regulations, are written in a style that is opaque to the layperson. So we need to translate them. Here's an example.

Suppose in your research you come across Cal. Code of Regulations § 2695.4(a):

---

1. There is a lesson here about the importance for plaintiff's attorneys of carefully defining their terms. In the first edition, we assumed the reader would use the same definition of "rule" that we had in mind: "a prescribed guide for conduct." But if you look at any dictionary listing of the acceptable definitions of "rule," another definition is "a usually valid generalization." (See, for example, the Merriam-Webster entry for "rule," definitions 1-a and 2-a.) Many of our readers obviously went with that second definition.

> Every insurer shall disclose to a first-party claimant or beneficiary, all benefits, coverage, time limits or other provisions of any insurance policy issued by that insurer that may apply to the claim presented by the claimant. When additional benefits might reasonably be payable under an insured's policy upon receipt of additional proofs of claim, the insurer shall immediately communicate this fact to the insured and cooperate with and assist the insured in determining the extent of the insurer's additional liability.

Which makes a better principle for the jury to use in judging the insurer's conduct?

- The language of the previous regulations?

or

- "The insurance company should assist the policyholder with the claim"?

That's an easy choice, isn't it?

Look at appendix B, "Sample Insurance Bad Faith Rules of the Road" and you'll see a Rule list from a commercial property case. Rule 2 is: "Company should assist the policyholder with the claim." This Rule is helpful in almost every bad faith case.[2]

Here's a principle from the failure-to-diagnose context. We found the following quotation in a leading internal-medicine textbook:

> The first kind of strategic error is to fail to weigh the consequences of being wrong. . . . Where the cost of error is high, even a slight risk of a false-negative result is unacceptable.[3]

---

2. Look at appendix A, "Annotated Rules of the Road." This is an example of what we call a master annotated Rules of the Road list. We will discuss the assembly and use of such lists later. For now, note that Rule 3 in appendix A is very similar to the Rule quoted above. The main difference is that the Rule in appendix A is annotated with sources for the Rule.

3. Johns, Fortuin, and Wheeler, *The Collection and Evaluation of Clinical Information, in* THE PRINCIPLES AND PRACTICE OF MEDICINE, at 6 (22d ed. 1988).

A juror-oriented way to express that principle as a Rule might be:

> A doctor facing a potential life-and-death situation needs to be really sure of his diagnosis before deciding it's safe to send the patient home.

In chapter 4, we discuss how to secure the defendant's agreement with your simple expression of a Rule. For now, it is enough to understand that your goal is to present the jury with the simplest, most understandable expression of the Rule that you can.

Attribute 3: Defense Cannot Credibly Dispute It

To be useful, a Rule of the Road either must be endorsed by the defendant and its witnesses or must be so persuasive that the defendant loses credibility by resisting it.

In a bad faith case, most claims handlers will readily agree that part of their job is to assist the policyholder with the claim. They may not believe it, but they know that is the right answer. They instinctively know that resisting that proposition puts them on the slippery slope to Witness Hell.

If the witness denies an obligation to assist the policyholder, he loses credibility, and so does his employer. You can decide how and when you take advantage of that. You can show him the regulations and ask if he agrees they apply to him. Or, you can get him further out on a limb, denying that he has a duty to reveal additional coverages to the insured (for example), or denying he has any duty to provide claim forms or instructions. *So the policyholder paid for this coverage, is entitled to it under the contract, but you can keep it secret from him? You know he wants to file a claim, but you can hide how he should go about it?* In the end, he either has to admit he has a duty to assist, or he looks like the representative of an unreasonable and recalcitrant insurance company.

In a malpractice case, the defendant doctor should concede her obligation to rule out serious, treatable problems before deciding that the patient has a benign condition. If she does not, she, too, is on the road to Witness Hell.

All good Rules are like this. There is no "safe" answer. Disagreeing with the Rule should hurt the defense as much as or more than agreeing with it. If a doctor endorses a text as authoritative—or has written it himself—he is going to look bad disagreeing with a simple, straightforward principle stated in that text.

In some cases, we can find a relevant principle that has such moral force that it can be used as a Rule, even if not written down anywhere. In this book, we call these Rule sources "common sense" or "moral imperative" sources. For example, relative to the bus stop case discussed in chapter 1, "Defining the Problem," we used the following Rule (see appendix C, Rule 4):

> If there is more than one reasonable and practical place to locate a waiting area, the one safest for the child should be designated.

When we first articulated this Rule in the case, it existed nowhere in writing (at least that we could find). Yet how could anyone possibly argue with it? In fact, the defendants did not. Each of their witnesses, without hesitation, endorsed this Rule.

Here are some other examples of "common sense" or "moral imperative" Rules that share the attribute of being impossible to credibly dispute:

- [Claims handlers] [doctors] [engineers] [accountants] should not destroy documents to hide or disguise their conduct.
- A doctor should always listen carefully to the patient's description of symptoms.
- An insurance company should not use biased consultants to assist in investigation or evaluation.
- Claims handlers should not use racially derogatory terms when communicating with policyholders.
- Company should pay the claim unless there is a good reason not to.
- A [type of defendant] should not lie to a [type of plaintiff].
- If a company can make its product safer at a modest cost, it should do so.

- A doctor should prescribe the lowest effective dose of a drug, to avoid dangerous side effects.
- A surgeon should not cut any internal structure without making sure what it is.

Anyone who resists any of these statements in front of a jury immediately loses credibility. Even in deposition, resisting a Rule will likely make a witness feel ridiculous and cause him to backtrack and agree with you.

Here is the deposition testimony of a surgeon who, in taking out a patient's gallbladder, mistakenly severed the connection between the patient's liver and the rest of the body (the common bile duct) instead of the connection between the gallbladder and the liver (the cystic duct). Actual transcript:

Q: Dr. Smith, is there a rule in gallbladder surgery that a surgeon should never ligate or divide any structure until he is absolutely certain what its identity is?

A: There is no such rule.

Q: Well, are you allowed to guess what you're cutting before you cut it?

A: You have to take reasonable precautions of identifying the structures and preserving them.

Q: So you have to take reasonable precautions of identifying structures before you cut them?

A: Yes.

Take a minute to think of one of your cases. Are there basic moral truths about your case that can be stated in simple, direct language? Will the defendant look ridiculous contesting the accuracy of the statement? You may have the beginning of your Rules of the Road list.

Let's pause and consider the intersection between two key Rule requirements: "easy to understand" and "defendant cannot credibly dispute." Because a good Rule must meet *both* of these requirements, we are doing more than translating technical terms from the defendant's business/profession into plain English. Ultimately, the most successful Rules do not merely allow the jury to enter the defendant's world; they also bring the defendant's conduct into the world of motive and character familiar to the jury. Human greed, arrogance, and thoughtlessness underlie so many instances of harmful conduct. That's why the search for clear moral imperatives, both easy to understand and dangerous for the defendant to resist, is a critical part of the Rules technique that we believe can pay off handsomely for plaintiff's lawyers. We explain this in more detail in chapter 4, "Developing a Working List of Rules."

Attribute 4: The Defendant Has Violated It

By "violated," we mean the defendant breached the letter or spirit of the Rule. Ideally, you will be able to prove, beyond all doubt, that the defendant violated a specific Rule in very definite ways. You never want to use a Rule with which the defendant can prove it complied. For example, you don't want to invoke a Rule that says, "Insurance company must disclose all possible coverages to the policyholder," if your claim file shows the company did just that.

On the other hand, you don't need absolute proof of violation to make a principle valuable as a Rule. If the spirit of the Rule was violated, that may be enough. Remember our original purpose in using the Rules technique: we are trying to make an ambiguous standard more specific, more meaningful. We are trying to bring clarity to a complex and confusing fact pattern. You should always ask yourself, "Can I prove this Rule was violated?"

One problem we will bookmark for now and return to later is this: when your Rules are too vague, you can believe the defendant violated them, and the defendant can sincerely believe she followed them, because your terms are so ambiguous that they mean different things to different people. For example, the "rule" "A doctor should always be careful" meets two attributes—easy to understand and hard to dispute—but it runs into trouble because it doesn't prescribe conduct and you cannot clearly prove that the defendant violated the Rule. The solution, when constructing a list of Rules for a case, is to never stop with a vague truism "rule" but to flesh it out with specific conduct that you can prove the defendant violated.[4]

Consider this next Rule, some version of which is often the first Rule in almost all our bad faith trials:

> Company must treat its policyholders' interests with equal regard as it does its own interests. This is not an adversarial process.

Case law in almost every state supports the first sentence. Almost every adjuster will agree with the second sentence. If the jurors find in our client's favor, chances are they will have concluded this Rule was violated. But it is included here, not because we can "prove" a violation, but because it sets the proper tone for the case. It provides a vehicle for educating the jury about the fact that insurance is not like any other business. "Buyer beware," "survival of the fittest," and "laissez-faire economics" have no place in the adjustment of claims. Again, by the end of the case, the jury should be convinced that the spirit of this Rule was violated because of the other specific Rule violations.

Attribute 5: The Rule Is Important

The Rule needs to be important enough in the context of the case that proof of its violation will significantly increase the chance of a plaintiff's verdict.

This attribute of a Rule should go without saying, but the mistake of ignoring it is made often enough to warrant discussing it here. Not every Rule violation is worthy of attention at trial.

---

4. In their path-breaking book, REPTILE: THE 2009 MANUAL OF THE PLAINTIFF'S REVOLUTION (Balloon Press 2009), our colleagues Don Keenan and David Ball suggest an archetype for a general Rule:

"A [type of defendant] must not needlessly endanger the safety of [type of plaintiff]."

We agree this is a good starting place for a Rule that might apply to your case, but we stress that you can never stop at this starting line, because Rules that are so general, and never get more specific, can be readily sidestepped by defendants at trial. We know Don and David agree with this.

For example, if you have only two minor incidents where the insurance company failed to assist the claimant with the claim, this Rule may not belong on the list you show the jury. This is not like issue-spotting in law school. Your case does not get better in proportion to the number of Rules you add to your list.

Defense attorneys make good issue-spotting lawyers because their fundamental job is to create problems, not solve them. The more problems that can be ginned up in a case, the happier the defense is. Remember complexity, confusion, and ambiguity?

Our job on behalf of the plaintiff is to solve problems, not create them. So we need to reduce our list of Rules to the basic core that is outcome-important to the case and hard to fight.

We've all heard the advice "Keep it simple." The reason the advice is sound in the Rules context is because we want to avoid handing the defense ammunition that they can use to create complexity, confusion, and ambiguity.

Usually, we will keep a running annotated list throughout the litigation, similar to those in appendix A, "Annotated Rules of the Road: A Master List," and appendix D, "Bus Stop Safety Principles Annotated." We finalize the jury copy in the days before trial. Often, it is only in these final days that we will know which Rule violations are important enough to include in the final, jury-ready list.

We also usually find that we need to keep editing and massaging our list of Rules as the case progresses, a process we will detail in these next several chapters.

4

Developing a Working List of Rules

Early in the case, you should begin constructing an annotated working copy of your Rules of the Road. The annotations form a quick reference to the various sources of support for each Rule. For example, take a look at appendix A, "Annotated Rules of the Road: A Master List," which is a master list Rick Friedman used as a starting point in several bad faith cases. Also, look at appendix D, "Bus Stop Safety Principles Annotated."

You will use your own annotated working copy in various ways throughout a case. The annotated list of Rules is a living, working document. Other chapters will discuss how to use this document; this chapter focuses on its construction.

Sources for Rules

Rules can be found in many places. Here are the common Rule sources:

- Statutes and regulations
- Case law

- Contracts between relevant parties or entities
- Court rulings in your case
- Jury instructions
- Testimony of your experts, their experts, or their lay witnesses
- Policy and procedure manuals
- Other training manuals, quality-control procedures, or operations manuals of the defendant
- Admissions in pleadings
- Textbooks and articles from the professional literature
- Industry guidelines or mission statements
- Ethical codes or guidelines
- Common sense or moral imperatives

We want to emphasize that while you will start your annotated Rules list early, you will regularly revise it throughout a case as new information comes to your attention. You found a new case or a new textbook? Court ruling in your favor? Major admission by a defense witness? Review your annotated list to see if you can add the new information—either as additional support for a Rule you have already drafted, or perhaps as an entirely new Rule.

Jury Instructions as Rules Sources

Jury instructions comprise a major source of Rules for your annotated list. And now (faint drum roll), the most important advice in this book:

> Draft proposed jury instructions at the beginning of every case.

Years ago, before cell phones, iPods, and continuing-legal-education courses conducted via the Internet, almost every CLE speaker would make this point: *at the very beginning of a case you should draft a set of proposed jury instructions.* We have become so preoccupied with the stealth, authoritative, antilawyer juror who will destroy our case no matter how perfectly we try it that we don't hear as much about the basics in CLEs anymore. Or maybe the instructors just gave up, the way some dentists give up telling patients to floss.

So let us tell you. This is basic: *at the very beginning of a case you should draft a set of proposed jury instructions.* The less experienced you are with the type of case you are prosecuting, the more important this is. The more complex the case, the more important it is.

Plaintiff's lawyers work hard. Many think nothing of routinely working nights and weekends. Tell plaintiff's lawyers that wearing the color brown to court will increase the chances of victory, and new suits in shades of taupe and chocolate will quickly sprout in courthouse hallways. Tell them PowerPoint will make them more effective in court, and soon a tangle of new projection equipment will crowd their trial tables. Tell them you recall a case from Arkansas in the 1960s, right on point . . . just can't remember the name right now . . . it should really help their case, and they will flog the search engines for hours to find the citation. But tell them they should draft jury instructions more than three weeks before trial, and you will get the same look you get from your dog when you try to explain the Rule Against Perpetuities.

Nothing focuses the mind of a trial lawyer like a set of jury instructions. The jury instructions are "the bottom line," as the MBAs like to say. They determine what evidence is relevant. They determine what you have to prove to win. They reveal what affirmative defenses can hurt you. They are the ultimate, strongest Rules.

Lawyers who say jurors don't pay attention to jury instructions:

- Are lazy and looking for an excuse to avoid the hard work of thinking about instructions.

- Lost a trial, don't know why, and are looking for an excuse.

- Don't have much experience trying cases.
- All of the above.

Do jurors sometimes misunderstand jury instructions? Yes. But whose fault is that? Do jurors sometimes ignore or disregard jury instructions? Yes, but often because the instructions have not been properly presented and argued by the lawyers. *Usually*, jurors pore over the instructions, looking for help in making their difficult decisions.

An often overlooked benefit of having the jury instructions clearly in mind early in the litigation is that they can influence the judge. Citing a pattern instruction in a brief dealing with summary judgment, motions *in limine,* or even discovery motions can effectively focus the judge on the appropriate issues. Yet citing instructions to the judge seldom occurs. We suspect this happens so little because the lawyers working on motions have not yet thought about jury instructions. Neither have the judges, but when you remind them, they will take notice.

Jury instructions can help with your experts too. In professional-negligence cases, for example, experts commonly trip over the concept of "standard of care." They often assume, wrongly, that a very large majority, even 99 percent, of their peers must practice in a certain way for that practice to become the "standard of care." When you tell experts to focus on the language from your state's jury instruction—what a "reasonably competent" or "reasonably prudent" practitioner would do in similar circumstances—the experts can focus on what competent care consists of and not worry about what a pollster might find in a survey.

If you have worked numerous cases in a particular area, maybe you don't need to prepare jury instructions before filing suit, because you already have memorized what the instructions will look like. In all other cases, *just do it.*

In the movie *Prelude to a Kiss* an old man and a young woman inadvertently exchange bodies. The mind and personality of the young woman reside in the old man's body, and vice versa. At one point in the movie, the old man reflects on how he would live differently if he could be young again. His conclusion: "I would floss more."

Doing your jury instructions early is like flossing. The benefits are provable, even obvious. Yet it brings no instant joy. So it is easy to put off.

Will your draft jury instructions change as the judge makes rulings, you add or drop causes of action, or the facts change? Of course. But you will always have, clearly in mind, in every deposition, conference, or oral argument, the elements necessary to win your case.

Will your friends and colleagues make fun of you? Will they think you are a nerd? Yes. But after you have litigated a case with a set of jury instructions in hand from the beginning, you may agree this is one of those good habits of litigation hygiene that should not be put off.

You might want to think about flossing more too.

Incorporate Jury Instructions into Your Rules

When you have finished drafting your jury instructions, you may be surprised to discover principles embodied in those instructions that you can incorporate into Rules of the Road.

This all-purpose negligence instruction can prove useful in almost any injury lawsuit:

> Negligence is a relative concept. A reasonable person changes [his][her] conduct according to the circumstances or according to the danger that [he][she] knows, or should know, exists. Therefore, as the danger increases, a reasonable person acts in accordance with those circumstances. Similarly, as the danger increases, a reasonable person acts more carefully.[1]

---

1. STANDARDIZED CIVIL JURY INSTRUCTIONS FOR THE DISTRICT OF COLUMBIA (1998 ed.) No. 5–3. Maryland puts it more succinctly: "If the foreseeable danger increases, a reasonable person acts more carefully." MARYLAND PATTERN JURY INSTRUCTIONS No. 19:3 (2004 ed.).

That last sentence can readily become the springboard to specific principles that can form the foundation for later Rules. For instance:

> As the danger to the patient increases, a doctor should act more carefully.

Or even more specific:

> Because a patient can't protect herself while under general anesthesia, the surgeon has to be much more careful than if the patient were awake.

Think about the idea for a minute. It's really a core concept of negligence law: "A reasonable person acts more carefully as the foreseeable danger increases."[2] Many states have cases approving such language in jury instructions.[3] And many of the Rules we will want to fashion in injury cases spring from this idea.

Pattern jury instructions give plenty of fodder for Rules of the Road in insurance bad faith cases too. Look at the following California Judicial Council's pattern instruction on first-party bad faith.

2332. BAD FAITH (FIRST PARTY)—FAILURE TO PROPERLY INVESTIGATE CLAIM-ESSENTIAL FACTUAL ELEMENTS

[Name of plaintiff] claims that [name of defendant] breached the obligation of good faith and fair dealing by failing to properly investigate [his/her/its] loss. To

---

2. A federal pattern instruction says: "Any increase in foreseeable danger requires increased care." O'Malley, Grenig & Lee, 3 FEDERAL JURY PRACTICE AND INSTRUCTIONS, No. 120.12 (5th ed. 2000).

3. A recent case reversing a trial court for failing to allow such an instruction is *Pannu v. Jacobson*, 909 A.2d 178 (D.C. 2006). For a list of some of the older cases from around the country approving similar language, see 3 Harper, James, and Gray, THE LAW OF TORTS (2nd ed. 1986) section 16.9 at 473 n.12.

establish this claim, [name of plaintiff] must prove all of the following:

1. That [name of plaintiff] suffered a loss covered under an insurance policy with [name of defendant];

2. That [name of plaintiff] notified [name of defendant] of the loss;

3. That [name of defendant] unreasonably failed to properly investigate the loss and [denied coverage/failed to pay insurance benefits/delayed payment of insurance benefits];

4. That [name of plaintiff] was harmed; and

5. That [name of defendant]'s unreasonable failure to properly investigate the loss was a substantial factor in causing [name of plaintiff]'s harm.

When investigating a claim, an insurance company has a *duty to diligently search for, and to consider,* evidence that supports an insured's claimed loss. An insurance company may not reasonably and in good faith deny payments to its insured *without thoroughly investigating* the grounds for its denial.[4]

From this, you could make a Rule that states: "Insurance company must properly investigate a claim." That is not much better than the vexing "reasonableness" language. But the last paragraph has the makings of one or two good Rules for your annotated list:

1. An insurance company must thoroughly investigate a claim before denying it.

Or, you could phrase it like this:

---

4. Emphasis added.

> 2. An insurance company must diligently search for and consider evidence that supports the claim.

Depending on your case, these two might be combined into a single Rule:

> An insurance company must thoroughly investigate a claim and diligently search for and consider evidence that supports the claim.

On the other hand, Rule 2 could itself be divided into two Rules:

> An insurance company must diligently search for evidence that supports the claim.

> An insurance company must diligently consider evidence that supports the claim.

How you ultimately phrase the Rule for the jury will depend on exactly what facts you have to present and how defense witnesses have testified regarding your various formulations. For example, if the claims people never interviewed people you claim they should have interviewed, you might prefer the first version of Rule 2, immediately above. If they interviewed people, but your claim is that they *ignored* what these people had to say, you might prefer the second version. You will also want to consider how strongly the defense witnesses agreed with or resisted each of these versions.

You might have the same or similar concepts expressed several ways on your annotated Rules list. Shortly before trial, you can decide what formulation to present to the jury.

However you divide up the Rules on this idea, the annotation in support of any of these Rules will include "CACI 2332," the original jury instruction. We say "include" because you will eventually get witnesses to endorse these Rules, and you will also include their testimony in the annotation.[5]

---

5. For an example of this, see appendix A.

Appendix E, "Proposed Jury Instructions in a Disability Bad Faith Case," is what we submitted in a case a few years back. If you compare it to appendix A, "Annotated Rules of the Road: A Master List," you will note how jury-instruction principles end up in the Rules of the Road, and the Rules of the Road end up in jury instructions. For example, some version of the second instruction in appendix E is commonly given in first-party bad faith cases.

> INSTRUCTION NO. ___
>
> An insurer's obligation of good faith and fair dealing includes *giving at least as much consideration to the insured's interest as to its own.* To meet the obligation of good faith and fair dealing the insurer *must fully inquire into possible bases that might support the insured's claim.* It may not in good faith deny payments to its insured without *thoroughly investigating* the foundation for its denial.
>
> Authority: *Egan v. Mutual of Omaha Ins. Co.,* 598 P.2d 452, 456, 457 (Cal. 1979).

The three italicized statements are also on our Master Rules of the Road list in appendix A, "Annotated Rules of the Road: A Master List."

> 2. Company must treat its policyholder's interests with equal regard as it does its own interests. This is not an adversarial process.[6]
>
> 5. Company must thoroughly investigate the claim.
>
> 12. An insurance company may not ignore evidence that supports coverage.

---

6. The first sentence comes from the *Egan* case. The second sentence is a "spirit" or "moral imperative" Rule. If an adjuster argues that adjusting a first-party claim is an adversarial process, then he is in effect saying that when you buy insurance, you are buying an adversary, and maybe, a lawsuit. They will never disagree with the second sentence.

Yet another could be added, based on the instruction:

> Company must seek out evidence that supports the claim.

Again, the exact formulation will depend on your facts and the testimony of the defense witnesses. The important point is that there will often be substantial overlap between principles in your jury instructions and principles in your Rules.

ADMINISTRATIVE REGULATIONS AS RULES SOURCES

An administrative code provision can form the basis for a Rule, as well as for a jury instruction. Some courts resist giving jury instructions on detailed provisions of law—even if the instructions accurately state the provision and the provision applies to the case. Still, proposing instructions based on regulations can be worthwhile. Let's look at one example, instruction #4 from appendix E.

> INSTRUCTION NO. ___
>
> The Alaska Administrative Code provides that any person transacting a business of insurance who participates in the investigation, adjustment, negotiation or settlement of a claim under any type of insurance *must document each action taken on a claim.* The documentation must contain all notes, work papers, documents and similar material. The documentation must be in sufficient detail that relevant events, the dates of those events, and all persons participating in those events can be identified. The documentation may include legible copies of originals and may be stored in the form of microfilm or electronic media.
>
> If you find that the defendant violated this law, you may consider this in deciding whether or not it breached its duty of good faith and fair dealing in this case.

Suppose the insurance adjuster claims he had the file materials reviewed by an in-house expert before denying the claim but the file contains no reference to this review. Knowing this, and knowing the administrative code provision referenced in the instruction above, you might draft a Rule that says:

> The claim file must contain detailed documentation of each action taken and all work performed on a claim.

So you now have both a proposed instruction stating this principle, as well as a Rule.

Avoid the Implied Cause of Action

When you are working with administrative regulations and statutes as sources of Rules and jury instructions, watch out for one trap the defense often tries to lay: confusing the judge by using a violation of a statute or regulation as *"evidence of negligence"* and using the same violation as an *"implied cause of action."* These are completely distinct legal doctrines. Plaintiffs almost always are better off on the familiar ground of using such violations as evidence of negligence (or deliberate misconduct). As one legal treatise classically puts it:

> The almost universal American and English attitude is that where legislation prescribes a standard of conduct for the purpose of protecting life, limb, or property from a certain type of risk, and harm to the interest sought to be protected comes about through breach of the standard from the risk sought to be obviated, then the statutory prescription of the standard will at least be considered in determining civil rights and liabilities.[7]

---

7. Fowler Harper, Fleming James, and Oscar Gray, The Law of Torts section 17.6 at 619 (2d ed. 1986). A good case that explains the distinction between implied causes of action and use of statutes and regulations to support common-law claims is *Zhou v. Jennifer Mall Restaurant, Inc.*, 534 2d 1268 (D.C. 1987).

In the bad faith context, for example, defendant may argue against our code-based proposed jury instruction on the ground that no cause of action exists for violation of this provision of the administrative code. We will tell the judge that we do not claim any separate cause of action exists; the code contains a standard relevant to claims handling. While there may not be a private cause of action under a state's unfair claim practices act and regulations, the terms of such act and regulations are properly considered in determining whether an insurer's conduct amounts to bad faith.[8]

Don't get too hung up on the distinction between "negligence *per se*" and "evidence of negligence" when putting statutory or regulatory violations into your lawsuit and your proposed jury instructions. The only difference is whether the court will find negligence as a matter of law (negligence *per se*) or leave the issue for the jury to consider (evidence of negligence). Most courts are reluctant to find a defendant guilty of negligence as a matter of law, so the modern trend is to allow the evidence of statutory or regulatory violations to come in for the jury's ultimate decision. This suits us fine. Leaving the decision to the jury gives the plaintiff more room to put in evidence of the purpose of the statute or regulation and thus drive home its importance as a Rule of the Road.[9]

---

8. Among many cases that support this view, see, for example: *Spray, Gould & Bowers v. Associated International Ins. Co.*, 71 Cal. App. 4th 1260, 84 Cal. Rptr. 552 (Cal. App. 1999); *MacFarland v. United States Fidelity & Guarantee Co.*, 818 F.Supp. 108, 110 (E.D. P 1993); *Weiford v. State Farm Mutual Automobile Ins. Co.*, 831 P.2d 1264, 1269 (Alaska 1992); *Walston v. Monumental Life Ins. Co.*, 923 P.2d 456, 461 (Idaho 1996); *Hart v. Prudential Property & Casualty Ins. Co.*, 848 F.Supp. 900 (D. Nev. 1994); *Ace v. Aetna Life Ins. Co.*, 139 F.3d 1241 (9th Cir. 1998); *Wailua Associates v. Aetna Casualty & Surety Co.*, 27 F.Supp.2d 1211, 1221 (D. Hawaii 1998).

9. For an instructive case showing how a plaintiff made a fatal misstep by failing to elicit testimony about the purpose of the statute at issue (the federal Food, Drug & Cosmetics Act) and how the defendant violated it, see *McNeil Pharmaceuticals v. Hawkins*, 686 2d 567 (D.C. 1996). (Judgment for the plaintiff reversed due to failure to have an expert testify as to each statutory and regulatory provision put before the jury, how it was violated, and why it was relevant.)

Never underestimate how hard a desperate defendant will fight to keep statutes and regulations from being incorporated into jury instructions. If they lose on the "no implied cause of action" tactic, defendants may still argue that the rules as expressed in statutes or regulations are not a proper subject for an instruction but should be addressed through testimony or other evidence instead. You can then argue:

1. The instruction accurately states the law regulating the defendant's conduct.

2. The standardized civil-jury instructions in your jurisdiction, which are usually the product of negotiation among leading lawyers on both sides plus judges, recognize that statutory violations are an appropriate subject for instruction.

3. Whether the regulation was followed by the defendant is relevant to numerous issues in the case (which may include the defendant's state of mind, interactions with government agencies, and normal operating procedures).

4. If we don't get an instruction, our expert certainly may testify about the statute or regulation.

5. If our expert may not testify about this law, he may certainly testify to the *standard* expressed in the law, which is also the standard in the industry.

6. Actually, we are entitled to *both* an instruction on this issue and to have our expert testify about it.

A smart, self-confident judge will recognize you are entitled to have your expert testify to how claims handling (or drug labeling, or whatever else is at issue) is affected by the law *and* to have jury instruction on the same laws. In a traffic case, it is common for the court to instruct on the legal speed limit where the accident occurred *and* allow the experts to testify to that speed limit. This is no different.

When you ask for your Rules of the Road to be expressed in jury instructions and present them through witnesses or exhibits, the wording may vary somewhat, but the Rules remain the same. The goal is for the jury to hear you sponsor a Rule throughout the trial and then hear the judge endorse that Rule when instructing the jury. Who could ask for more?

A final word about using violations of statutes and regulations to construct Rules: you may have come across a statute or regulation (or case law, for that matter) that contained relevant ideas for your case but did not seem necessarily appropriate for a proposed jury instruction. Put those ideas in your annotated Rules. Ask your expert and the defense witnesses about them. You may get them to endorse a concept as a Rule that the judge would never give as an instruction.

Caution: don't go overboard. Only include legal concepts relevant to the facts or disputes in your case. You are not creating an academic list; you are creating a working lawyer's litigation tool.

OTHER SOURCES OF RULES

Now that you've formulated some Rules from your draft jury instructions, it's time to look at the myriad other sources of Rules.

Textbooks, Articles, and Industry Guidelines

Texts, academic articles, industry trade publications, industry mission statements, codes of ethics, and similar material are all great sources for Rules. Principles that seem applicable to your case should be formulated into Rules and added to your annotated Rules list.

A lot of elbow grease needs to be applied in sifting through this source material. We talk about this more in chapter 7, "The *Daubert*-Proofed Expert," because good objective literature is critical to *Daubert* motions. For now, a few principles can be emphasized:

- First, do the research yourself, or use a trusted assistant. *Never* delegate this task solely to your testifying expert. While an expert may be helpful, an obsessive plaintiff's lawyer finds more good gems than any expert. Why? Because you know (or should know) more about the entire case and how it needs to be argued than an expert ever will.

◆ Second, never limit your search to what you can get with a few Google clicks. The Internet has a great cache of information, no question. But some of the best material hasn't made it online yet. You or your assistant must make the trek to the old-fashioned library, sit down, and crack open the books.

◆ Third, follow the footnote trail. You are likely to find sort-of-relevant material before you find the really good stuff. Persistence pays. Once you get close to your goal, start checking all the footnotes and references carefully. This is where the best source material often hides.

Contract Provisions

Surprisingly, plaintiff's lawyers often overlook contract provisions. Used as Rules of the Road, they can be powerful offensive weapons.

Contracts between your client and the defendant may contain duties or standards that were breached by the defendant. *Read the contract carefully.* The contract may incorporate by reference public laws and codes that themselves contain duties or standards breached by the defendant.

Contracts with third parties may also contain provisions that help formulate Rules. This is particularly true of contracts with public entities, which you can usually find through informal discovery such as Freedom of Information requests to the contracting agency. These contracts may articulate standards and designate responsibility between entities.[10] If one of those entities is a defendant, and a standard was breached, you may have a new annotated Rule.

In the school bus stop case, for example, the bus company originally claimed the parents determined where the child should

---

10. Licensing applications and certificates of authority for insurance companies may contain an agreement to conduct all aspects of the business with high standards, which may be expressed in ways that lead to Rules of the Road.

wait for the bus. The contract between the school district and the company, however, showed the company had that responsibility. Defense witnesses had to admit this, and the court eventually ruled as a matter of law that the company had the duty to designate bus stops. This ruling supported rules 2 and 3 of our Bus Stop Safety Principles (see appendix D).

Even if contract provisions don't create an official legal duty, they likely create standards, which a party to the contract would have trouble disclaiming as unfair or inapplicable. So, be alert for all contracts in the vicinity of your case, and read them carefully.

Admissions in the Answer to the Complaint

If you have drafted proposed jury instructions and an annotated Rules list, you are now ready to draft the complaint. Draft your complaint with an eye toward gaining more support for the Rules on your list, or *adding* more Rules to your list.

Suppose in the bus stop case, for example, you have a Rule that looks like this:

> Children should be trained not to cross the arterial road until after the bus arrives and driver gives signal.

Annotations to this Rule would look like the following.

> School Bus Safety Curriculum Guide (Ex. 37, p. 2)
> National Association of State Directors of Pupil Transportation position paper on "Transporting the Nation's School Children." Says: "Stopping traffic in areas where children get on and off school buses, and are often crossing the street has proven to be beneficial in protecting students who must cross the street to reach the bus or go home. Stopping traffic creates a safer environment for young children who are not as adept as adults in negotiating their way through traffic."

Alaska School Bus Driver Training Manual: "Drivers of school buses have full responsibility for the safety of students while they are boarding the bus, on the bus, leaving the bus, and *crossing the road.*"

National Standards for School Transportation, page 276, appendix E: "Pupil shall cross the road or street in front of bus only after bus has come to a complete stop and upon direction of the driver."

One section of your complaint might look like this:

1. Defendant [school bus company] is a member of _____, which publishes "National Standards for School Transportation." The standards articulated in this publication represent "_____" [insert statement from standards explaining high goals of the standards].

2. Defendant subscribes to and attempts to follow the standards articulated in this publication.

3. On page 276 of this publication, the following is stated: "Pupil shall cross the road or street in front of bus only after bus has come to a complete stop and upon direction of the driver." This standard applied to the stop where the plaintiff's accident occurred.

Another section of the complaint might look like this:

1. Defendant requires all of its drivers to attend the Alaska School Bus Driver Training class, sponsored by the State of Alaska. It requires all drivers to pass this class before being allowed to drive its school buses with children aboard.

2. The training manual for this class provides, at page ___, that "Drivers of school buses have full responsibility for the safety of students while they

are boarding the bus, on the bus, leaving the bus, and crossing the road." Defendant's drivers are taught this principle by the State of Alaska. Defendant's drivers are taught and reminded of this principle by defendant's own instructors and publications.

Our goal is for the defendant to admit some or all of these allegations and thus give more support for our statement of the Rules.

Not every Rule of the Road should be addressed in your complaint. You may not want to alert the defendant early that you believe it has violated industry standards. You may want to ask about a principle for the first time at a deposition, or even at trial. But you should think about incorporating Rules into the complaint. It may surprise you how many Rules the defense will endorse early in the case, before they know better.

By now you should have a good start on your annotated Rules of the Road. It is time to clarify the critical distinction between a "principle" and a "Rule."

5

Why Rules and Principles Need to Be Kept Distinct

The first edition of this book failed to draw a clear distinction between "principles" and "Rules." In fact, at times, we used these terms interchangeably. This has become a source of trouble for some lawyers applying Rules techniques to their cases. In fact, it may be the single greatest source of difficulty.

To address this problem, we must first clarify our terms. A "principle" is a major truth about the defendant's activities or conduct. It does not prescribe conduct, but describes conduct that might lead to injury or some other serious trouble. For example, in a case where a miner was hurt because a railroad did not take appropriate safety precautions, the following would be principles:

> Accumulated debris that is not removed from a railcar can injure a miner working around the railcar.
>
> A partially open railcar door can cause injury to a miner working around the railcar.

A partially open railcar door could be holding back accumulated debris in the railcar.[1]

These are all true statements. They can be important starting points for questioning witnesses and formulating Rules, but notice that they are not, in themselves, Rules. They do not say what a railroad should or should not do—though that might be inferred.

"Rules" are statements that directly say what a defendant should or should not do. From the *principles* of railroad safety, certain Rules may follow:

1. A railroad should perform a safety inspection of each railcar whenever railcars are placed in a train, before the train is moved.

2. A railroad must fix any defect or potentially hazardous condition found during the safety inspection.

3. If a railroad discovers accumulated debris in a car during premovement inspection, it should remove the debris before placing the car in the train.

4. A railroad must warn anyone who may come in contact with a railcar of any uncorrected or unavoidable potential danger.

Notice you should be able to prove whether these Rules were violated. The railroad either did or did not do these things.

In some cases you may want to put your principles on a board or screen to show the jury, but that is usually not necessary. On the other hand, you always want your Rules on a board or screen. These are the things the defendant should or should not have done—their violation is what led to your client's injuries.

Let's look at another example to solidify this distinction. Suppose you have a case where the treating doctor did not have an important medical record in his chart. Your first task is to think about why medical records are important. This essential

---

[1]. These principles and Rules of railway safety appear here courtesy of Fred Harrison of Wyoming.

step of ruminating about fundamental assumptions is skipped by many lawyers. Only by ruminating about fundamental assumptions can you dig out the principled foundation of your case.

What principles can we come up with about medical records? Why are they important?

> Medical records assist the doctor in remembering facts about the patient so he can provide proper care.

These can be the patient's history as related by the patient or others, test results, or treatment given by other doctors. These facts also include the treating doctor's reasoning process, so subsequent care providers can understand what was done and why.

> Medical records assist other health-care providers treating the patient.

These can be other doctors or nurses who are contemporaneously treating the patient or people who will treat the patient in the future—even decades in the future.

From these two principles, another logically follows:

> The availability of accurate medical records is essential for patient safety.

Notice again these are not "rules." They may imply that certain actions should be taken or not taken, but they do not directly and clearly require or prohibit action. You cannot show that any of them were or were not violated. But Rules follow naturally from these principles:

1. All important medical facts, discussions, and decisions should be documented in the patient's chart by the health-care provider making the entry.

2. The doctor and his employees are responsible for keeping a complete and accurate chart.

3. The doctor should take, or review with patient, the patient's prior history.

4. If a patient refuses a prescribed test or treatment, the doctor must document the refusal in the patient's chart.

These rules were formulated in a case where the doctor was the only defendant, and he was trying to blame the hospital for lack of information in the chart.

If the case involved a claim of lost medical records, another principle could be added to the first three above: "Losing medical records creates a serious danger to the patient." The follow-up rule could be: "The hospital must keep a set of backup records," or "The hospital must have a records-retention policy," or some other specific do or don't that you claim would have prevented the loss of the records.

As you construct your annotated Rules of the Road list, put important principles at the top, and annotate them as well.

Your annotated principles are important to your own clear thinking about the case. It is because of these principles that many of your Rules exist. For that reason, they are often a good starting point for questioning defense witnesses—or your own. Who can disagree with this principle: "Accumulated debris that is not removed from a railcar can injure a miner working around that railcar," especially when everyone knows your client was in fact hurt by accumulated debris?

Why Our Cases Need Rules and Not Just Principles

The problem with principles is that they can float in the atmosphere of a case without stinging the defendant directly. When we state the principle "A miner can be hurt by accumulated debris," it's not clear whose job it is to prevent that harm. Is it the miner's? Someone else's? This introduces an ambiguity to the case, and ambiguity never helps the plaintiff. That is why it is the Rules that hurt the defendant most. Rules are squarely aimed at the defendant and leave no ambiguity about what the defendant is required to do (or refrain from doing).

For the same reason, it is also a good idea to formulate your Rules into active voice statements rather than passive voice, because in the passive, the identity of the actor who needs to take the action is obscured. For example, "medical records should not be lost" is more ambiguous than "a doctor should not lose his patient's medical records." The latter makes the better Rule.

Principle/Rule Hybrids

Some statements can serve as both principles and Rules. A good example is our first Bus Stop Safety Principle:

> Child safety is always the primary consideration in any decision concerning pupil transportation.

This can easily be a principle. Who will argue with it? It is a good aspirational statement. But it doesn't really state what specific conduct is required of the defendant. So it does not make a good Rule.[2] Or does it?

Suppose you have an internal memo from the bus company that says, in effect, "putting the stop here is less safe, but it will save us money." Now you can directly prove that the company broke the Rule that safety should be the primary consideration. Without such a memo, probably better to keep this statement in the "principle" section; with such a memo, it becomes a powerful Rule.

Using Principles

Even though not a Rule, a principle can set up nice lines of cross-examination. For example, once a school-bus executive or defense expert has acknowledged that child safety is always the primary consideration, you can go through the facts with that principle in mind.

Q: Was child safety the primary consideration when the bus stop was located across the street from the child's house?

---

2. It's also perhaps better phrased like this: "A bus company should always make child safety its primary consideration in any decision concerning pupil transportation." That at least puts the principle into solid Rule format, although it still doesn't cure the generality problem of the Rule.

Q: Was child safety the primary consideration when Shellbus discontinued its annual inspections?

Q: Was child safety the primary consideration when the drivers told the children to cross the street before the bus arrived?

Or consider an example from the context of informed consent: the doctor's duty to give the patient all the information a reasonable patient would want in order to make an informed decision about undergoing the proposed treatment.

We're not just talking about the narrow kind of informed-consent claim that many plaintiffs lawyers decline to pursue, in which the patient claims he would have refused the proposed treatment if only he had been informed of the risks. There is another kind of informed-consent claim, where the doctor withholds information about an alternative treatment that would have been safer than the one undertaken. These claims can be powerful, because they implicate basic issues of self-determination and freedom.

In just about every aspect of medical care, but especially concerning informed consent, everyone should agree:

> Doctors are trained and take an oath to always put the patient's interest ahead of their own.

This is a universally accepted principle. What if the surgeon fails to disclose his own lack of experience performing the procedure and the fact that other surgeons have better track records?

Medical journals have published reams of data proving that experience and volume go hand in hand with better outcomes in surgical procedures, yet the issue has barely hit the radar screen of the law.[3] The plaintiff's lawyer who takes a Rules of the Road approach will be able to show the following:

---

3. Besides our own case of *Goldberg v. Boone,* 396 Md. 94, 912 A.2d 698 (2006), we have found only two other appellate decisions on the issue. Both said these can be valid claims depending on the proof of how much additional risk the plaintiff was put to by the lack of disclosure of the defendant's inexperience and the alternatives. *Howard v. University of Medicine and Dentistry of New Jersey,* 172 N.J. 537, 800 2d 73 (2002); *Johnson v. Kokemoor,* 199 Wis.2d 615, 545 N.W.2d 495 (1996). The Maryland Court of Appeals in Goldberg said the issue was what would be relevant to a reasonable patient, which is ordinarily a fact issue.

1. When informing the patient about alternative ways to proceed, the doctor should always put the patient's interest first (general rule).

2. The more experience a surgeon has in performing a particular procedure, the better the chance of a good outcome (general principle proven by the medical literature).

3. The defendant surgeon had little experience with this procedure, and other surgeons were available who had significantly more experience (our facts).

4. A surgeon should tell a patient of choices he has that might lead to better outcomes (our case-specific rule).

A General Principle of Injury Prevention

One principle underlies many personal injury cases:

    _____ is dangerous unless basic safety rules are followed.

Go ahead, fill in the blank:

- Operating a swimming pool is dangerous unless basic safety rules are followed.

- Operating a tractor-trailer is dangerous unless basic safety rules are followed.

- High school football is dangerous unless basic safety rules are followed.

- Doing janitorial work at a grocery store is dangerous unless basic safety rules are followed.

- Cardiac surgery is dangerous unless basic safety rules are followed.

A defendant in the last example will be quick to point out that there are unavoidable dangers to cardiac surgery, even if basic safety rules are followed. In that case the principle can be modified slightly to: "Cardiac surgery becomes more dangerous when basic safety rules are not followed."

The principle that an activity is dangerous unless basic safety rules are followed deserves to be the starting point for all of your thinking about Rules of the Road in your case. Other principles may follow from this principle, as will basic safety rules. *But if you can't make that fundamental statement of principle, you likely have no case.*

It could be argued by the defense that there are inherent risks in any of these activities—swimming pools, tractor-trailer operation, football, and so forth—but does that really help the defense? If there are inherent risks in these activities, all the more important to follow basic safety rules. *If those rules are followed, there is no negligence; if they are not followed, defendant has needlessly—and negligently—increased the danger.*

If your case involves only harm to the plaintiff's wallet, and not to the plaintiff's bodily or mental integrity, the fundamental principle might not be cast in terms of "danger," but it's still basically the same thing. For example, in an insurance bad faith case, where the failure to pay a claim does not result in physical injury, the fundamental principle will be something like this: "When a claim is made, the insured is particularly vulnerable and dependent on his insurance company for fair and just treatment." You may be able to articulate this better, but you get the idea. It is from a principle like this that all the claims-handling rules flow.

A final thought: we believe plaintiff's attorneys need to spend a lot of time, in discovery and at trial, painting in the backdrop for their Rules, so that by the time the jury is deliberating, they not only know the reasons behind the Rules, but they become invested in the case as safety guardians for the community. Rules gain their moral force from the possibility of future harm if they are not followed.

Indeed, this is the real power of the Rules system—not merely clarifying the case, but showing the relevance of the plaintiff's case to the jurors' own lives. Plaintiff's lawyers who use the

Rules of the Road approach are putting forward—explicitly or implicitly—a simple paradigm to the jury. It goes like this:

1. We live in a dangerous world. Anyone can get hurt.

2. Rules are set up to protect against danger and reduce the risk of injury.

3. People who engage in dangerous conduct need to follow the safety rules to protect the public.

4. A defendant who (a) knows the danger in what she does, (b) knows the rules to protect against that danger, (c) but breaks those rules, (d) is a person who can hurt anybody.

5. Enforcing the rules against a rule breaker protects the entire community.

The Rules system is designed to make it easy to set up the paradigm outlined above, even if it is not spelled out exactly this way to the jury. Once you have your first tentative, working set of Rules for your case, the next step is to try out those Rules on the defendant, the defendant's employees, and the defendant's expert witnesses. You want to ask the defendant to agree with your Rules or redefine them in a way the defendant can agree to. We will talk about how to approach the defendant's witnesses after first discussing the plaintiff's experts.

6

THE PLAINTIFF'S EXPERTS

A lack of focus permeates all aspects of litigation and trial. Our three enemies—complexity, confusion, and ambiguity—scatter dust onto all participants. The dust falls heaviest on the plaintiff's lawyer, but a heavy accumulation can also be found on the expert witness. Just as it can for the plaintiff's lawyer, the Rules of the Road can wipe the dust off expert witnesses and help focus their thinking and testimony.

A good expert witness loves his subject area and loves to talk about it. The intricacies and minutiae fascinate him. He may be so familiar with the basics of his subject area that he forgets to even mention them; he takes them for granted and assumes everyone else does too.

Your first job is to have a thorough discussion with your expert on the fundamental principles of his field that apply to your case. This conversation needs to happen early in the case. The ideal time is before you file the complaint but certainly before you have started discovery.

Take the expert back to the basics of her field. Does she agree that child safety is always the primary consideration in any decision concerning pupil transportation? Show her the contract between the school district and the bus company. Show her the provision dealing with selection of bus stops. Does she agree that the bus company had the duty and responsibility to select the bus stop locations? Show her the industry publications. Does she agree with the principles you have extracted from them?

The same is true with an insurance expert. Show her the relevant state statutes and regulations. Does she agree they apply to the claim handling here? Can a regulation be stated in a simpler, more understandable way that is still acceptable to the expert?

The approach with medical experts is similar. The sources of their rules will be a little different: consensus statements of medical-specialty societies rather than codified regulations will dominate the inquiry. But the basic building blocks of the doctor/patient relationship—the duty to put the patient's interests ahead of the doctor's, for example—remain the same.

In whatever field the expert specializes, you want to ask him what basic industry or professional principles he believes are at stake in the case and which safety rules follow from those principles. Push the expert for the source (or sources) of every principle and rule, and push the expert to state the principle or rule as simply as possible. Push the expert to explain to you why violation of the rule is important. The expert's testimony will be stronger, even unshakable, if the expert's testimony is well within his comfort zone—one that is rooted in solid foundational principles and rules of conduct.

Now, explain to the expert the Rules of the Road concept. Ask her what other sources might exist for basic principles and rules—and then go look at those sources for yourself.

Remember, some of the basic principles and rules may be so ingrained in your expert's professional soul, so basic and intuitive, that they are not easily articulated. If fish could talk, they probably would still have a tough time explaining hydrodynamics. But once the principles and rules of the profession are coaxed out into the open, they can become some of your best, most unshakable Rules of the Road.

Once your expert has set out the basic principles and rules, ask her to help you refine them into Rules of the Road that meet the criteria we discussed in chapter 3, "Identifying the Rules of the Road."

A Rule of the Road should be:

1. A requirement that the defendant do, or not do, something.

2. Easy for the jury to understand.

3. A requirement the defense cannot credibly dispute.

4. A requirement the defendant has violated.

5. Important enough in the context of the case that proof of its violation will significantly increase the chance of a plaintiff's verdict.

Chances are the expert's list will lack some principles or Rules you believe are important. Don't be afraid to discuss that. The expert may well have simply overlooked them. Explain why you believe them important. Explain that at this stage it is better to be overinclusive, because it's easier to later subtract principles or Rules from an expert's list of opinions than to add new ones.

Conversely, there is a good chance that the expert's list will contain some principles or Rules you believe lack importance. If this is because the expert misunderstands a fact or a principle, clarify the issue. If she just has some ideas you don't consider central to your case, don't worry about it; at this stage, you want to be overinclusive. But if your expert's list is overstuffed with so many "basic principles" or "Rules" that it appears the expert has missed the whole point of this exercise, start over with the expert or get a new one.

In jurisdictions where an expert must write a disclosure report, you will want all of the basic principles and Rules stated in the report. The two of you can decide whether these should be presented as a list at this time. The important point is that they be stated in some form that can be used at trial.

We want to emphasize that you are not asking the expert to endorse anything she does not believe. You are trying to get her to focus on articulating the principles most material to the case.

Working with an expert to do that is completely proper and, we believe, essential.

The expert's testimony will be discussed in chapter 17, "Direct Examination of Your Expert." For now, just know that you will use expert testimony to present and explain eight to twelve (sometimes fewer) of your most important Rules to the jury. If you have other experts in the same or similar fields, they need not testify to these Rules in detail. Still, when your Rules expert has completed the list, you should run the list by your other experts to make sure no one disagrees. If anyone does, you must resolve that disagreement.

It's almost time to start discovery. But first, we need to address the specter that haunts many plaintiff's cases: the *Daubert* motion that seeks to kill your case by knocking out your critical experts.

7

THE *DAUBERT*-PROOFED EXPERT

We can't leave the topic of hiring and working with your experts without addressing *Daubert*[1] motions, because that's when you need to be thinking about them: right from the start of the case. We believe some simple rules that fit with our Rules of the Road theme can go a long way toward *Daubert*-proofing your experts.

Do *not* skip this chapter if your state hasn't yet adopted *Daubert*. Courts all over the country are giving more and more critical scrutiny to experts, even if they have not explicitly adopted a *Daubert*-style gatekeeping standard.

Ironically, *Daubert* motions are the one area of trial practice in which the defense has adopted a Rules of the Road approach, and with great success. When they attack your expert as a junk scientist or junk engineer, all they are really claiming is that the expert doesn't measure up to the rules of the profession for analyzing data and coming up with opinions. If we show that, no, the expert *is* following professional rules in the development of

---

1. *Daubert v. Merrell Dow Pharmaceuticals Inc.*, 509 U.S. 579 (1993).

her opinions, the *Daubert* motion will be defeated. That requires focusing on the expert Rules early in the case.

As now codified in Fed. R. Evid. 702, the *Daubert* standard requires trial courts to allow opinion testimony from a qualified expert only if three requirements are met (in addition to the expert's qualifications):

- First, the testimony must be "based upon sufficient facts or data."

- Second, it must be "the product of reliable principles and methods."

- Third, the witness must have "applied the principles and methods reliably to the facts of the case."

Many gallons of ink have been spilled by legal writers trying to puzzle through what "reliable" and "sufficient" mean for expert testimony. Some states still use the *Frye* test of admissibility: that the expert's methodology must be "generally accepted" in his or her field to be admissible.[2] Whatever the standard, the ideas in this chapter will help to shore up your own experts' admissibility and attack adverse experts.

RULE 1: FIND A METHODOLOGY APPROPRIATE FOR THE EXPERT'S FIELD, AND MAKE SURE THE EXPERT FOLLOWS IT

Here is the key language from the last of the Supreme Court's three *Daubert* cases, *Kumho Tire Co., Ltd. v. Carmichael*, 526 U.S. 137 (1999). Justice Breyer crystallized what *Daubert* is all about: the purpose of a trial court's gatekeeping, he wrote, "is to make certain that an expert employs in the courtroom the same level of intellectual rigor that characterizes the practice of an expert in the relevant field."

---

2. *Frye v. United States*, 293 F. 1013 (D.C. Cir. 1923).

If your expert is an engineer analyzing why a piece of machinery collapsed, you need to know the rudiments of the science of failure analysis, and your expert needs to conform her work to these basic methods.

If your expert is a physician, he must know and apply differential diagnosis to determine what caused the plaintiff's injury. If the expert has failed to exclude some reasonably possible cause of injury, the differential diagnosis is incomplete, and many courts will exclude the expert.

If your expert is a pharmacologist analyzing whether a drug is capable of causing a certain class of injuries (in *Daubert* jargon, "general causation"), he needs to employ the methods of medical evidence synthesis, which draws from the fields of epidemiology, toxicology, and other medical disciplines.

In short, every expert must have a methodology. That methodology must have a lineage traceable to some nonlitigation techniques used by experts in that field. The methodology will have been published somewhere, although not necessarily in one place. (Nonscientists are frequently chagrined at how the basic methods of a scientific discipline are assumed much more than spelled out by those working in the field.)

The Federal Judicial Center's *Reference Manual on Scientific Evidence* (2d ed. 2000) is a good place to start in looking for methodologies. See, for example, the summary on p. 469 of the types of evidence to be considered in a general causation study.

Sometimes your best evidence of a scientifically accepted methodology is an example that's similar to your case. The Food and Drug Administration published a lengthy justification in the Federal Register for why it banned the herb ephedra from dietary-supplement products. Its analysis wove together the basic pharmacology of the active ingredient of the herb, the adverse-event reports the agency had received, and the peer-reviewed literature.[3]

---

3. FOOD AND DRUG ADMINISTRATION, *Final Rule Declaring Dietary Supplements Containing Ephedrine Alkaloids Adulterated Because They Present an Unreasonable Risk*, 69 FED. REG. 6787 (2004).

A similar approach should stand up in court when an expert analyzes any drug's dangerous propensities.

Of course, the experts in some fields do not rely upon a scientific methodology. The cases recognize this. For example:

> Concerning the reliability of nonscientific testimony such as Caliri's [the insurance expert], the *Daubert* factors (peer review, publication, potential error rate, etc.) simply are not applicable to this kind of testimony, whose reliability depends heavily on the *knowledge and experience* of the expert, rather than the methodology or theory behind it."[4]

What then? First, you emphasize the knowledge and experience of your expert. The court has broad discretion to find the testimony is reliable (thereby satisfying *Daubert*) based upon this knowledge and experience. Second, you use the Rules approach to come up with a set of Rules for how experts in this field approach their jobs and reach opinions. Having an established set of Rules of the Road can be a big help here.

If all experts agree that the claim file should contain documentation of every major action on the claim, and state regulations say the same thing, the question becomes one of the expert's experience. Does he have knowledge and experience in evaluating claim files and ensuring that they document all major action on the claim?

Similarly, if you are handling an accounting malpractice case, you would start with Generally Accepted Accounting Principles (GAAP) and other sources for your Rules of the Road. Then, the question becomes, what experience does your expert have in applying these Rules in situations similar to that presented in your case.

---

4. *Hangarter v. Provident Life and Acc. Ins. Co.*, 373 F.3d 998, 1017 (9th Cir. 2004)(emphasis in original) citing *U.S. v. Hankey*, 203 F.3d 1160, 1168 (9th Cir. 2000), cert. denied, 503 U.S. 1268, 120 S.Ct. 2733 (2000).

In short, for the nonscientific expert, the Rules of the Road you draft for liability purposes will take you a long way in withstanding a *Daubert* challenge.

RULE 2: FIND LITERATURE SUPPORT FOR THE EXPERT'S THEORY

Good literature is the holy grail of *Daubert/Frye* motions. Textbooks, pamphlets, journal articles, online publications—anything that was not written for litigation—can be absolute gold in defeating a *Daubert/Frye* motion. Plaintiff's lawyers make three big mistakes with professional literature:

- First, they turn over the job of finding good literature to the expert.

- Second, they give up too soon on the search for supporting literature, assuming that nothing out there could be relevant to the unique circumstances of their case.

- Third—and this is a modern affliction—they limit their searches to whatever is available on Google or another search engine in a quick online search.

Literature searches should never be delegated to a testifying expert. They are too busy and their hourly rates are too high. The plaintiff's lawyer, or a trusted designee, must do the heavy lifting. That means an actual trip to a real library to find all the relevant textbooks that do not appear in any online format. That means repeated and layered searches. Sometimes the best nuggets appear in an article that was found only because it was referenced in a footnote in another article.

You may not find direct support for your expert's case-specific opinion. However, you should always be able to locate some literature supporting the expert's methods used in reaching her opinion.

Some lawyers believe that feeding literature to your expert can taint the expert. We say, better a small taint than a useless expert. Most experts worthy of the name are familiar with the key literature, but their ability to put their hands on it and cite it is usually lacking. Plus, there is a vast body of "secondary literature," the treatises and review articles that are published every year summarizing the findings of the primary literature, concerning which no expert is likely to have a complete catalog. Support for your expert's opinions in any kind of literature—primary or secondary—can be critical to the admissibility of that expert's opinion. So be assertive about doing these literature searches. As for the "taint" issue, your expert can help minimize or eliminate any problem by directing you where to focus your literature search on behalf of the expert. Then, whatever you find can be honestly said to be a part of the expert's work on the case. *Caution:* don't be sneaky and try to maneuver your expert into saying that she personally found a key article that you actually found for her. If the expert has delegated literature searching to you and your assistant, let the expert say so honestly.

Rule 3: Make the Expert Read the Relevant Literature

Once you have identified literature that you believe supports one or more Rules of the Road for your case, you must make sure your expert reads and endorses the literature before being deposed. If you let the expert go on record as not being able to identify supporting literature, you face an awkward, and potentially fatal, problem if you try to cure that after the deposition transcript has been locked up.

The *Daubert/Frye* landscape is littered with the bodies of experts who tried to wing it by vague references to a body of literature that they had read sometime in the distant past but could no longer cite with precision. This vagueness, at a minimum, makes the expert look bad in front of the jury, but it also exposes the expert to a motion to strike his or her testimony.

Rule 4: Go to the Top in Your Search for Experts

We live in an era where professionals sub-sub-subspecialize. Take advantage of this. When you can make the other side concede that your expert is preeminent in the field, *Daubert* motions tend to lose steam.[5]

Rule 5: Avoid Experts Who Won't Explain the Basis for Their Opinions

Some experts, especially those with long experience testifying, are used to bluffing their way through challenges to their opinions. They invoke their many years of practice in their profession—and little else—in support of their opinions. Avoid such experts at all costs. They are a *Daubert* disaster waiting to happen.

Rule 6: Enlist Help from the Other Side's Experts

At deposition, you should explore to what extent the defense experts will concede key points where you might have *Daubert/Frye* exposure. That will go a long way toward neutralizing a *Daubert* attack. Even a concession that reasonable experts can differ over a point is valuable, because the *Daubert/Frye* doctrine is all about eliminating only those opinions that are so far out that reasonable people don't entertain them.

One focus with defense experts is to obtain their agreement that the methodology used by the plaintiff's expert is sound, and that their quarrel with the plaintiff goes only to certain particulars

---

5. As the Second Circuit observed in a lead paint case: "Although stating that 'it is undisputed that Dr. Rosen is one of the preeminent experts in his field' and has 'vast credentials,' [the defendant] 'suggests that the theory advanced by Dr. Rosen in order to prove the plaintiffs' case is not adequately based on prevailing methods of assessing lead poisoning.' We disagree." *Campbell v. Metropolitan Prop. & Cas. Ins. Co.*, 239 F.3d 179, 184 (2d Cir. 2001).

of the analysis. Most true experts in a field should be able to settle on an agreed methodology to approach a problem, even if they disagree about the conclusions reached from that methodology. Remember, a defensible methodology is a core concern of *Daubert*.

RULE 7: ATTACK THE OTHER SIDE'S EXPERTS

This is not a contradiction of rule 6. Even if you obtain some concessions from the defense experts, consider attacking their opinions to level the playing field. There are good reasons and bad reasons for holding back on filing your own *Daubert/Frye* motion attacking the defense experts. If you contend that any weaknesses in your expert's opinion are up to the fact finder to resolve, then you can hardly take a different position about the other side's experts. *However*, it's a big mistake to allow your own experts to become the sole focus of a *Daubert/Frye* battle. If you do that, you have made a potentially huge psychological concession. The defense experts become enthroned as authorities—just by the sheer lack of attack from your side—and the whole issue for the court becomes whether the plaintiff's experts are courtworthy.

You don't have to file your own *Daubert* motion to even the playing field. It can be enough to file affidavits and spend time in your opposition brief showing the deficiencies in the defense theories. Then the judge can see that the case revolves around a true "battle of experts" with pluses and minuses on both sides that the jury will have to sort out. Bottom line: don't give defense experts a free pass in the *Daubert/Frye* wars.

Once you've focused on the *Daubert* issues in your case both defensively and offensively, you're in good shape to take discovery.

8

Discovery

Now you are on the hunt. As far as the Rules are concerned, you are looking for four things:

1. New Rules to add to your annotated list
2. Support for Rules you have already drafted
3. Clear agreement or disagreement from defense witnesses regarding your Rules
4. Violations of any Rules

Also keep alert for new foundational principles—and support for them—but this is secondary to your Rules hunt.

Requests for Production of Documents

Just as in any case, you want to ask for all the policy and procedure manuals, training manuals, personnel policies, and other internal company documents that describe how the company conducts its activities—or says it does. Also ask for any contracts you think might be in existence and might possibly contain helpful standards applicable to your case.

When you're writing a request for documents, use the plainest English you can. Remember that ultimately the defense lawyer is going to turn over your request to one or more nonlawyer employees of the defendant to gather responsive documents. If the nonlawyers find it hard to wade through masses of legalese to figure out what you're asking for, you're less likely to find the good stuff in their files. Plain English means more than plain words. It also means keeping each numbered document request to a single topic. Remember, someone is going to be checking off each item. Each of your important topics deserves its own paragraph.

In a case against an individual defendant for professional malpractice, you will want to see the defendant's library of documents and books that he or she trained with or uses for references. Be prepared for various excuses resisting this production. Strategies we like to use to overcome resistance include:

1. Notice if the defendant's deposition is to be held at her own office, and if the deposition is conducted in a conference room, ask to see the defendant's personal office. Read into the record a list of the texts you see on the shelves, and ask the defendant about them. (Typically a defendant will claim she hasn't used the text in years, that it's out of date, and so on.) You will of course want to look up those texts in a library after the deposition. What better cross-examination and closing argument material can you get than to be able to say, "Ladies and gentlemen, the answer was right on her own shelf in a book that she just hadn't bothered to read in years"?

2. If you cannot do the inspection at the time of the deposition, or if the defendant tells you that he also keeps treatises in a home office or some other location, send an interrogatory after the deposition asking the defendant to list all such materials.

3. File a motion if necessary to get this material. Any Rules of the Road that you find in the actual possession of the defendant are pure gold for your case.

Whatever material you get from Requests for Production, don't let it sit on a shelf in your office. You know what you are looking for: principles or standards that may have been violated in your case. When you find them, add them to your annotated Rules list.

Interrogatories and Requests for Admission

Your interrogatories must be very specific and factual to have any hope of turning up useful support for Rules of the Road. Defense lawyers are never going to volunteer chapter and verse on the Rules of the Road in an interrogatory answer. It's not in their nature. So about all you can hope for by way of interrogatory answers is a list of specific documents that might be sources of Rules—texts and treatises kept on shelves or stored in computers, for example. (One other important use of interrogatories is described in chapter 18, "Cross-Examination," to block the defense from surprising you at trial with its own "reliable authority" literature, which it did not identify in discovery.)

Requests for Admission can be quite useful in gaining support for Rules of the Road. A good set of requests for admission is like a good leading cross-examination. You control the words; the witness must simply admit or deny.

Here is an example to get your creative juices flowing:

1. Please admit that when it adjusts claims originating from the State of Alaska, Acme Insurance Company is required to comply with all applicable provisions of A.S. 21.36.125 [Alaska's Unfair Claims Practices Act].

2. Please admit that Acme Insurance Company trains its claims handlers to comply with the provisions of A.S. 21.36.125 when adjusting claims in Alaska.

3. Please admit that Acme Insurance Company does *not* train its claims handlers to comply with the

provisions of A.S. 21.36.125 when adjusting claims in Alaska.[1]

4. Please admit that it is standard in the insurance industry for claims departments to adjust claims in a manner that does not violate the substantive provisions of A.S. 21.36.125.

Or how about this, for the bus stop case:

1. Please admit that Exhibit 3 to these requests, Bates numbered pages 0557–0590, is a true and correct copy of the contract between the School District and Shellbus Bus Company, in force at the time the accident occurred.

2. Please admit that section VII(A) at Bates numbered pages 572 and 573 states in part: "Thirty days before the start of each school year, the Company shall notify the District of the areas it has selected as student waiting areas."

3. Please admit that according to the contract between the School District and Shellbus Bus Company, in force at the time of the accident, Shellbus Bus Company had the duty and responsibility to select safe waiting areas for students to wait for the school bus.

Depositions

You will depose three types of witnesses: 30(b)(6) witnesses (corporate designees), lay witnesses, and expert witnesses. Because your approach will be similar with all three types, we will discuss each type briefly and then move on to deposition strategy and technique.

---

1. An admission of not training is an admission of violating the standards that require training.

Corporate Spokespersons: 30(b)(6) Witnesses

One of the most underutilized tools at the plaintiff's lawyer's disposal is the 30(b)(6) deposition. Under Federal Civil Rule 30(b)(6), and the civil rules in most states, you may require a corporation to designate a witness to testify for the corporation on a particular topic.[2] What the witness says about that topic binds the corporate defendant.[3] The witness may be required to testify not only to facts, but also to subjective beliefs and opinions.[4] The courts have held that a corporation has a duty (through its designated witness or otherwise) to research and investigate the corporate knowledge about the designated topic before the depo-

---

2. Federal Rule of Civil Procedure 30(b)(6) provides: "A party may in the party's notice and in a subpoena name as the deponent a public or private corporation or a partnership or association or governmental agency and describe with reasonable particularity the matters on which examination is requested. In that event, the organization so named shall designate one or more officers, directors, or managing agents, or other persons who consent to testify on its behalf, and may set forth, for each person designated, the matters on which the person will testify. A subpoena shall advise a non-party organization of its duty to make such a designation. The persons so designated shall testify as to matters known or reasonably available to the organization. This subdivision (b)(6) does not preclude taking a deposition by any other procedure authorized in these rules."
3. *Rainey v. American Forest & Paper Ass'n*, 26 F.Supp.2d 82 at 94 (D.D.C. 1998) ("not permitting a corporation to proffer new or different interpretations or allegations by affidavit testimony 'unless it can prove that the information was not known or was inaccessible' at the time of the 30(b)(6) deposition."); *See, A&E Prods. Group, L.P. v. Mainetti USA, Inc.*, 2004 U.S. Dist. LEXIS 2904 (S.D.N.Y. 2004) (collecting cases and discussing varying views on the effect of admissions of 30(b)(6) deponent).
4. *Lapenna v. Upjohn Co.*, 110 F.R.D. 15, 20 (E.D. P 1986); *see also Alexander v. FBI*, 186 F.R.D. 148, 151 (D.D.C. 1999).

sition is conducted and testify to all matters "known or reasonably available to the organization."⁵

The opportunities when using the Rules of the Road approach should be obvious. Any Rule you get this witness to endorse is established as a standard for the rest of the litigation.

When noticing your 30(b)(6) depositions, be as specific and narrow as possible. For example:

> Pursuant to Federal Rule of Civil Procedure 30(b)(6), plaintiff requests that you designate and make available for deposition at the below stated time and place, a person or persons to testify on behalf of Acme Corporation about:
>
> a. The reason or reasons plaintiff's claim was denied on February 23, 2005.
>
> b. The standards to which Acme claims handlers are expected to adhere in handling claims.
>
> c. Written materials Acme provides to its claims handlers to assist them in handling claims.
>
> d. What material is ordinarily contained in the personnel files of claims handlers.
>
> e. Any efforts Acme makes to ensure that its claims handlers comply with Alaska's Unfair Claims Practices Act, when handling claims originating in Alaska.

---

5. *Alexander v. FBI*, 186 F.R.D. 148, 152 (D.D.C. 1999); *Mitsui & Co. v. Puerto Rico Water Res. Auth.*, 93 F.R.D. 62, 67 (D.P.R. 1981); *The Paul Revere Life Insurance Company v. Jafari*, 206 F.R.D. 126 (D. Maryland 2002); *Canal Barge Co. v. Commonwealth Edison Co.*, 2001 U.S. Dist. LEXIS 10097 at * 8 (N.D. Ill. 2001) ("The Court agrees that if none of defendant's current employees has sufficient knowledge to provide plaintiffs with the requested information, defendant is obligated to 'prepare [one or more witnesses] so that they may give complete, knowledgeable and binding answers on behalf of the corporation.'")

In a product liability case, your 30(b)(6) notice may look like this (some items have been eliminated):

> PLEASE TAKE NOTICE that, pursuant to Superior Court Rules of Civil Procedure 26 and 30(b)(6), plaintiffs, through counsel, will take the deposition of defendant Wyeth on November 26, 2002 at 10:00 a.m. in the offices of plaintiff's counsel at [address].
>
> Defendant Wyeth is advised that it must designate one or more persons to testify on its behalf regarding the following matters:
>
> 1. The name, current and former, of any entity involved in the research, development, testing, marketing, sales, and promotion of the pharmaceutical product Prempro since 1995.
>
> 3. The defendant's document destruction and retention policies with respect to any documents requested in the first request for production of documents.
>
> 6. All protocols, guidelines, rules, regulations, standards, policies and practices at Wyeth regarding the research, development, testing, marketing, sales, and promotion of the pharmaceutical product Prempro since 1995.
>
> 7. All persons, organizations, and entities involved in the research, development, testing, marketing, sales, and promotion of the pharmaceutical product Prempro since 1995.
>
> 8. All efforts by Wyeth since 1990 to study the relationship between combination estrogen-progesterone hormone replacement drugs including but not limited to Prempro and thromboembolic disease, cerebral vascular accident, stroke risk, and intravascular coagulation.

You get the idea. None of the examples in this book are meant to be exhaustive. They are intended to illustrate concepts. The 30(b)(6) deposition is your chance to put your "wish list" together and get straight, binding answers to your questions. Use it. And use it often. The rule has no limit on the number of topics you can designate, the number of spokespersons you can force the defendant to produce, or the number of times you can require a 30(b)(6) deposition in one case.

When you start using this device more often, you will quickly learn that defense attorneys hate 30(b)(6) depositions. For all the reasons you hate having your client deposed, they hate it when a 30(b)(6) deposition occurs. Their side is bound by the answers, and a bad answer can really mess up their case. Courts, on the other hand, recognize these depositions as an efficient way to get to the heart of litigated issues. The case law is clearly aimed at promoting the efficacy of this rule.

Corporate health-care defendants (hospitals, HMOs, and the like) particularly dislike 30(b)(6) deposition questions that ask for the corporation's knowledge of the basic facts that happened to cause the plaintiff's injury. Because the rule requires them to divulge not only the knowledge they have, but what is "reasonably available" to them, you can force the defendant to investigate the case for you and turn up witnesses you might not otherwise have discovered. Hospitals and other health-care corporations much prefer the posture that only the individuals involved in the care know what happened. But if those individuals are employees (or even former employees) of the corporation, and if they have knowledge readily available to the corporation, you can insist that the corporation find out what they know and tell you.

The Know-Nothing 30(b)(6) Witness

Sometimes, defense attorneys think it is cute to produce a 30(b)(6) witness who knows little or nothing about the designated topic. You have several tactics to meet this.

First, you can ask questions to determine what the witness did to inform himself on the topic. When you establish a record that the witness did little or nothing—and *knows* little or nothing—you can file a motion asking (1) for sanctions,[6] (2) that a new witness be provided and be required to be knowledgeable, and/or (3) that the issue upon which the witness was designated be determined adverse to the defendant.[7]

You also should ask the "know-nothing" 30(b)(6) witness who among the defendant's staff *does* have the information and how simple it would be to find that person. You can often thoroughly map the various divisions and personnel that deal with the subject area, which will make future discovery easier.

Proving a Negative with a Know-Nothing Witness

Motions for sanctions can work just fine with the know-nothing spokesperson. But sometimes we file motions in the heat of the moment out of anger with an obstreperous opposing counsel. Since revenge is a dish best served cold, we may want to consider another approach. Let's use some of the examples designated above in our 30(b)(6) notice to illustrate.

> The reason or reasons plaintiff's claim was denied on February 23, 2005.

Q: You are the person designated to testify on behalf of Acme Corporation with regard to why plaintiff's claim was denied?

A: I guess so.

Q: Well, didn't we go over that at the beginning of your deposition; you *are* the person designated by Acme to respond to

---

6. See *Black Horse Lane Assoc. v. Dow Chem. Corp.* 228 F.3d 275, 303 (3d Cir. 2000); *Resolution Trust Corp. v. S. Union Co.,* 985 F.2d 196, 197 (5th Cir. 1993); *United States v. Taylor,* 166 F.R.D. 356, 363 (M.D.N.C. 1996); *Marker v. Union Fidelity Life Ins. Co.,* 125 F.R.D. 121, 126 (M.D.N.C. 1989).
7. *Groat v. Equity Am. Ins. Co.,* 884 P.2d 228 (Ariz. App. 1994) (court properly imposed sanction of striking answer; 30(b)(6) deponent had no knowledge of subject areas).

the deposition notice we have marked as Exhibit 1, aren't you?[8]

A: Yes.

Q: And if I understood what you have said over the last few minutes, you have some ideas as to why the claim might have been denied, but you don't really know for sure; is that a fair summary?

A: Yes.

Think of the implication here. The witness designated to speak for Acme on this topic doesn't know why the claim was denied. *That means Acme doesn't know why the claim was denied.* When the inevitable summary judgment motion comes, arguing that the defendant acted in good faith, you have a ready response: how can the defendant establish no genuine issue of material fact about its good faith when it can't even establish why the claim was denied?

> The standards to which Acme claims handlers are expected to adhere in handling claims.

Q: You have been designated to testify on behalf of Acme as to the standards Acme claims handlers are expected to adhere to?

A: Yes.

Q: And what are those standards?

A: We have on-the-job training by experienced claims representatives.

Q: And what standards are communicated by the experienced claims representatives?

---

8. Note the technique. It's a good idea to mark the deposition notice with its list of topics as an exhibit at the beginning of the deposition, and then confirm that the witness knows that he or she was called in to testify about each item and is prepared to do so.

A: Good claims practices. How to document the file. How to read the policy.

Q: What are the standards for documenting the file?

A: Just document what you do.

Q: What are the standards for reading the policy?

A: Depends on the policy.

Q: Well, let me ask you this: Are you aware of any written standards for the handling of claims that Acme communicates or makes available to its claims handlers?

A: No.

Q: Are you aware of any uniform standards for the handling of claims that Acme communicates to its claims handlers, either orally or in writing?

A: What do you mean by uniform?

Q: Standards that all claims handlers are expected to follow.

A: No.

So Acme knows of no uniform standards, written or otherwise, that Acme has for the handling of claims. The law in most states *requires* a company to have such standards.[9] Now that you have the admission from the person designated to speak for Acme that the company has no written standards, you can formulate a Rule of the Road, based on this state law requirement:

> An insurance company must adopt and communicate to its claims handlers written standards for the handling of claims.

Later, you can ask this witness, or another witness, if she believes Acme is required to follow the state insurance regulations.

---

9. *E.g.*, 10 CAL. CODE OF REGULATIONS § 2695.6(a) ("Every insurer shall adopt and communicate to all its claims agents *written standards* for the prompt investigation and processing of claims.") (emphasis added)

You can ask if the standard in the industry is to comply with these regulations in handling claims. In short, you now have a provable standard (the regulations) and a binding admission that it was violated (from your know-nothing 30(b)(6) witness).

The point here is that with a 30(b)(6) witness, you can often prove a negative. That is, there are no standards or there is no known reason for denial of the claim. That negative can often be powerfully useful. So, if you get a negative admission, don't be too quick to run to court asking for help. The negative admission may be just what you want.

Expert and Lay Witnesses

Defense expert witnesses frequently suffer from the same lack of focus as plaintiff experts. Even when focused and precise, they do not want to discuss the principles and standards that support your case. The Rules of the Road can work well in eliciting favorable testimony from defense experts.

Many of the lay witnesses you depose will have expertise relevant to Rules of the Road, even if they are not designated as experts under the Civil Rules. Someone who has been a claims handler or a bus driver for the defendant has expertise in the industry standards and the defendant's own standards and practices. They may also shed light on whether the standards were violated in your case. Accordingly, in many respects, your questioning of these witnesses will be similar to your questioning of 30(b)(6) and expert witnesses.

Planning and Conducting the Deposition

Let the games begin! Your depositions will deal with other topics besides the Rules. But with respect to the Rules of the Road, you want to explore the following four areas:

1. Finding new sources of standards, both in-house and outside the defendant organization.

2. Securing the witness's agreement or disagreement to your existing annotated Rules.

3. Seeing if together you can't come up with some new Rules.

4. Finding out whether any Rules were violated.

We will consider them in this order. But first, an important point: you will almost always want to go over the Rules of the Road with the witness before talking about the facts of the case. You will have an easier time getting endorsement for your Rules when talking about the basic principles of the industry than when you get to the specifics of the case. And once you have those principles nailed down, the witness has less wiggle room when talking about the facts of the case and defending the company's conduct.

Area 1: Find New Sources of Standards

The first area to explore is finding new sources of standards, both in-house and outside the defense organization. You know how to do this already. But let's review the touchstone questions:

- What books, articles, and documents does the witness refer to in the course of her work?[10]

- Does her employer have standards, policies, and/or guidelines?

- What organizations does she belong to? Does the organization have standards, guidelines, or ethical codes? Periodicals?

- Who are the leading authors in the field?

- What are the leading texts in the field?

- What texts did she train with?

- What texts does she regard as authoritative? If not authoritative, reliable?

---

10. Consider giving the defendant detailed interrogatories and requests for documents that force production of Rules of the Road material from their employees and experts. Samples of these interrogatories and document requests appear in appendix H, "Discovery Requests."

- Are there any ethical codes or rules of conduct applicable to the field or subject?

The "There Is Nothing Authoritative" Answer

Often, defense witnesses are coached to say there are no standards, there are no leading texts in the field, there is nothing authoritative. This frustrates beginning lawyers. Our advice is to simply change your approach:

Q: You are here as an expert in _____?

Q: You can't identify the leading authors in the field?

Q: You can't identify the leading texts in the field?

Q: You can't identify a single text in the field you would regard as reliable?

Q: Do you even own any books in the field? Why do you own them if they are not reliable?

Q: In the course of doing your job, do you ever have to look any information up? Where do you go to look it up?

Q: Do you subscribe to any journals in your field? Why do you subscribe if they are not reliable?

Q: When you say "nothing is authoritative," does that mean that anyone's opinion in this field is as good as anyone else's? Does that mean there's nothing that experts in your field agree on? How exactly are you using the word "authoritative"? *[The witness usually has an extreme definition, that to be authoritative, something must be perfect, infallible, and not subject to any disagreement.]*

Most witnesses get uncomfortable with this line of questioning very quickly and will begin to provide substantive answers. If not, you have laid a nice foundation for a good section of cross at trial, or perhaps a motion to exclude the witness entirely.

In dealing with reluctant adverse experts, it helps to keep your eye on the ball. Remember your ultimate goal: to prove Rules of the Road at trial that the defense must concede or look foolish in not conceding.

Once a witness has identified new sources of Rules, be sure to read through them. We are looking for additional Rules, or additional support for existing Rules. Make sure to note on your annotated list each time the witness endorses a source. It might look something like the following.

> The bus company should locate a child's designated waiting area on the same side of the arterial road as the child's home, unless it would be unsafe to do so.
>
> Annotation: Alaska School Bus Driver's Manual, p. 10. Defense expert John Smith says this is a good "teaching" tool. (Dep. p. 64)

Then, when you depose the next defense witness, you can ask:

Q: John Smith has testified that the Alaska School Bus Driver's Manual is a good "teaching tool"; do you agree?

Q: At page 10 of the manual, it states: "_____." Do you agree?

Area 2: Secure Agreement or Disagreement

The second area to explore is securing agreement or disagreement with your existing annotated Rules.

By now you should have an annotated list that looks something like appendix A, "Annotated Rules of the Road: A Master List," or appendix D, "Bus Stop Safety Principles Annotated." You want the defense witness to agree with the statements on that list—or to lose credibility by disagreeing. You have two basic approaches to accomplish these goals. First, you can simply ask the witness if she agrees with the Rule. Alternatively, you can ask the witness about the source of the statement first.

Example 1

Q: Would you agree that part of the claim examiner's job is to assist the policyholder with the claim?

Example 2

Q: Are you familiar with the NAIC[11] model regulations?

A: Somewhat. I don't have them memorized.

Q: Let me hand you a copy of Model Regulation Section 6D. It reads: "Every insurer, upon receiving notification of a claim, shall promptly provide necessary claim forms, instructions and reasonable assistance so that first-party claimants can comply with the policy conditions and the insurer's reasonable requirements." Would you agree that this is a recognized standard in the insurance industry?

A: It depends what you mean by "recognized standard." These model regulations have not been adopted everywhere.

Q: Would you agree that it is generally recognized in the insurance industry that insurance companies should provide "reasonable assistance" to their first-party claimants?

A: Yes, of course.

Q: That's part of every claims handler's job, isn't it?

A: Yes.

There is no right or wrong answer to this tactical choice. Every witness is different, and every plaintiff's lawyer is different. There are innumerable combinations and variations on these approaches as well. Here is an approach that often works well:

When you reach the point in the deposition where it is time to talk about the Rules, begin with the two or three Rules you believe are the least controversial and supported by the most authority. Don't start with the Rule, but with the authority, just

---

11. NAIC stands for the National Association of Insurance Commissioners.

like in example 2 above. By talking with the witness about the source or authority, you are showing the witness (1) you are familiar with the sources and authorities in his field, and (2) if he disagrees with you, he will be disagreeing with the sources and authorities. Remember, the goal is to get him to endorse the rule, not necessarily the source.

After securing agreement to a few of the Rules by walking him through the sources, you might try a shortcut or two. He knows you have done your homework. He knows you can make him look foolish if he fights. You might continue the questioning from example 2 like this:

Q: That is because assistance is one of the things an insurance company sells, isn't it? Assistance with the claim?

A: Yes.

Q: Most people need assistance because the business of insurance is highly specialized, isn't it?

A: Depends on what you mean by "specialized."

Q: What I mean is that the average policyholder knows a lot less about how the claim process works than an insurance company or a claims handler?

A: Yes, that's usually right.

Q: And the process can be quite hard for the average person to understand, unless the insurance company explains it to the policyholder?

A: True.

Q: So the average policyholder is dependent on the insurance company to treat him fairly and assist him in the process.

A: True.

Q: And that's understood within the insurance industry, isn't it?

A: It should be.

Q: And insurance companies know that they should treat the insured's interests with equal regard as to their own interests?[12]

A: That's generally understood.

Q: This is not supposed to be an adversarial process, where the insurance company plays "hardball" with the claimant?

A: No, it's not.

We now have support for three of our Rules:

1. Business of insurance is highly specialized, with policyholders particularly vulnerable and dependent on their insurance company.

2. The company must treat its policyholder's interests with equal regard as it does its own interests. This is not an adversarial process.

3. Part of the claim examiner's job is to assist the policyholder with the claim.

Is it always this easy? No. Sometimes it is even easier, sometimes much harder. But you are fighting on your preselected high ground. If you can't come out ahead, your case may have a serious flaw. Or your lawyering may need more work.

Polarizing the Combative Witness

What if the witness really wants to fight? Then try a technique we call "polarizing" the witness.[13] Let's use our example again, with different answers leading to different questions.

Example 3

Q: Are you familiar with the NAIC model regulations?

---

12. This principle is so prevalent in the case law that just about all insurance people will readily acknowledge it. It is a good principle to use to remind the witness you have a basis for your questions, without showing him the source.
13. For more information about the polarizing technique, see POLARIZING THE CASE by Rick Friedman (Trial Guides 2007).

A: Somewhat. I don't have them memorized.

Q: Let me hand you a copy of Model Regulation Section 6D. It reads: "Every insurer, upon receiving notification of a claim, shall promptly provide necessary claim forms, instructions and reasonable assistance so that first-party claimants can comply with the policy conditions and the insurer's reasonable requirements." Would you agree that this is a recognized standard in the insurance industry?

A: It depends what you mean by "recognized standard." These model regulations have not been adopted everywhere.

Q: Would you agree that it is generally recognized in the insurance industry that insurance companies should provide "reasonable assistance" to their first-party claimants?

A: No, not really.

Q: That's part of every claims handler's job, isn't it?

A: No, not necessarily.

Q: Do you think claims handlers have any responsibility for assisting the policyholder with the claim?

A: In what way?

Q: In any way?

A: No.

This witness has staked out an unreasonable position. You may want to leave it as is, for further exploration at trial. Or you may want to push him with questions like these:

Q: Claims handlers don't have a responsibility to assist the policyholder with the claim by providing claim forms?

Q: By responding to requests for information?

Q: By informing the policyholder of the status of the claim?

You get the idea. If the witness responds to these questions by saying there *is* a responsibility to assist in these ways, you might follow up like this:

Q: So there is a responsibility to assist the policyholder, at least to the extent of providing claim forms?

A: I just said that.

Q: Any other ways in which a claims handler should be assisting the policyholder with the claim?

A: Like what?

Q: You're an expert in handling insurance claims?

A: Yes.

Q: Then tell us some other ways a claims handler should help a policyholder. If you don't know of any others, I am happy to accept that answer.

You are forcing the witness either to take an extreme position, or move toward the middle—closer to your Rule of the Road. Remember one of our big-three enemies: ambiguity. Don't let the witness hide there. Is there a duty to assist or isn't there? If the answer is "sometimes," then ask when *is* there, and when *isn't* there a duty.

In essence, you are giving the witness three choices:

1. Completely agree with your principle or Rule.

2. Completely disagree with your principle or Rule.

3. Define some middle ground.

Complete agreement is great. After all, you selected this Rule believing you can prove it was violated and that it will help your case. Complete disagreement is often great too. In our example, complete disagreement means the witness is saying there is no responsibility to assist the policyholder. This is the epitome of the type of stonewalling many jurors expect from insurance companies. The witness is putting on the black hat. The defendant will pay for this at trial.

Finally, the witness's efforts to define a middle ground often result in his ultimate agreement with your original Rule—or something very similar to it—or creating yet another good Rule for you. Again, root out ambiguity; make him be specific.

One problem lawyers sometimes have in securing agreement with a Rule is that they get caught up in a game of semantic hide-and-seek with the witness. To combat a witness who wants to play semantic games, you need patience and flexibility. First, remember you are not wedded to any of the language in your Rules. Your annotated list is just a starting point.

Suppose, for example, the witness balks at the word "assist" as used in the above examples. You can either try to get him to adopt your word, or suggest a synonym: "Well, would you agree a claim examiner has a responsibility to *help* the policyholder with the claim?" You would be surprised how often the witness is satisfied with such a simple change. Fast-forward now to trial. Maybe you changed your Rule to say claims handlers should "help" the policyholder with the claim. Or maybe your Rules of the Road still contain the word "assist," and he has only acknowledged a responsibility to "help." Think he is going to want to fight about that difference with you in front of the jury?

Another approach to the semantically challenged witness is to go to your sources, like this.

Example 4

Q: Would you agree that part of the claim examiner's job is to assist the policyholder with the claim?

A: What do you mean by "assist"?

Q: Help?

A: In what way?

Q: Any way?

A: I don't understand what you are asking me.
[Time to run to your sources.]

Q: Are you familiar with the NAIC model regulations?

A: Somewhat. I don't have them memorized.

Q: Let me hand you a copy of Model Regulation Section 6D. As an expert in insurance claims practices, do you think you are capable of understanding this regulation?

A: Yes.

Q: It reads: "Every insurer, upon receiving notification of a claim, shall promptly provide necessary claim forms, instructions and reasonable *assistance* so that first-party claimants can comply with the policy conditions and the insurer's reasonable requirements."

Do you believe you understand that?

A: Yes.

Q: In that context, what does "assistance" mean?

• • •

Q: You have already told us that the California Insurance Regulations were applicable to this claim. As an insurance expert, do you believe you are capable of understanding these regulations?

A: Yes.

Q: I would like to hand you section 2695.4(a), which reads: "When additional benefits might reasonably be payable under an insured's policy upon receipt of additional proofs of claim, the insurer shall immediately communicate this fact to the insured and cooperate with and *assist* the insured in determining the extent of the insurer's additional liability."

What does "assist" mean in this context?

• • •

Q: Here is section 2695.5(e)(2): "Upon receiving notice of claim, every insurer, . . . shall immediately . . . (2) provide to the claimant necessary claim forms, instructions, and *reasonable assistance,* including *but not limited to,* specifying the information the claimant must provide for proof of claim."

Do you understand what "assistance" means here?

A: What?

Stay loose; stay flexible. Again, remember, you have done your homework and are fighting on your best ground. Pretty soon the witness will realize that too.

Area 3: See If You Can Create New Rules

Whether deposing a 30(b)(6) witness, the defendant's employee, or a defense expert, you have a golden opportunity to come up with new Rules. Just like your experts, many of these people enjoy talking about the basic principles in the areas in which they work. In resisting agreement to your Rules, responding to your "polarizing" efforts, or just discussing the witness's personal philosophy on the subject, there is a good chance the defense witness will articulate a principle not on your list. Discuss this on the record. Make the principle specific and clear; remove the ambiguity; and you may have a new Rule of the Road.

In reading depositions taken by other lawyers using Rules of the Road techniques, we've noticed a common problem we refer to as the "Mush-Mouthed Witness." This is the witness who simply can't answer a question because all of your Rules are too general or contain words he doesn't understand. The problem is perhaps best illustrated by the medical-expert witness who answers any question about rules or standards with an "it depends" answer.

This witness will insist that your Rules cannot possible apply to all situations and that the matter under consideration is always a question of medical judgment, dependent on a vast array of factual circumstances that need to be taken into account.

Lawyers get frustrated with such a witness, trying to wear him down into admitting to one or more of their Rules, as they have stated them. In our view, the better approach is to get the witness to help you to draft new Rules.

Simply stated, the approach is this: instead of trying to drag the witness into your world, enter into his. If he can't accept your Rule because it raises questions reserved for medical judgment, don't fight that; accept it. Your questions might go like this:

Q: So in dealing with _____ a doctor must exercise medical judgment?

Q: In exercising medical judgment in this situation, what aspects of the patient's history should be taken into account?

Q: What other factors should be taken into account?

Q: So you are saying that in exercising medical judgment when dealing with _____, a doctor should take, x, y, and z into account?

Notice what happened? The doctor just wrote a Rule for you.

What if the doctor responds to your last question by saying, "He doesn't need to always take x, y, and z into account, but just when appropriate." Your rejoinder?

Q: When is it appropriate to take x, y, and z into account?

Q: So when a, b, and c are present, a doctor should take x, y, and z into account?

You have a Rule again.

In essence you are forcing the witness to take one of two positions. Either the decision making is entirely unprincipled, or he needs to tell you what the principles are. This takes patience—especially with a witness determined not to give you Rules. But if you listen carefully and are persistent, any witness will sooner or later give you principles and Rules. They may not be the ones you hoped to establish as you walked into the deposition, but they may work just as well.

If you feel like you are getting nowhere, try these questions:

Q: Are there any principles or standards that apply to _____ [the relevant activity]? What are they?

Q: Are there any safety rules or standards that apply to _____ [the relevant activity]? What are they?

If the witness says there are none, then you go to trial with two competing worldviews for the jury's consideration: in one, there are principled safety standards to guide conduct; in the other, those who control the instruments of injury and death admit to no principled standards that can govern their behavior.

Area 4: Find Out Whether Any Rules Were Violated

The witness has either agreed or disagreed with the Rules on your list. It is now time to talk about the facts of your case. You have a choice of two approaches. Do you refer back to the agreed-upon Rules as you question the witness about the facts? Or do you get a detailed explanation of what occurred and whether it was right or wrong, leaving the question of Rule violation for trial?

This is a tactical issue for which no hard-and-fast strategy exists. Our general approach is to pry a detailed, specific statement of facts out of the witness and seal off any escape hatches for later changes in the facts. We also stay away from linking these facts back to the Rules we have already established with the witness. If you start a discussion of whether a particular Rule was violated, you risk the witness's withdrawing his agreement to the Rule. You may start hearing answers like, "Oh, you misunderstood what I was saying about assistance." At best, you will spend a lot of deposition time trying to preserve the admissions previously secured. The same attempts at trial to qualify or retract agreement to the Rules will sound evasive or disingenuous.

With some witnesses, however, securing agreement that Rules were violated may be worth a try. Does the witness seem unusually honest? Independent? Not taking the defense attorney's objection hints? Not well prepared to spout the party line? If so, go for it. If you do try, start with your clearest examples of violations. These give you the best chance of hitting a home run.

Handling Deposition Objections

When the objections come, as they almost always do, you need to have clearly in mind what you are doing. You are *not* asking the witness for a legal opinion. Nor are you asking for speculation.

You are asking for the standards, customs, understandings, guidelines, or agreed-upon principles in the industry or profession.

You can fence out many deposition objections by aggressively enforcing the rules against speaking objections and instructions not to answer. In federal court, and in many state courts, it is against the rules to instruct a witness not to answer a question, except to preserve a privilege or to make a motion to stop the deposition.[14] Until you know this by heart and can quote the rule verbatim, defense lawyers will try to block some of your best questions by bogus instructions not to answer. Or the defense lawyer will make a "speaking" objection that hints to the witness why she should play dumb on your question. The *first* time a speaking objection happens in the deposition, you must cut off the lawyer and insist that any objections explaining the objection be stated outside the witness's presence.

One instance where objections come up in bad faith cases is when you start asking about the case law, which is, of course, one source of bad faith Rules. The same issue can arise when asking a witness about a regulation or statute in some other type of case. Let's look at an example of how this might play out.

You are addressing Rule 2 in appendix A as you question a defense expert witness:

> Company must treat its policyholder's interests with equal regard as it does its own interests. This is not an adversarial process.

Q: Insurance is a heavily regulated industry, isn't it?

A: Yes.

Q: In the state of California, there are statutes and administrative regulations that set standards for how a claim should be handled?

A: Yes.

---

14. See Fed. R. Civ. P. 30(d)(1).

Q: Are you familiar with those statutes and regulations?

A: I believe so.

Q: Is it standard in the industry for insurance companies adjusting claims in California to be familiar with those statutes and regulations?

A: Yes.

Q: There is also case law in the state of California that sets standards for how claims should be handled?

A: I'm not sure what you mean.

Q: Are you familiar with the case of *Egan v. Mutual of Omaha Ins. Co.*?

DEFENSE COUNSEL: Objection, this witness is not a legal expert and is not here to give legal opinions.

Q: I am not asking for a legal opinion. I am just asking him if he is familiar with the case.

A: Yes, I am.

Q: Would you agree that this case discusses important obligations for claims handlers in the state of California?

A: Yes.

Q: Would you expect most insurance companies adjusting claims in California to be familiar with that case?

DEFENSE COUNSEL: Objection, calls for speculation.

Q: You are an expert in claims practices in California, aren't you?

A: Nationwide, actually.

Q: Including California?

A: Yes.

Q: And you told us earlier today about all of your experience working with different California insurance companies in various claims departments?

A: Yes.

Q: Based on that experience, do you have an opinion as to whether most insurance companies adjusting claims in California should be familiar with *Egan*?

A: I would expect they would be.

Q: Would you expect that most insurance companies adjusting claims in California would teach their claims staff about this important case?

A: Probably.

Q: Are you familiar with the portion of *Egan* that says an insurance company should treat its insured's interests with equal regard as its own interests?

DEFENSE COUNSEL: Objection, you are asking him to interpret a legal case, which is beyond the scope of his expertise and beyond the scope of what he is offered for.

Q: Mr. _____, I don't want a legal opinion from you. Let me start again. Have you read *Egan*?

A: Yes.

Q: And do you recall there is discussion in *Egan* to the effect that an insurance company should treat its insured's interests with equal regard as its own interests?

A: Along those lines, yes.

Q: Do you agree that within the insurance industry, the concept that an insurance company should treat its insured's interests with equal regard as its own interests is well accepted?

A: Yes.

Q: Regardless of the state of the law, that is a recognized principle in the insurance industry?

A: Yes, it is well understood that that is our obligation.

Note the position the witness is in. He knows *Egan*, and he knows you know *Egan*. If he wants to take the position that the company has no obligation to treat the insured's interests with equal regard, he knows his testimony is going to be contradicted by the jury instructions. If he wants to go there now, he will have to go there in front of the jury—or capitulate and give you what you want.[15] If he won't accept this principle in front of the jury, you can point out that his testimony is directly contradicted by the judge's instructions.

Note also that you now have a record from which to argue an important distinction to the judge. "Yes," you say to the judge, "*Egan* says the company should treat the insured's interest with equal regard to its own. But the defendant's own expert acknowledges that that is a recognized principle in the industry, regardless of the state of the law." This distinction will be important when you argue objections about the opening statement (see chapter 16, "Opening Statement").

When dealing with objections, be flexible. You don't care if the witness calls your Rule a standard, custom, understanding, guideline, or agreed-upon principle in the industry or profession. Be ready with other ways to start or end the same question:

Q: Would you agree it is *commonly understood* in your industry that _____?

Q: Would you agree that a *basic principle* of [claims handling, medicine, product design] is that _____?

Q: Is it *standard* in your business to _____?

Q: Is this sort of obligation *well recognized in your profession?*

---

15. It is not uncommon for witnesses to fight against endorsing Rules in deposition but to quickly agree with them in trial. By then it has sunk in how foolish they will look if they persist in resisting the Rule.

Q: Are you the only one in the _____ business who holds this view, or is this a *commonly accepted guideline?*

Get agreement to *some* form of your Rule, if you can. The exact wording is usually not that important. Again, if he won't agree at all, get him to state the opposite; that is, there is *no* obligation to treat the insured's interests with equal regard, and no one in the industry, much less the defendant, thinks there is; or, there is *no* obligation for a surgeon to identify what he is cutting before he cuts it.

Don't Forget to Ask "Why?"

You want to ask the defendant to agree with your Rules, or redefine them in some way the defendant can agree to. Then you ask the magic question, Why? Why does that rule exist? And if you question persistently, the defendant will agree—reluctantly but eventually—that the Rule exists to reduce the risk of harm to people like your client—and even like those sitting in the jury box.

In a case about a railroad crossing that is missing a flashing crossing signal, it may seem obvious that the flashing lights are a safety device, but there is more work to be done here.

- Why put lights at a crossing?
- Why make them flash?
- Why flash only when a train is near?
- Why cover both directions of travel?
- How often do you test to make sure flashers work?
- If power is out to the lights, what does the train engineer do when approaching an unlit crossing?
- Why aim the flashing lights at drivers?
- Why make sure that those flashing lights are functioning and visible to drivers?

◆ Why, if a crossing had the lights burned out, or misaimed, or not installed at all, would that affect automobile drivers and their passengers? Would you expect someone in a car eventually to be hurt or killed?

All these questions are aimed at a single goal: to get the witness to admit, in his own words, that crossings are fitted with flashing lights to protect the safety of people crossing the tracks in cars.

Questions for the End of a Deposition

Here is an important deposition technique that should be used, even without a Rules of the Road approach to the rest of the case.

Give every defendant and every defense witness a choice: did you make mistakes or not? If the answer is yes, you, of course, want to know what those mistakes are, why they were made, and what is being done to keep similar mistakes from being made in the future. If, as is almost invariably the case, the answer is some variation of "no, there were no mistakes made," then you have accomplished at least two important goals:

1. You have deprived the defendant of what is often its best defense: "Mistakes were made, and because we are an honest, caring corporation, made up of honest, caring employees, we are really sorry, and it won't happen again—and by the way, no real harm was done."

2. You have the material to make the defendant look recalcitrant and unreasonable at trial by getting the witness, at the beginning and end of your exam, to repeat that neither she nor the defendant did anything wrong.

Here are some sample questions, to give you the general idea:

Q: To the best of your ability, did you handle this claim the way you understood Acme Insurance Company trained you to handle claims?

Q: Did you handle it the way you understood Acme Insurance Company wanted you to handle claims?

Q: In your opinion, did you make any mistakes in the way you handled this claim?

Q: From what you have seen, did anyone at Acme make any mistakes with regard to the handling of this claim? What were they?

Q: Have you ever been reprimanded or criticized by any of your supervisors for the way you handled this claim?

Q: Have you ever heard that anyone has been reprimanded or criticized for the way they handled this claim?

Q: If a similar claim came in tomorrow, would you handle it in a similar manner?

Similar questions should be asked of any defense expert witnesses:

Q: Did Acme do anything wrong in its handling of this claim?

In a malpractice case, similar questions should be asked. The only difference is that in most jurisdictions, if any "peer review" hearings were held into your incident, their results are privileged and nondiscoverable. But that shouldn't stop you from asking the defendant, the defense fact witnesses, and the defense experts whether any mistakes were made in the patient's care by any of the caregivers.

Conclusion

You have conducted discovery and refined your annotated Rules list as new information came in. Defense witnesses were pinned down; they either agreed or disagreed with each Rule. The defense witnesses were committed to their version of the facts. By now, you should have a plan for how you can prove key Rules were violated. But first, let's show how to troubleshoot the wording of your Rules to make it easier to find provable violations of them.

9

TROUBLESHOOTING YOUR RULES

This chapter, new to the second edition, will help anyone who has tried the Rules technique and been disappointed. It is also important for first-time readers. The process of devising powerful Rules to fit all five of our Rule requirements is not as easy as it looks. This chapter addresses some of the most common problems and discusses how rules can be improved in a variety of cases.

A common problem is what we could call "rule fade-out." The trial starts with a set of Rules that seems to meet all our requirements for good rules, but then somewhere along the way, usually not long after opening statement, the Rules fade away and the trial lurches to its end with the focus (if there is one) on a variety of other topics.

It could be, of course, that the plaintiff's attorneys are simply letting the defense counsel take charge of the trial agenda and so get overly caught up in chasing all the rabbits typically unleashed in a trial by clever defense counsel. Experience and persistence with the Rules technique will go a long way toward preventing that.

But there is another problem that happens when we don't do the job we should before trial of making our Rules specific enough. As a result, the defense is able to undercut the Rules' power by saying one or more variations of:

- "That's not a real rule that applies to this case."

- "We followed that rule."

- "It doesn't matter because breaking that rule didn't make any difference."

The answer to each of these defense moves is to go back to square one and make sure our Rules meet all five criteria for a good Rule. In particular, make sure each Rule requires that the defendant do, or not do, something. This process of troubleshooting your Rules will pay big dividends. You will have exposed why the defendant should be liable by creating an easy-to-understand Rule of positive conduct that the defendant has violated and that is important to the case.

Make Your Rules Specific

One of the quickest defense escape routes is to argue that he or she complied with the Rule—at least the way the defendant defines the Rule. If that happens in a trial, the Rule quickly becomes irrelevant to the case. The real art in Rule writing is making the Rule easy to understand *and* hard to argue with *and* provably violated by the defendant. This requires you to tighten up your Rules to make sure they are specific enough for your case. That will block the escape routes that were created unintentionally when you left undefined generalities in your Rules. So always ask yourself, *Can I make this Rule more specific and concrete in terms of what it requires of the defendant?*

Here is an example of how we worked with our Rules in one case to make sure they were specific enough. A recent particularly tragic case we prosecuted involved a forty-six-year-old man whose doctors missed multiple chances to remove a mole from his back before it turned into deadly melanoma. The dermatologist wrote the internist, who had sent the patient to the specialist to lance a painful boil on his back, that the patient also needed to have a mole, about the size of a pencil-head eraser, removed from his lower back. Somehow, it never got done. Then a few years later, when the patient returned with another painful cyst on the upper back, another dermatologist in the same office dutifully recorded the same mole and recommended it for periodic monitoring. Only now it was twice as big. This dermatologist didn't realize the mole had doubled in diameter because the office had a five-year rule for throwing out old records, in compliance with Maryland law for the minimal time medical records must be saved. Two more years went by, and when our client's wife noticed the mole had changed color, he returned to the internist, and then to the dermatologist, but now it was too late. He died in agony a year later from metastatic cancer in his brain.

In the conservative venue where the case was prosecuted, we could easily have lost if the trial had focused on the conflict between the patient's insisting he had never been told and the doctors' responding, "We must have told you and you just forgot." What we needed were some simple Rules that applied to both the internist and the dermatologist, which shined a spotlight on their duty to coordinate with each other to make sure recommended care took place.

Here is how the editing process went on Rules for the internist:

Version one:

> A primary doctor should not let a patient fall through the cracks.
>
> *Problem: The defendant agrees with the Rule but says he met it.*

Version two:

> A primary doctor needs to make sure a patient gets follow-up care recommended by a specialist.
>
> *Problem: The defendant doesn't agree with the Rule, and the rule doesn't meet the "agree or look foolish" requirement.*

> A primary doctor should keep track of his patient's treatment needs.

We could force the defendant to agree with this Rule because his records contained a face sheet—like any competent primary doctor should have—with a preprinted form headed at the top, "Problem List," and with boxes arrayed below to allow for brief recording of all injuries, immunizations, specialist referrals, new disease diagnoses, and so on—in short, a patient's entire treatment needs summarized on one sheet.

But notice the generality of this Rule. What does it mean to "keep track" of a patient's treatment needs? Specifically, what was the doctor required to do?

We spelled this out in a series of Rules. We put up a poster at trial with the headline "Primary doctor's standard for skin care." Immediately below that was the basic Rule:

> A primary doctor should keep track of his patient's treatment needs.

Below that, we had the following bullet points to spell out what the Rule meant:

General:

- Do regular skin checks of patients at risk for skin cancer, *or* refer to a specialist for regular checks.

- Keep track of treatment needs with an updated "problem list." Include specialist treatment plans on the "problem list."

- Review the "problem list" with patient.

- Develop and document follow-up plans for items on the "problem list."

Notice these rules each require a doctor to *do* something. And these are all things the doctor admittedly did not do. The same is true of additional Rules we called:

Specific after specialist recommendation:

When a specialist proposes treatment, the primary doctor should consult with the specialist, and together they should decide how to implement the plan.

1. Inform the patient of the treatment need.
2. Follow through: write referral.
3. Document patient's awareness.

We showed how following these simple rules would result in coordinated care with an educated patient and would prevent the kind of needless tragedies that had occurred to our client.

Don't Quibble

Another common problem encountered by lawyers employing the Rules approach is the failure, at trial, to focus on important Rules and important violations. Remember the final requirement for a useful Rule:

Important enough in the context of the case that proof of its violation will significantly increase the chance of a plaintiff's verdict.

You may have a working list of twenty-six Rules arguably violated by the defendant. You may use that list throughout the litigation. But before trial you need to take a hard look at your list. How many of these are important rules in the context of your case? Remember, this is not law-school issue-spotting. You are trying to convince a jury that fundamental safety rules were violated and that your client was injured as a result. If it looks like you are playing a lawyer's "gotcha" game, you will lose every time.

Eliminate from your final list any Rule whose violation you cannot claim played a major role in causing your client's injuries. This is difficult to do. You have cultivated each Rule on your list for months, perhaps even years. You've grown attached to them all, as if they were your children. But they are not your children; get rid of the unimportant ones.

The Causation Defense

The causation defense is another place where defendants like to hide from the power of the Rules approach to liability. Faced with your list of carefully honed Rules, the defendant and her attorneys simply shrug and say, "Well, these rules didn't matter. Something else caused the unfortunate injury to the plaintiff."

When this happens, the plaintiff's lawyer's biggest mistake is to rush too quickly to the defendant's chosen battleground before first making sure the Rules-violation battle has been fought and won in the jury's presence. Carefully exploring the Rules will go a long way toward defusing the causation defense and getting the fact finder to see that the causation defense is nothing more than a fancy excuse.

When the defendant wants to run from the Rules by putting up only a token defense to them (or even admitting them) but saying the violation didn't matter, the plaintiff's attorney must force the defendant and his experts to admit, in detail, the reason for the Rules' existence: *to prevent the kind of harm that happened to the plaintiff here.*

For example, in one of our cases, the patient's heart stopped beating in the middle of a cosmetic-surgery procedure, and she suffered severe brain damage before it was finally restarted. One of the drugs given for local anesthesia is known to stop the heart if given in a high overdose. That is exactly what we alleged happened. The defendant wanted to say that the overdose didn't matter because the patient had actually suffered an idiosyncratic reaction to another drug given in a normal, acceptable dose, something for which, conveniently, he could not be accountable. We focused our liability attack first and foremost on why a surgeon should never give an overdose of local anesthesia, because of the predictable bad reaction that can occur. Only after we had this well established did we go to the more arcane issue of proving why the heart stoppage did not fit the known pattern of what happened with the other drug he gave in the ordinary dosage.

When confronted with a causation defense, it is helpful to draw out exactly what the excuses are for breaking Rules, when a Rule violator is caught red-handed. Those excuses include:

1. It's okay to break this Rule because lots of other people do so also.
   [After age fifteen, this is not a convincing excuse to use.]

2. It was okay to break this Rule because the victim could have been hurt anyway by some other cause.
   [Does that make any sense? If somebody rear-ends a farmer's truck carrying eggs and leaves a sticky pile of egg shells, yolks, and whites, it's no excuse that there were some bad potholes further down the road that could have broken those same eggs.]

3. It was okay to break the Rule because no one had been hurt before under similar circumstances.
   [If no one is hurt when a safety rule is violated, that is luck—not a legitimate excuse. And of course, in our case, someone was hurt, and the defendant is not able to say no one was hurt.]

All of these excuses (and probably others you can think of) have one thing in common: they rely on convincing a jury that the Rule was not that important in the context of your case. But if your client was hurt in exactly the way the Rule was meant to prevent, fighting causation should be an uphill battle for the defense. Jurors don't like rule breakers—especially ones who try to argue that safety rules are not important.

Other Common Mistakes

- **Expecting this to be quick and easy.** Drafting Rules of the Road can be fun—if you're a certain kind of person—but it is slow, hard work. Rick recently worked on a set of Rules for a product liability case for two solid weeks. He now has a rough draft in need of more work. The Rules approach is a framework for helping you think more clearly about your case; it is not a substitute for thinking about your case.

- USING SOMEONE ELSE'S RULES. If you are doing, let's say, a medical malpractice case on a baby's shoulder being stuck in the birth canal, looking at Rules someone else did for a similar case can be extremely helpful in jump-starting your brain to compose your own set of rules. But it is not a substitute for tailoring rules for the facts of your own case. Facts and testimony will differ from case to case. It is virtually legal malpractice to simply take someone else's Rules from another case and attempt to use them, unmodified, in yours.

- BEING RIGID. Don't rigidly cling to your own, original formulation of Rules and principles. As the litigation proceeds and defense witnesses express themselves, you will need to modify the wording of your Rules. That is not only acceptable but desirable. Every time a defense witness quibbles with your wording and gives you a synonym, it is a gift. It would be foolish not to accept it.

IMPROVING YOUR RULES

Here is an example of a set of Rules we received from Maryland attorney Jon Pels, from a case many of us might not have seen: property damage to hundreds of clients in a class-action case. Pels told us that his case against mobile-home installers "was like jumping into a John Grisham novel." He crawled under dozens of mobile homes to inspect their anchors, held clandestine meetings in cheap taverns with former industry insiders whose consciences were nagging them, and faced the usual fog of corporate excuse-mongering from his dark-suited adversaries. He wanted to know why so many mobile homes were slipping off their moorings. Pels and his partner Larry Anderson proved that the installers were not driving the piers down to the frost line as Maryland state regulations had required since 1985. The defendant installers wanted to make the issue more complicated than it really was, invoking the failure of county inspectors to call them out for their failings.

Pels wrote a set of Rules, with the help of the first edition of this book, which he credits for helping to drive his case to victory. We think they are excellent, and we reproduce them here with our comments about how we might edit them to make them even better.

1. You should build your house on rock, not on sand (with thanks to Matthew's gospel, 7:24–27).
   [This is a nice introduction to the Rules applicable for this case, because it helps bring the idea into the world with which jurors are familiar, but since the defense can quibble that the requirement is to go to the frost line, not rock, it's probably most helpful as an anchor for closing argument, not a centerpiece of a list of Rules for examining witnesses.]

2. A mobile home must have anchors extending down to the frost line to prevent dangerous heaving from the freezing and thawing of the ground.
   [This is a good Rule. Can we make it better by specifically identifying who should do what? Try this:

   An installer must extend anchors down to the frost line.

   [The "why" of this rule—to prevent heaving from the freezing and thawing—can be explained by the lawyer and witnesses and does not need to be in the Rule.]

3. A mobile home without footers down to the frost line is unsafe for occupancy.
   [As written, this is a principle, not a Rule. We could change it to a Rule: No one in the mobile-home industry should allow occupancy of a trailer if they know it lacks footers down to the frost line.]

4. A mobile-home installer is required to ensure compliance with all applicable building codes related to site installation.
   [This is a good Rule. You could consider substituting "must comply" for "is required to ensure compliance," but that is certainly not necessary. In addition, if there are particular building-code sections that were violated other than the frost-line requirement, those could be made separate Rules, or subparts of this Rule.]

5. Failure of a county inspector to notice a violation of the code is not an excuse for the home installer's code violation.
   [This is not a Rule, but a principle. But like Pels and Anderson, we would be inclined to leave it on the Rule list. It is too important a concept to be left off. If we wanted to change this to a Rule format, how about:]

   An installer must follow the building code, regardless of whether the county inspector catches the installer's violations.

   or,

   . . . regardless of the competence of the county inspector.

   or,

   . . . regardless of whether or not the county inspector insists.

On this last point, Pels and Anderson turned back the blame-shifting effort of the mobile-home installers and their experts by pointing out that both Maryland common law and statutes required compliance with all building codes in effect at the time of construction, with no exceptions, even when inspectors had issued building permits without noticing the violations. Old-fashioned legal research once again proves invaluable in defining the Rules applicable to a defendant's conduct.

Jon Pels won a "lawyer of the year" award from the Maryland Association for Justice for his work on these cases. He's proud of that, but he's more proud that the industry was required to retrofit more than one thousand mobile homes in the state to meet the ground-anchoring requirements that had not been regularly enforced before his lawsuit.

10

FITTING THE RULES INTO YOUR CASE STORY

The Rules of the Road approach can do many things for your case, but not everything. It can give you a clear, well-focused liability theory, with intellectual integrity. It can help the jury see what is important, and what is a distraction. As we'll discuss later, it can give you a wonderful blueprint for various lines of direct and cross-examination. What this approach cannot give you is your story. And that's what trials are about—competing stories. You have your story of what happened; the defense has theirs. Which is more believable to the jury? Which is more compelling because it fits with the jurors' life experiences?

At trial, you need to answer questions. What happened? Why did it happen? Why did the people involved act as they did? Are they good, responsible people? Irresponsible? Why is this case important? Why should I (the juror) care about the case? How could this case affect me or my community? All of these questions will be on the minds of jurors as the trial opens and as the two sides battle for whose story grabs the jurors.

There is no one-size-fits-all method for fitting your Rules into the story of your case. We can only exhort you to get it done. Most of the time, the Rules in and of themselves are *not* the story of your case. Instead, they are the foundation that helps make your story convincing.

In a recent bad faith trial against an insurance company, the plaintiff was a doctor seeking disability benefits after an auto accident. Before the accident, the doctor had led an exemplary life. By everyone's account, he loved his job and was hardworking, honest, and kind. The insurance company sent him to three so-called IME doctors, all of whom opined that the doctor was faking his disability. They called him a liar and a cheat. The "story" of the case became the doctor's treatment at the hands of the insurance company: "If they can do this to someone like him, they can do it to anyone." The Rules violations illustrated and highlighted the unfairness of how this plaintiff was treated—but they were not the story itself.

Most good stories are very much concerned with *motivation* and *character*. Most juries are very much concerned with motivation because it helps them make sense out of confusing arrays of facts. They judge a party's character because it helps them decide who deserves their judgment in a moral sense. And character, too, fills in the story. The Rules of the Road will not give you the defendant's motivation; you have to find it. Once you have it, the Rules of the Road will help you prove it. The same goes for character.

Sometimes we have to sift through layers of Rules about the conduct in a case to find the ones that fit with the story we want to tell. In professional-negligence cases, too often this task isn't done at all, because the lawyers get too wrapped up in the technical "standard of care" violations to see the important Rules violations that can fit into a compelling story. We make a mistake if we think that formulating Rules is satisfied by just translating technical professional standards into plain English that a jury can understand. That's enough if our job is only to bring the jury into the world of medicine. But our task, if we want to win with a compelling story, is to bring the case into the jury's world.

We represented the family of a forty-five-year-old woman whose primary-care doctor misdiagnosed her as suffering from two unrelated benign conditions (the flu and a vaginal yeast infection) when she actually had only one thing: a bacterial infection that killed her a few days later. On the technical level of "standard of care" violations, we could show that the doctor had (1) failed to consider that the patient might have had one condition explaining all her symptoms, (2) failed to rule out a potentially fatal condition, and (3) failed to culture the vaginal discharge for possible bacterial infection. Any of these failures could have lent themselves to our formulating fairly straightforward Rules, such as:

> A doctor should take a culture of any possibly infected body fluids to see if there is a treatable infection.

And,

> A doctor should not conclude a patient has two unrelated benign conditions if it's possible the patient has a single potentially fatal condition.

But neither of these, despite being relatively accessible to an intelligent jury, gets anywhere near motivation or character. This one gets a little closer:

> If a simple test is available that can confirm what is really wrong with a seriously ill patient, a doctor should not skip the test just because he's fairly sure he already knows what is wrong.

This rule frames the issue in a way that the jury can more readily grasp, in part because it hints at character and motive. Only an arrogant, prideful doctor would insist that he does not need to use available tests that are easily carried out. (Notice we say "hints at." We want the jurors to discover these deeper currents of the case for themselves, which they will resist if we are overly obvious.)

In the same case, the patient's diary entry for the day of the fateful office visit showed that she had listed several symptoms that didn't appear in his office record. Her husband testified that she always wrote notes and took them with her to any sick visit to the doctor's office. So we could argue that these symptoms were available to the doctor. The expert witnesses were not quite sure what difference it would have made if the doctor had paid attention to these unrecorded symptoms. But his failure to do so fit very nicely into the picture of a prideful, arrogant doctor who didn't listen carefully to his patient. So another Rule we put forward in the case was:

> A doctor should listen carefully to all his patient's symptoms, should document them, and should consider all of them before deciding what is wrong.

We couldn't prove strict "causation" for the violation of this Rule, but emphasizing the Rule in our case fit into the story we were trying to tell, and it also meshed with the other Rule about not skipping a simple confirmatory test. So the listening rule became something to put on the board at trial. It helped bring the case into the jury's world, where we knew that at least one juror would have a similar story to relate in the jury room from her own life about an arrogant doctor who wouldn't listen because he was so sure what the problem was.

So the reason our revised Rules work better in this case than our original translations of the standard-of-care violations is that they play into a story the jury has seen and experienced before. We could have framed another story—"this is a case about a doctor who violated the rules of diagnosis"—but that is less compelling because it signals to the jury immediately that it will be asked to judge something with which it is not familiar. This is another way of saying that Rule violations themselves never should be the whole story.

Sometimes, as in the above example, the Rules need to be rethought and reshaped to build a bridge from the Rule violations to the familiar world of motive and character that the jury inhabits. Other times, as in a bad faith insurance claim denial, the motive for the Rule violations becomes obvious once the profitability of claims denials becomes clear to the jury. Then the compelling story of the good person being unfairly maligned solely out of corporate greed becomes all too real.

Now let's turn to how the Rules fit into a case where the Rules themselves are already very familiar to the jury.

11

A Special Problem: Rules of the Road in Automobile Cases

As used in this book, the term "Rules of the Road" is not only a technique, but also a simile. In effect, we say to the jury, "The rules for safe brain surgery [or railroad operation or product design] are as straightforward and easy to understand as the rules for driving your car."

When using the Rules of the Road approach for a typical car crash case, it's no longer a simile; we really are talking about the "rules of the road"—literally. Because jurors already understand, or think they understand, the rules for safely driving a car, unique challenges and opportunities appear in auto cases.[1] Lawyers who don't recognize this can run into trouble when they try to apply Rules of the Road to auto cases.

Here are some of the most common mistakes we have seen.

---

[1]. Trucking cases are a different story. Most jurors are not commercial truck drivers and are not familiar with the safety rules for that occupation. The same is true for highway-design cases or product liability cases involving passenger cars. Most jurors are not highway engineers or automobile designers and do not know how those jobs should be performed safely.

Excessive Complication

Remember who complexity helps? Not you. Rules for a rear-end collision can be as simple as:

- Driver should always look where he is going.

- Driver should leave enough distance between himself and the car ahead so that he can safely stop if the car ahead suddenly stops.

Yet, we have seen lawyers use lists that have seven to ten Rules for simple cases like this. That is a big mistake. To list that many Rules in a simple auto case, you are either splitting hairs or finding rules the jurors themselves are not familiar with. They are likely to excuse a defendant driver for breaking a rule they themselves were unaware of. They may also conclude that you have a weak case if you need to point to these obscure rules to support liability.

Loss of Perspective

Most—though certainly not all—auto accidents result from relatively minor deviations from acceptable behavior. A driver is looking at his radio, changing the stations, when the car ahead comes to a sudden stop and he hits it. Is this negligence? Yes. Is it a war crime? No. Conducting the trial as if the defendant driver is despicable is a sure path to a defense verdict.

The driver's attention wandered. He did not want to hurt anyone. He may even have been operating within the scope—or barely outside the scope—of normal driver behavior. Unless you convey an understanding of these realities, you are likely to lose.

Beating a Dead Horse

In most cases where Rules of the Road are employed, the jury needs to be educated about the Rules. This education includes explaining the Rule, what it requires, why it is fair, why it is important, and what harm can be caused if it is violated.

A Special Problem: Rules of the Road in Automobile Cases

In the typical auto case, however, the jurors already know all this. You can simply start the trial by saying something like:

> This case involves a rule we all know so well that we often take it for granted: the driver of a car must keep enough distance between himself and the car ahead of him, so that if the car ahead stops suddenly, he can still avoid a collision. A year ago, on Smith Street, Mr. Jones failed to do that and rammed into the back of Mr. Taylor's car.

If you emblazon this rule onto a poster board and keep preaching about it throughout the trial, you run a very real risk of appearing like you are patronizing the jurors. Give the jurors credit for understanding the difference between negligent and nonnegligent driving, and show them why the defendant's conduct was beyond what most of us do most of the time.

What else can you do to increase your chances of winning a typical auto case? A complete answer is beyond the scope of this book. But let's look at the nature of the typical problem and discuss some possible solutions.

These cases are not difficult when the defendant has deviated substantially from acceptable rules for driver behavior. The jurors are more than willing to find liability and award damages when the defendant was drunk or was driving sixty-five miles an hour in a school zone. The problem arises when the defendant appears not to have done anything different than the jurors themselves have done numerous times: he was going too fast for conditions and slipped on ice; he looked down at his radio and didn't realize your client had suddenly stopped ahead of him; he didn't react quickly enough when a child ran into the street.

These are difficult cases. If the case is about making the defendant's accidental and minor deviation from the rules appear to be a major transgression, you will lose. You must make the case about something else. Here are some ideas.

Emphasize the Differences

In the trial of a "child dart-out" case, Moe Levine asked the jurors in *voir dire:* "How many of you have had a child suddenly and unexpectedly rush out in front of your car?" Most of the jurors raised their hands. "How many of you hit that child?" was his next question. This encouraged the jurors to think about the *differences* between their conduct and the defendant's, instead of thinking about the similarities.

It is easy to adapt this approach to your case: "How many of you have ever skidded on ice unexpectedly?" "How many of you struck another car at forty-five miles an hour when you did so?" The trial then becomes an inquiry into what this defendant did that was different from what the typical driver does in these circumstances.

Polarize the Case

Often the defense will admit liability in the typical auto case and focus on damages. Then the case is not about the defendant's driving transgression—he has admitted he is 100 percent at fault. The trial is now about how the case is being defended. Rick wrote an entire book about how to handle this situation.[2] One approach is to point out that:

- The defendant broke the rules we all have to follow and hurt the plaintiff.

- The defendant admits the plaintiff did nothing wrong and in no way contributed to the accident.

- Now, the defendant has the gall to call the plaintiff an exaggerator, a liar, or a cheat. He wants a discount for the harm he created.[3]

---

2. Rick Friedman, Polarizing the Case: Exposing and Defeating the Malingering Myth (Trial Guides 2007).
3. David Ball's book David Ball on Damages (National Institute for Trial Advocacy 2005) has a variety of techniques for making the case be about damages rather than about the defendant's minor deviation from the rules of conduct.

As Rick points out in his *Polarizing the Case,* the more open the defendant is in attacking your plaintiff, the less it matters that the defendant's rule violation may seem minor. The trial will be about the plaintiff's credibility and the defendant's irresponsible attack upon it.

Breach of Contract

Try this approach, explained in one of Rick's other books:

> When we get our driver's license from the state, we are entering into a contract with the State of Oklahoma and all other drivers on the road. The laws of the state are the contract we all agree to follow. Among other things, all of us promise not to follow the car ahead of us too closely. A year and a half ago, at the corner of Elm and Shuster, Mr. Simpson broke that contract.[4]

Jurors, like all of us, put a lot of stock in contractual obligations. Everyone makes mistakes. But if you break a contract, even by mistake, you have to pay. This approach has worked well for many lawyers.

You will come up with other strategies for auto cases. Our point here is simply to warn that applying the Rules outlined elsewhere in this book, without taking into account the unique features of simple auto cases, can get you into trouble.

---

4. Rick Friedman, RICK FRIEDMAN ON BECOMING A TRIAL LAWYER 123 (Trial Guides 2008).

12

MOTIONS AND THE RULES OF THE ROAD

Complexity, confusion, and ambiguity are our undoing with judges, as well as with juries. Here, too, the Rules of the Road can bring focus and clarity to the issues—which is exactly what our cases and our judges need.

Let's start with a basic truth: judges need to be spoon-fed. What do we mean by spoon-fed? We mean:

1. You can't assume the judge knows anything about the applicable law. We mean *anything*.

2. You can't assume the judge remembers anything about your case, even if she just had a hearing on it last week.

3. You can't assume the judge cares a whit about your case.

4. You can't assume the judge is the first-line decision maker. Often, the law clerk makes the initial decision and the judge signs off on it. Law clerks are usually relatively inexperienced and are as busy as judges.

This is not because judges are evil, stupid, or lazy. Psychological and institutional factors are at play here that go far beyond the scope of this book.

Spoon-feeding is *not:* smothering the judge with every possible detail about the case. That's a good recipe for disengaging the judge's brain.

Spoon-feeding is: telling the judge quickly and directly only those facts and legal principles she needs to decide the issue before her.

Not *all* judges need to be spoon-fed, just the ones listed below:

- BUSY JUDGES. They have a lot of work to do and not much time to do it in. In a brief, you need to quickly give them the tools for decision making. Busy judges often rely heavily on law clerks. All law clerks need to be spoon-fed.

- LAZY JUDGES. They often think they are busy judges, but they're not. The thought of having to look up and read a case or parse a technical argument or statute either (1) irritates them or (2) makes them sleepy. The easiest thing for a lazy judge to do is dismiss your case or deny your motion. You need to make it easy for him to understand your argument and decide in your favor. Lazy judges rely heavily on law clerks. All law clerks need to be spoon-fed.

- CONFIDENT JUDGES. They, rightly or wrongly, believe they can get to the essence of a case or issue quickly. They trust their instincts. This means the confident judge will read the first few pages of your brief and start making up her mind. By page five, she will have made her decision. Better get some ideas that favor your position into her head quickly.

- INSECURE JUDGES. They get lost in clouds of complexity, confusion, and ambiguity. Remember who benefits from these?

- SMART JUDGES. They have inquiring minds. Things interest them that you may have missed. You had better keep the focus of the brief where you want it, from start to finish, or things could spin out of control.

- Dumb judges. You know why.

- Trial judges. They are generalists, working in all areas of the law. If your case involves specialized, complex areas of law (such as insurance bad faith) or complex facts (such as with medical malpractice or product design), it is your job to boil down the stew into simple, easily digestible bites. If "the judge just didn't get it," that is often due to the lawyer's failure.

- Appellate judges. If your jurisdiction keeps track, look at the caseload statistics of your appellate-court judges. Chances are they spend most of their time deciding cases involving family law and workers' compensation (if state court) or immigration and federal sentencing (if federal court). Also, they rely heavily on law clerks, who need to be spoon-fed.

Spoon-Feeding the Judge

Being a bad judge is a pretty easy job. Everyone defers to you, and you call the shots. Being a good judge is one of the most difficult jobs we know. Time pressures are huge, and distractions are readily available to derail fair decision making. A good judge must constantly guard against influences that could cause an unfair decision. These influences include, but are in no way limited to:

- Inadequate time to read the briefs and exhibits.

- Incompetent briefing and argument by attorneys.

- Personality factors—that is, this attorney is obnoxious and rude; the judge thinks, *I would like to rule against him, but does he have a good argument?*

- Inexperienced law clerks.

- Genuine uncertainty in the law.
- Personal biases, conscious or unconscious.

Your job is to make it easy for the judge to decide in your favor. Your job is *not* to impress the judge with how hard you have worked, what a long, complicated brief you can write, or how strongly you believe in the righteousness of your cause. Let us repeat: *Your job is to make it easy for the judge to decide in your favor.* The Rules of the Road are ideally suited for this task.

Why do almost all appellate courts now require a brief to state up front: "the question(s) presented"? Why do they also require the brief to state as to each question, "the standard of review"? For two reasons: (1) judges need to know these points of focus early on to begin understanding the case and how it should be decided, and (2) lawyers omit these points of focus from their briefs.

Stated another way, *you need to quickly tell the judge (1) what he needs to decide and (2) what standard he should apply.* Here, we are using the word "standard" in a looser sense than it is used in "standard of review" or even "legal standard." It may include those concepts, but it also encompasses standards of the industry. We are using "standards" in the same sense we have been using that term throughout this book: the factual rules or standards that govern the defendant's conduct.

Take a summary-judgment motion by the defense, for example. The legal issue may be: "Are there genuine issues of material fact" as to whether the defendant acted unreasonably in denying the claim? The defendant's conduct, as recited by the defense, may sound completely reasonable to the judge. He needs to quickly hear from you that the "standard" in the industry is for the claims handler to assist the insured with the claim—if that is one of the Rules you can show was violated. Chances are, he doesn't know that.

Let's get more specific. You have in hand your annotated Rules. Perhaps you have fifteen to twenty Rules listed. These are important tools for writing your brief. Do you want to use them all? Probably not. Maybe eight are relevant to the brief you must write. Get those eight Rules *with annotations* as close to the front of the brief as you can. This is the lens through which you want your judge to view the facts and the law.

Keep in mind that at this stage of the case, your annotated Rules list is still a flexible, living document. You may use a Rule in a motion to convince the judge to allow you discovery in a particular area but abandon that Rule before trial because discovery led nowhere. Similarly, you might use a Rule to oppose summary judgment, because it works well on paper or otherwise will be convincing to the judge, but abandon it before trial because it is not needed or helpful to the trial presentation.

Here is an example from a motion to compel we filed in a Nevada bad faith case. After a two-paragraph overview of the issues presented by the motion, we wrote:

> B. Underlying Legal Principles: With respect to plaintiff's substantive claims the following principles are important for the court to keep in mind while considering this motion to compel.
>
> - An insurer has a duty to disclose all significant facts to its insured. *Albert H. Wohlers and Co. v. Bartgis*, 114 Nev. 1249, 969 P.2d 949 (1998).
>
> - Bad faith occurs where an insurer denies a claim without a reasonable basis for doing so and with knowledge that there is no reasonable basis. *Pemberton v. Farmers Ins. Exch.*, 109 Nev. 789, 793, 858 P.2d 380, 382 (1993).
>
> - An insurer's unreasonable interpretation of its contract may amount to bad faith. *Albert H. Wohlers and Co. v. Bartgis, supra.*
>
> - An insurer may not rely on its own ambiguous contract as the sole basis for denying a claim. *Ainsworth v. Combined Ins. Co. of America*, 763 P.2d 673, 676 (Nev. 1988).

- An insurance policy is a contract of adhesion and should be interpreted broadly, affording the greatest possible coverage to the insured. *Farmers Ins. Group v. Stonik By and Through Stonik*, 110 Nev. 64, 867 P.2d 389 (1994).

- In determining the meaning of an insurance policy, the language should be examined from the viewpoint of one not trained in law or in the insurance business; the terms should be understood in their plain, ordinary and popular sense. *National Union Fire Ins. Co. of State of Pa., Inc. v. Reno's Executive Air, Inc.*, 100 Nev. 360, 682 P.2d 1380, 1382 (Nev. 1984) (citations omitted).

- Any attempt by an insurer to restrict insurance coverage must be done clearly and explicitly. *Farmers Ins. Exchange v. Young*, 108 Nev. 328, 832 P.2d 376 (1992).

- An insurer has an obligation to fairly and completely investigate a claim. *Ainsworth v. Combined Ins. Co. of America*, 763 P.2d at 675.

- An insurer has an obligation to fairly evaluate a claim. *Id.* at 676.

- Punitive damages are appropriate where a defendant has been guilty of fraud, malice or oppression. *Id.* at 675.

- Oppression includes conscious disregard for the rights of others that subject them to cruel and unjust hardship. *Id.*

- Punitive damages are also appropriate where a defendant has engaged in willful and intentional conduct with reckless disregard of its possible results. *Id.* at 676.

- As demonstrated below, the plaintiff's discovery requests are directed at developing facts related to these principles. Accordingly, the discovery should be permitted.

What have we given the judge? A one-page primer on bad faith law in Nevada? Not really. We have given him a one-page primer on those aspects of bad faith law in Nevada relevant to our motion to compel. With these principles in mind, he can see how our broad discovery requests are justified. The brief goes on to show him how we can tie each of our discovery requests to one or more of these principles. If we can do that, the discovery should be allowed.

A few more points worth noting here: First, we have not referred to these principles as Rules, or Rules of the Road. This particular brief is informing the judge of specific legal standards. Each standard is supported by case law. Referring to these legal standards as Rules would, at best, confuse and distract. At worst, it invites dispute from the defense.

Note also there are no citations to admissions by defense witnesses acknowledging the correctness of the principles. This is because, at this stage of the case, we had not yet conducted depositions.

Finally, note the brief makes no references to other sources of authority beyond the Nevada cases. We were fortunate that all principles we needed for this brief were supported by Nevada law. So why complicate things? We are trying to communicate to the judge that these principles are not complicated or controversial. The more authorities from other jurisdictions, the more opportunities for the defense to "distinguish" and confuse.

This is not to say you would never cite authorities from other jurisdictions. In some instances you might want numerous authorities to show the judge that this is a universally accepted principle.

Here is a portion of a summary judgment brief in which we included citations to authorities outside the jurisdiction as well as citations to other sources supporting these principles, including the testimony of witnesses. Notice how this section of the brief looks very similar to an annotated Rules of the Road list. This excerpt begins at page two of the brief.

II. Uncontested Principles and Standards

An insurer is liable for bad faith where it unreasonably delays or denies payment of benefits. *Best Place Inc. v. Penn American Insurance Company*, 82 Haw. 120, 920 P.2d 334, 347 (1996). An insurer that acts maliciously toward its insured may be held liable for punitive damages. Id. at 347–48.

In evaluating whether a jury could find Acme's conduct "unreasonable," the court should bear in mind certain long-standing, indisputable standards governing the handling of insurance claims. Significantly, defendant's claims manager, John George, has testified to the validity and applicability of many of these standards to the claim at issue here.

- An insurer must treat its insured's interests equally with its own. *Egan v. Mutual of Omaha Ins. Co.*, 598 P.2d 452, 456 (Cal. 1979); Ex. 1, George Dep. at 57–58.

- It is improper for an insurer to misrepresent facts or policy provisions relating to coverages at issue. H.R.S. Ch. 431:13-103(11)(A);[1] *United Fire Ins. Co. v. McClelland*, 105 Nev. 504, 515, 780 P.2d 193 (Nev. 1989) (insurer may not mislead or deceive its insured with respect to pertinent facts or insurance benefits); George Dep. at 59.

- An insurer has a duty to thoroughly and objectively investigate claims made. *Egan v. Mutual*

---

1. Under this court's ruling in *Wailua Associates v. Aetna Casualty & Surety Co.*, 27 F.Supp.2d 1211, 1221 (D. Hawaii 1998), evidence of violation of statutory standards may be considered as evidence of bad faith.

of Omaha Ins. Co., 598 P.2d 452, 456–57 (Cal. 1979); *Ainsworth v. Combined Ins. Co. of America*, 763 P.2d 673, 675 (Nev. 1988) (insurer has obligation to fairly and completely investigate claim); *Mariscal v. Old Republic Life Ins. Co.*, 50 Cal. Rptr.2d 224, 227–28 (Cal. App. 1996) (insurer may not ignore facts which support coverage); CAL. PRACTICE GUIDE: INSURANCE LITIGATION ¶¶ 12:848, 866 (The Rutter Group 1997); Ex. 2, International Claims Association, Statement of Principles, ¶ 2; Ex. 1, George Dep. at 58.

- It is improper for an insurer to deny claims based on speculation and conjecture. *Industrial Indemnity Co. of the Northwest, Inc. v. Kallevig*, 792 P.2d 520, 526 (Wash. 1990) (en banc); *Rawlings v. Apodaca*, 726 P.2d 565, 572 (Ariz. 1986) (fair debatability not raised where insurer failed to make adequate investigation), citing, *Farr v. Transamerica Occidental Life Ins. Co.*, 699 P.2d 376 (Ariz. App. 1984); *Deese v. State Farm Mutual Automobile Ins. Co.*, 838 P.2d 1265 (Ariz. 1992); 15A Couch, CYCLOPEDIA OF INSURANCE LAW, § 58:180 (2d rev. ed. 1983); Ex. 1, George Dep. at 58.

- An insurer must have a reasoned basis for resolving factual issues in its favor and against its insured. *Industrial Indemnity Co. of the Northwest, Inc. v. Kallevig*, 792 P.2d 520, 526 (Wash. 1990) (en banc); *Rawlings v. Apodaca*, 726 P.2d 565, 572 (Ariz. 1986) (fair debatability not raised where insurer failed to make adequate investigation), citing, *Farr v. Transamerica Occidental Life Ins. Co.*, 699 P.2d 376 (Ariz. App. 1984); *Deese v. State Farm Mutual Automobile Ins. Co.*, 838 P.2d 1265 (Ariz. 1992); 15A Couch, CYCLOPEDIA OF

INSURANCE LAW, § 58:180 (2d rev. ed. 1983); Ex. 1, George Dep. at 60.

- ◆ It is bad faith for an insurer to impose requirements on an insured that are not contained within the policy. *Amadeo v. Principal Mutual Life Ins. Co.*, 290 F.3d 1152 (9th Cir. 2002); *Ace v. Aetna Life Ins. Co.*, 139 F.3d 1241 (9th Cir. 1998); Ex. 2, International Claims Ass'n, Statement of Principles ¶ 3.

As outlined below, a reasonable jury could conclude each of these principles was violated by the defendant in its handling of the claim. This creates a genuine issue of material fact as to whether the defendant's conduct can be considered "reasonable."

Once you are done with your list of Rules for the judge, it is time to show him how a jury could conclude that these Rules were violated. Often, the best way to organize that section of the brief is to repeat a Rule as an argument heading, and then inventory the evidence establishing the violation.

This approach to brief writing also works well on appeal. You give the judges a framework for thinking about the case. If these accepted, well-recognized standards were violated, how can the defendant's conduct be "reasonable"?

Your motions work is done. It is now time for your final trial preparation.

13

FINALIZING THE
RULES OF THE ROAD

It is shortly before trial. You are focusing on your presentation to the jury. It is time to finalize your Rules of the Road. Hopefully, you have a good command of the facts and an annotated list of Rules you are comfortable with.

All good trial lawyers look at the jury instructions for the elements (standards) they must prove, then pick and choose from the available evidence to maximize their chances of proving those elements. As outlined in chapter 4, "Developing a Working List of Rules," you should write your jury instructions early in the case to facilitate this process.

The Rules technique requires that you *also* engage in the reverse of this process. That is, you look at the facts at your disposal as you decide what standards you want to present to the jury.

To illustrate, let's look at the elements of a claim for defamation of a private figure in California. CACI 1702 provides the following:

1702. Defamation per se—Essential Factual Elements

(Private Figure—Matter of Public Concern)

[Name of plaintiff] claims that [name of defendant] harmed [him/her] by making [one or more of] the following statement(s): [list all claimed per se defamatory statement(s)]. To establish this claim, [name of plaintiff] must prove all of the following:

1. That [name of defendant] made [one or more of] the statement(s) to [a person/persons] other than [name of plaintiff];

2. That [this person/these people] reasonably understood that the statement(s) [was/were] about [name of plaintiff];

3. That [this person/these people] reasonably understood the statement(s) to mean that [insert ground(s) defamation per se, e.g., "(name of plaintiff) had committed a crime"];

4. That *the statement(s)* [was/were] *false*; and

5. That [name of defendant] failed to use *reasonable care* to determine the truth or falsity of the statement(s).[1]

We have to prove the statement was false. That is an unambiguous legal standard. We will go through our inventory of facts to see how we can prove the statement was false. The Rules of the Road won't help us much here, except to formulate the following statement for our list of principles:

> It's wrong to publish false statements that make someone look bad.

---

1. Emphasis added.

We also have to prove the defendant failed to use "reasonable care to determine the truth or falsity of the statement(s)." This is *not* a clear standard and, therefore, is one that *can* be shaped by our Rules. Suppose we have an annotated list that includes:

> Journalists should always attempt to check the credibility of their source before publishing information conveyed by the source.
>
> Journalists should ask the subject of a story about negative facts before publishing those facts.

We know that the journalist in question did neither of these things. We will, therefore, select these two "standards" to go with our facts. They meet our criteria in that:

- They are easy for the jury to understand.
- They require that the defendant do something.
- Presumably, we are comfortable with our annotations and feel the defense cannot credibly dispute the requirement.
- We know they were violated by the defendant.
- They will be persuasive to the jury in evaluating whether the defendant exercised "reasonable care."

We have done two things by selecting these standards. First, as a practical matter, we have gone a long way toward defining "reasonable care" for the jury. Second, we have provided a definition we know was violated. In other words, in addition to the usual process of selecting facts to fit our standards, we have also selected standards to fit our facts.

Look at your annotated Rules list. You want to select eight to twelve Rules to put on a large board to show the jury, judge, and witnesses.

Remember our criteria for Rules:

1. Require that the defendant do, or not do, something.
2. Be easy for the jury to understand.

3. Be a requirement the defense cannot credibly dispute.

4. Be a requirement the defendant has violated.

5. Be important enough in the context of the case that proof of its violation will significantly increase the chance of a plaintiff's verdict.

Think about each Rule in the context of these criteria. Think about opening, direct exam, cross-exam, and final argument. Which of your annotated Rules will be most helpful in advancing your case? In constructing your trial Rules board, here are some guidelines to think about.

Guideline the Authors Disagree On

Despite having distinctly different backgrounds and experiences, we, the authors of this book, have had a relatively easy time reaching agreement on the advice in the book. On the first point in these guidelines, we could not reach agreement. Rather than reach some wishy-washy compromise or avoid the point altogether, we have elected to present both points of view, and allow you to decide which makes the most sense in your particular case.

- Rick's Guideline 1. Never call your Rules "Rules" or "Rules of the Road." Not on your chart, not to opposing counsel, not to the witnesses, not to the jury. It is too easy for the defense to interpose invalid objections that can distract and confuse the judge. It can look too much like you are attempting to instruct the jury on the law. The judge is supposed to say what the "rules" are, not some lawyer or expert—or so the argument goes. When many of your Rules are in fact based upon legal principles, this is dangerous territory. It is dangerous, not because you are doing anything wrong, but because the judge may not understand what you are doing. The word "rules" blurs the distinction between a legal standard and an industry standard.

Remember, you are expressing "well-recognized standards in the industry," or "basic principles"[2] or similar concepts. My experience has been that using the term "Rules" buys you needless and unnecessary trouble.

Since publication of the first edition, I have become even more convinced about this advice. Defense lawyers are filing motions *in limine* to prevent the use of the words "Rules" or "Rules of the Road." To my knowledge, none of these motions has ever been granted, but why risk confusing the issue? Before the trial is over, these standards will be treated by the witnesses, lawyers, and jurors as rules—as they should be. Who cares what we call them?

♦ PAT'S GUIDELINE 1. I like the word "Rule." It's good, plain English. But we all know that courts and defense counsel sometimes have a perverse reaction to words that are too plain. So you need to be careful about labeling charts with red-flag words like "Rules" or "Rules of the Road." For a chart, it is probably better to use the label "industry standards" or "basic principles" or "standards of care."

Another approach I like is to put the headline as a rhetorical question: "What are the industry standards?" Yet another approach is to skip the headline. However, I disagree with the idea that the word "Rule" should never cross your lips at trial. I do think you have to use it, at least the first few times, in close proximity to a more legalistic term like "standards," until the judge is educated to what you're talking about. The advantage of using the "R word" is that everyone knows what it means. But you have to be careful in using any potent weapon. Is this one of those "rules" made to be broken? You have to find your own comfort zone on this one.

---

2. Here, we are using the term "principle" differently than discussed in chapter 5. There, we made clear that a principle is different than a Rule in that it does not explicitly require a particular conduct. Now, when we present our Rules to the judge and jury, we may call them principles in order to avoid objection, even though they, in fact, require particular conduct from the defendant.

Guidelines the Authors Agree On

- **Guideline 2.** Don't use the word "duty" on your chart, or in any other way in court when referring to the chart. "Duty" is a legal term. While many judges don't have trouble with an expert witness testifying to established law in relevant areas, others have a very hard time with it. Why invite objections? You don't need the term "duty." Use words like "should," "responsibility," even "must," as in: "a reasonable investigation must include . . .

- **Guideline 3.** Never make any direct references to the law on the list shown to the jury. You may have a Rule such as "Company must give equal regard to the insured's interests as it does to its own." This comes right out of a case, but you will have witnesses who will testify that this is a standard in the industry. Your Rules list will be discussed with the court, the jury, and the witnesses as: (a) a summary of the testimony, and/or (b) a summary of the basic principles or standards in the industry—with which everyone agrees. The law is for jury instructions only.

- **Guideline 4.** All the Rules should fit on one poster board. You will be using this board a lot. It must be easy to access and easy to read. That is why we recommend no more than twelve Rules on your final list. This is a guideline. We know of one lawyer who had over twenty Rules that took up three pages. It worked quite well for her, given the case she was trying. Still, remember, complexity and confusion are our enemies.

- **Guideline 5.** Try to make your Rules even simpler. One last time, go through each Rule and see if the Rule can be expressed in a still simpler way. The simpler and shorter, the better.

- **Guideline 6.** Make sure your Rules are absolutely clear and without ambiguity. Pronouns are one source of ambiguity. Is "he" a reference to the plaintiff, or the defendant? What does "it" refer to? Use concrete words.

- GUIDELINE 7. Create three versions of your list. The first is the jury list. It will look like those in appendix B, "Sample Insurance Bad Faith Rules of the Road," or appendix C, "Bus Stop Safety Principles." No annotations. The jury list will be shown to the jury and the witnesses. You will cross-examine and argue from it.

The second list is the judge's list. Early in the trial, the defense may start objecting to your use of the Rules.[3] The judge's list will have annotations of all the *evidence* that supports each Rule or principle. If your expert supports the Rule that a claims handler should assist the insured with the claim, the expert's name, and the page number of his deposition should be noted under the Rule. If the company claims manual also supports the Rule, that portion of the claims manual should be cited. Any admissions by defense witnesses that support the Rule should be noted as well. We tell the judge it is proper for the jury to see the jury list, because it is really just a quick and efficient way to distill and present the evidence they are going to hear. Most judges have no problem with that. *No legal authorities should be on the judge's list.* If we have legal authorities, it looks like we are trying to "argue the law," before closing argument. That can be a problem for some judges. We will discuss how to use the judge's list in the next chapter.

Finally, you should have your own annotated list. It includes all the Rules you believe could possibly become relevant during trial. It includes Rules you may never show the judge or the jury, but which you *might* show them, depending on how the trial goes. On this list will be *all* annotations to those Rules, including the legal annotations. This way, you will have at your fingertips any citations to facts or law you might need when discussing your Rules with anyone at trial.

---

3. In our experience, the defense objects to the Rules of the Road about half of the time. To date, these objections have never been sustained in any significant way.

COORDINATING THE EVIDENCE WITH YOUR RULES

Now, how do you coordinate your list of Rules with the evidence? Among the many ways to do this, here is one we've found effective:

1. Make sure all the key documents from the defendant's files are enlarged onto poster boards that are legible to both the witness and the jury. Not every single page, mind you, just the ones that contain a violation of one or more Rules. Deposition transcripts of defense witnesses can get the same poster board treatment.

2. With your expert on the witness stand, show the list of rules on one easel at the same time as, on a second easel, you display a defense document or transcript illustrating a violation of a rule.

3. Now, as each violation is identified, mark the exhibit with a small round red sticker—the kind of sticky-backed bullets you buy in sheets at an office-supply store. Three-quarters or one inch in diameter is a good size.

4. If you can get defense witnesses to agree with Rules violations, you can add another red sticker when they're on the stand.

5. If you red-sticker each Rule violation on all the exhibits and deposition transcripts throughout the trial, you should have used several sheets of stickers by the end. Now you have a powerful visual tool for closing argument. Array the red-stickered poster boards around the well of the courtroom, wherever the judge lets you put them, and show them to the jury. You won't need to spend much time on each. The visual impact is the key.

14

Motions *In Limine* About the Rules

Defense lawyers have begun filing motions *in limine*, seeking orders preventing lawyers or witnesses from using the terms "Rules" or "Rules of the Road."

It is impossible to catalog every argument the defense might make and the appropriate responses, but here are a few responses you might consider:

- These are well-recognized standards in the industry or field. We expect experts to testify about principles and standards in their field; they do it every day. The defense is just uncomfortable that we are pointing out that they violated such a standard. They are free to argue there is no such standard or that they didn't violate it—that's what trials are for.

- We are calling them Rules because they *are* rules. They are standards of conduct that actors in this field or industry are supposed to follow. Even some of the defense witnesses admit these are valid standards of conduct. If the defense wants to argue with the word "Rules," they are free to do so in front of the jury.

- The jury knows the difference between an industry rule or standard and the "law" the court will instruct on at the end of the trial. Neither we nor our witnesses will directly or indirectly suggest these Rules are the "law."

- Yes, some of these Rules have their basis in law. But that does not mean an expert should not be allowed to talk about them. The law on the highway is a 65 mph speed limit. It is the tractor-trailer industry standard to follow that law. An expert can certainly talk about the speed limit where the accident occurred. A construction-site safety inspector can talk about the law contained in the building code or in OSHA regulations. Our experts are doing the same thing. The fact that something is the law does not mean witnesses cannot mention it. Obviously, the court will instruct on the law at the end of the case.

You can certainly think of other responses. For a very nice brief opposing a motion *in limine* to prevent reference to "rules," see appendix L, "Response to Motion *In Limine*."

15

Voir Dire

Voir dire is a very personal matter. Everyone has his own style and attitude toward the process—largely influenced by the customs where he practices. What is allowed varies from state to state, and even courtroom to courtroom. What would be brilliant in one courtroom could be disastrous in another. Here are our ideas on *voir dire* with respect to Rules of the Road. Try what seems helpful and ignore the rest.

First, in our view, there is no need to talk about your Rules of the Road with the jury during *voir dire*. Most of the time we don't. Even when the judge allows it, you run the risk of sounding like you are arguing your case at a time when jurors can feel that is improper.

It can be helpful to get the jurors thinking about the importance of safety rules in general. Again, most of the time we don't do this. Virtually all jurors believe in the importance of safety rules and the importance of following them. Why waste valuable *voir dire* time talking about something everyone agrees on?

There are occasions when asking about Rules in *voir dire* seems called for. In our view, this most often occurs when we are afraid the jurors will excuse Rule violations. Then, it can be helpful to have an early discussion about the reasons for safety rules and what excuses their violation.

A medical malpractice case was tried in a town of less than ten thousand people. The defendant had lived there for thirty years, delivering close to half the babies born during those years. One of the jurors was a coast guard commander in charge of a large ship with 135 crew members. The Rules portion of *voir dire* went like this:

- Are there safety rules that you are required to enforce as commander of this vessel?

- Are those safety rules important? Why?

- Do you sometimes have to enforce those rules and discipline a sailor, even when he did not intend to break those rules? Is that personally hard for you sometimes? Why do you still do it?

- What would happen if you decided to let a crew member get away with breaking a safety rule?

Other jurors heard the commander give an eloquent explanation about the importance of enforcing safety rules, even when it is personally uncomfortable to do so.

You could also ask:

- If Dr. Smith had run a red light in this case and caused an accident, does anyone think he should not be responsible for the harm he caused? Even if he lived here thirty years? Should he be held responsible, even if he didn't mean to hurt anyone? Even if it was just a moment of neglect or carelessness?

- If we prove that Dr. Smith violated medical safety rules—as basic as the driving safety rule of not running a red light—when he treated Mrs. Jones, does anyone feel as though he shouldn't be held responsible? Even if he lived here thirty years?

Sometimes we will ask if there are any pilots on the jury and then ask:

- Are there basic safety rules you have to follow in every single flight? Like what?

- Once you have enough hours of flying time, is it okay to no longer do a preflight checklist? You are now so experienced, can't you just rely on your judgment and experience?

You get the idea. Watch for jurors who have to follow or enforce safety rules at their jobs. Get them talking about why those rules are important to the safety of co-workers and, more important, to the general public.

You are making the point that we all need to follow safety rules. Then when the jury sees the Rules in opening, it will be prepared to accept them—especially if you can say where they come from and that the defense agrees with most of them.

16

Opening Statement

In chapter 13, we talked about how to finalize your Rules into three lists, one for the jury, one for the judge, and one for yourself. Now that you are almost ready for trial, it's time to outline an opening statement.

Your opening statement should not be a mechanistic recitation of the Rules and their violation. Instead, as we discussed in the chapter on fitting the Rules into your case story, you use the Rules to support the story you are telling and to undermine the defense story.

There is no single right way to use the Rules of the Road in an opening statement. We can show you what has worked for us and explain why it has been effective. But because every case is different, you will need to find what works for your cases.

Generally, here is the format we follow in the liability portion of our opening:[1]

---

[1] Damages are an essential topic for the plaintiff's lawyer, which we don't say much about in this book. Damages deserves a book of its own, and it has a masterpiece, in DAVID BALL ON DAMAGES—THE ESSENTIAL UPDATE: A PLAINTIFF'S ATTORNEY'S GUIDE FOR PERSONAL INJURY AND WRONGFUL DEATH CASES (2nd ed. National Institute for Trial Advocacy 2005).

- ♦ BRIEF OVERVIEW OF THE FACTS. We start in a neutral, just-the-facts way. Remember, premature advocacy can be a credibility turnoff to skeptical jurors. You want to win them over with the facts.

- ♦ DESCRIPTION OF THE RULES. We like to describe in some detail how the defendant's industry or profession is supposed to work, but in a general way, focused on what matters for this case. In a medical case, for example, you might focus on the importance of teamwork and clear communication among the members of a patient's hospital care team.

- ♦ WHY THE RULES ARE IMPORTANT AND MAKE SENSE. This usually is part of the Rule description but deserves special emphasis. Some people will follow a rule simply because it is the rule. Most people need to understand the reason for a rule before they are willing to follow it—or hold others to it. Jurors are no different. At some point during the trial, you must explain to the jury *why* the Rule or standard makes sense. Opening statement is a logical place to do that. It's also very helpful to talk about the history of the Rule if you have a credible history to tell.

- ♦ HOW THE DEFENDANT BROKE THE RULES. Here we transition back to the case by saying that the plaintiff is suing the defendant for breaking the standards (Rules). Then we go back through the chronology of the case, in more detail than in the introduction, explaining at each point how the defendant violated industry/professional standards. Here, we might first preview testimony of experts.

- ♦ UNDERMINE THE DEFENSE EXCUSES. Then we will go through the defenses in detail and explain why they are wrong: because they don't fit with the basic standards/rules.

We like this structure because it gives us the chance to go through the critical facts at least three times (introduction, Rules violations, and defenses-undermining) but in a nonrepetitive way. By the time we sit down, the jury has become familiar with the basic chronology of the case and will know all the plaintiff's theories and the plaintiff's response to the defense excuses.

We also like this structure because it capitalizes on a basic strength of the Rules approach: *it keeps the focus on the defendant and its conduct.* Repeated social-science studies (including extensive work by AAJ) have confirmed that the more time spent with the spotlight on the defendant, the greater the chance of a victory for the plaintiff. Implicitly, if not explicitly, we tell the jury that all of us have gathered in this courtroom because of the conduct of the defendant, because the defendant broke the Rules and hurt someone.

Some Rules are so basic you may want to start your opening with them. In personal injury cases, jury consultant David Ball likes to coach the plaintiff's lawyers to make these the first words out of their mouths when they stand up to talk to the jury:

> Ladies and gentlemen. There's a rule that you're going to hear a lot about in this case. If you are careless, and you hurt someone, you are responsible for all the damage that you have caused.

In a malpractice case, you might add:

> It doesn't matter if you're an important person *[or, in a products case, an important company]* or if you are busy doing good work. If you are careless, and you hurt someone, you are responsible for all the damage that you caused.

Of course, no opening in a big case is complete without a blizzard of defense objections. Let's talk about some of the predictable ones.

Handling Objections to Opening

In opening statement, you want to introduce the jury to the Rules of the Road. You have your board with your list of Rules.

154   *Rules of the Road*

You want to show it to the jury. The defense is likely to object. Here are some of the common objections and responses.[2]

OBJECTION: This has not been premarked as an exhibit.[3]

RESPONSE: It is not intended to be an exhibit and go to the jury. It is illustrative. It is a summary of the testimony the jury is going to hear in this trial. It will save a lot of time to present the information this way, as opposed to my discussing each witness and what each is going to say about these things.

[These standards are not controversial—even the defense witnesses agree with them.]

OBJECTION: Counsel is instructing the jury on the law; that is the court's function at the end of the case.

RESPONSE: These are not legal standards, these are insurance (or bus or medical or aviation) industry standards. The testimony will be that these are basic principles accepted by everyone in the industry. Some of them may also be incorporated in the law, but that is not what I intend to talk to the jury about—nor will the witnesses who will testify as to these standards.

---

2. With regard to the responses, we are not suggesting you use all those described for a particular objection. You need to figure out what will be most persuasive to your judge: some, all, or none of the responses.
3. This is the kind of objection that you can sometimes head off by adroit pretrial maneuvering. Think about proposing a list of stipulations to be agreed to at the pretrial conference, including boilerplatelike authenticity of exhibits and a few others that give both sides more flexibility at trial, such as:
- Demonstrative aids are enlargements of evidence or argument that are intended to help educate the jury but are not being offered into evidence as exhibits.
- Demonstrative aids containing medical illustrations will be exchanged ___ weeks before trial.
- Demonstrative aids consisting of enlargements of documents with explanatory text or markings need not be exchanged before trial.
- Demonstrative aids consisting of text only need not be exchanged before trial if they are intended to help educate the jury but are not being offered into evidence.

OBJECTION: This is argumentative.

RESPONSE: This is not argument, this is evidence. Your Honor, I have put together an annotated chart for you, so you can see the evidentiary source of each principle. I am not making this up. I am not arguing. I am telling the jury what the evidence will show: that Acme's own manual and claims manager agree that Acme has a duty to assist the policyholder with the claim. This is a quick, efficient way to give the jury an overview of the evidence they are going to hear. That is the purpose of opening statement.

If the judge seems to be leaning toward the defense on this issue, ask if there would be any problem with your writing these principles on a blackboard as you give your opening. Say that using the board is the same thing, just written out ahead of time, in neater script.

You can also argue that clearly you can say to the jury, "The testimony will be that everyone in the insurance industry, including Acme's witnesses, recognizes that insurance companies should assist the policyholder with his claim." If you can say it to the jury, why not show it? *It will make things go much faster.*

If the judge still will not let you show the board to the jury, say something like this in opening:

> During this trial you are going to hear that there are nine basic principles that apply to the type of surgery that was performed in this case. These principles are so basic and commonly accepted that I don't believe you will hear a single witness disagree with them. Some of these principles are stated right in the hospital's own manual. The first is . . .

Then, just discuss each principle as if the board were there.

Concluding Thoughts on Opening Statement

The Rules approach can help you avoid a mistake we frequently see in openings.

The trial books and CLE speakers all tell us we must show the jury how much we believe in our case. Many lawyers misinterpret this to mean they must be emphatic and emotional in opening statement. This is a big mistake.

At this stage of a trial, the jurors do not trust you. They have no reason to. Everyone knows "lawyers can't be trusted." They will see your emotion as a cheap parlor trick.

Stated another way, at the opening-statement stage, jurors are still trying to decide if they can trust you—and your emotions. The best way to show them they can trust you is to show them standards that cannot be disputed (your Rules) and evidence that shows those standards have been violated.

Emotion at this stage accentuates your bias. Better to show the jury that you can back up everything you are saying. Show them the documents; show them pages from depositions. Show them they don't have to take your word for anything—it's all here in black and white.

This doesn't mean you should adopt a flat, detached tone. You should be animated and involved with your story. If you don't sound interested in what you're saying, no one else will be interested either.

Show the jurors you care about your case by showing them you cared enough to do the work, to be meticulously prepared, and to back up everything you tell them. You must trust them to understand and have the appropriate emotions. You don't have to tell them how to feel or what to think.

17

Direct Examination of Your Expert

Testifying to the Rules of the Road

Early in your case in chief, an expert should introduce the Rules to the jury. The defense now has its last opportunity to shut down your use of the Rules, so expect objections similar to those discussed in the previous chapter.

Your responses to these objections are similar: (1) the expert is knowledgeable about the industry; (2) she is testifying to well-recognized standards in the industry; (3) all reasonable industry participants recognize and follow these standards; and (4) for the expert to state her opinion as to the wrongfulness of the defendant's conduct, she must first explain the standards to which she is holding the defendant.

Appendix F, "Direct Examination of Plaintiff's Insurance Expert in a Bad Faith Case," is an excerpt of a bad faith case. This is from the same case as the opening statement in appendix I, "Bad Faith Case Opening Statement." A few shorter excerpts are printed here to illustrate specific points.

Explaining Reasons for the Rule

As mentioned in our discussion of the opening statement, the jury needs to hear not just the Rules themselves, but the reasons behind them. As the witness testifies, the board with the list of Rules sits in front of the jury. In the following excerpt, the **bold type** is a paraphrase of the Rule or standard on the board.

Direct Examination Continued by Mr. Friedman

Q: Mr. Prater, when we ended yesterday, we were talking about whether or not there were certain claims handling standards or principles[1] that were well accepted in the industry and that you considered applicable to this case?

A: Yes.

Q: Could you tell the jury what some of those principles are?

A: Sure. One of the principles is that **an insurance company is supposed to treat its insured's interests at least equal with its own. It's not supposed to be an adversarial process** when you're dealing with what we call a first-party claim, where you pay an insurance premium to your own insurance company for homeowner's or auto, and something happens. You don't pay the premium, expecting to have to get into an adversarial relationship, and insurance company claims handlers are trained with first-party claims to try and not be adversarial, and to give the insured's interest at least as much consideration as they give themselves.

• • •

Q: Other standards or principles?

---

1. Here again, we are using the term "principle" differently than discussed in chapter 5. There, we made clear that a principle is different from a Rule in that it does not explicitly require a particular conduct. Now, as we present our Rules to the jury, we may call them principles in order to avoid objection, even though they, in fact, require particular conduct from the defendant.

A: **An insurance company has a duty to assist an insured with a claim** because, you know, insurance policies are written with complex phraseology that's written by the insurance company, and a lot of times people don't understand what they are entitled to or understand what the insurance company needs. And so it's an insurance company's obligation to assist the insured in any way necessary to help the insured receive everything they are entitled to. They have to point out other kinds of coverages that the insured might not know about, or if something is needed or necessary, they have to assist the insured in obtaining it if they can't get it themselves, those kinds of things.

Explaining That the Rule Is Well Recognized

Remember, we selected these Rules because we believe the defense cannot credibly argue with them. Now we start rubbing their noses in it.

Q: Let me just ask now before we go through the other standards: are the standards that you're talking about today—are they standards that are Professor Prater's standards, or are these well accepted in the industry?

A: No, these are not my standards. These are concepts that are well known and understood by claims handlers around the United States. These are basic elementary claims handling standards that people are trained in.

Q: And, in fact, were some of the claims handlers in this case asked about many or most of these standards?

A: Yes, many of the people in their depositions that worked on this claim were asked if they agreed with these standards, these concepts, and they all unanimously basically agreed.

Notice that in these examples, the witness was not questioned about the sources for these Rules. In part, this was because many were legal sources. We did not want to provoke objections that the witness was testifying as to the law. In addition, we did not want to bog down the jury with minutiae. The Rules, as explained by the expert, made sense and seemed fair. We knew the defense would concede these Rules. We didn't need to go into the sources.

Setting Up Evidence from Learned Treatises

What if the defense doesn't concede your Rules? Then you may need to establish the pedigree of your Rules by discussing their sources. Of course, your experts can give citations for all the Rules they discuss, at the risk of boring the jury with numerous oral footnotes. Another approach is to confront the defense experts with the citations and annotations that prove your Rules really are the Rules. This is obviously more interesting to the jury. We discuss this in detail in the next chapter on cross-examination. Here, in a discussion of direct examination of plaintiff's experts, only one point needs to be made, but it is critical: you should consider having at least one of your experts on direct examination identify statements from treatises and literature that they regard as "reliable authority," so that you are then set up to cross-examine defense experts with this material. It can be done as quickly as this:

Q: Let me show you exhibits X, Y, and Z, which are excerpts from medical textbooks. Did you look at these exhibits before trial?

A: Yes.

Q: Do you consider these exhibits as reliable authority?

A: Yes, I do.

That is all you need to do on direct examination. You don't offer the exhibits into evidence. You don't even need to read from them at this point. But you have set yourself up for important cross-examination of defense experts and important reinforcement of the validity of your Rules, which are expressed in these treatises.

Testimony About Sources of Rules

Other times, you will want a fairly detailed explanation from your expert about the sources of Rules. For example, in the bus stop case, we did not know what the defense witnesses would say at trial about the Rules, because we did not get involved in the case until after the defense witnesses had been deposed. Accordingly, it seemed to us more important to show the jury early in the case that we had sources for our Rules. Still, we did not want to bog down. Appendix G, "Direct Examination of Plaintiff's Bus Stop Expert," shows you how we handled this in the trial testimony of the plaintiff's expert. As you will see, the bases for some of the Rules were discussed in detail. For others, that were less disputable, we elicited little or no discussion of sources.

Rules Violations and Plaintiff's Experts

After the plaintiff's expert explains the Rules of the Road, you have some tactical choices to make—choices you need to think about before trial. Having had one expert—perhaps an academic—explain the Rules, do you want a more hands-on expert to discuss how they were violated? Or do you want the same expert to explain the Rules and their violation? Still another option is to have no expert explain how the Rules were violated; simply establish their violation with fact witnesses or through cross-examining the defense experts. This latter approach can make for a disjointed and confusing presentation, unless the underlying facts are fairly straightforward. For that reason, we often like to have our first expert witness walk the jury through a detailed chronology of the case and the main Rules violations. A strong, sympathetic fact witness can sometimes serve the same purpose of orienting and anchoring the jury. Usually, though, an expert needs to do this heavy lifting.

There is no right answer about how to present Rules violations, only questions to consider. One important consideration is how you expect the cross-examinations of the defense witnesses to go. So let's look at that.

18

CROSS-EXAMINATION

One of the joys of the Rules of the Road approach is the opportunity to cross-examine defense witnesses about the Rules. In essence, you have been preparing this cross-examination throughout the case.

Well-honed Rules of the Road provide a structure for the first part of your cross-examination—if not all of it. As with depositions, you have the tactical choice of talking to the witness first about the source, and then about the principle, or the reverse. If you have prepared your Rules well, there is usually no danger in going right to the principle. If the witness fights, go to the source of your principle to secure agreement.

Obviously, you should not cross-examine every defense witness on the Rules of the Road. After one or two defense witnesses have acknowledged the applicability of your Rules, it may be overkill to ask others about them. And some fact witnesses will know nothing of the standards in the industry.

This chapter will be divided into two major sections. In the first, we address the examination of expert or lay witnesses who *will* concede at least some of your Rules or standards. These witnesses retain at least some integrity. In the second section, we address the handling of witnesses who concede next to nothing. Bear in mind the scope of this book: we treat only those aspects of cross-examination for which the Rules of the Road technique provides significant help.

INTELLECTUALLY HONEST WITNESSES

If you routinely depose defense experts and defense fact witnesses at the managerial and policy-making levels, you will have a sense, long before you stand up to cross-examine them, of their honesty and the likelihood that they will give you favorable material without too much of a fight. Sometimes, of course, a kitten at deposition turns into a tiger at trial. If you have a basically honest witness who starts to fight out of fear (fear of the courtroom, fear of you, fear for her job), the Rules can help tame the witness quickly. Here is the basic technique.

First, remember a priority of cross-examination: seek favorable concessions first. If you obtain agreement from the witness on anything significant, you may not have to do anything else. You don't have to try to hurt any witness—by exposing bias, prejudice, or lack of credibility in general—unless the witness has first hurt you.

So it makes sense to first have in front of you the annotated Rules and start your cross-examination with the Rules themselves. Remember, your annotated Rules are your cheat sheet marked with your Rules sources, including all the favorable concessions already obtained in discovery.

Take the witness through the principles set out in your Rules one by one. Which ones you focus on first will depend on the witness's area of knowledge and your own priorities in the proof. Generally, you can make your life easier and look stronger to the jury by starting with the Rules the witness is most likely to concede.

If the witness agrees with a Rule, great; move on to the next principle. If he disagrees, review your annotations and pick appropriate follow-up questions:

- Is he familiar with the statute or regulation (or policy statement or literature, and so forth) that is the source of your Rule?
- Does the witness know that another employee of the defendant agreed that this principle is well understood and accepted in the industry?

- If she disagrees with the principle—for example, that the company should treat an insured's interest with equal regard as its own—then ask what is the accurate way to express the principle? That the company can put its interests ahead of the insured?

Here we can unleash our polarizing technique again.

Q: So you do *not* believe it is your job to assist the policyholder with the claim?

Q: You think it is all right for you, as a claims handler, to misrepresent facts or policy provisions?

Q: You do *not* believe it is necessary for the claims handler to document all important activity in the claim file?

In other words, get him to *disagree* with your Rules. That means he is disagreeing with your expert and all your other sources. You decide whether or not to point that out to him.

If you have the witness's agreement to the Rules, the cross-examination is easy. Let's use the first three Rules in appendix A, "Annotated Rules of the Road: A Master List," as an example:

1. Business of insurance is highly specialized, with policyholders particularly vulnerable and dependent on their insurance company.

2. Company must treat its policyholder's interests with equal regard as it does its own interests. This is not an adversarial process.

3. Part of claim examiner's job is to assist the policyholder with the claim.

The witness has agreed to these Rules, and it is now time to compare these standards with the company's performance. Any cross-examination is going to be heavily fact dependent; the examples below are to stimulate your own thinking.

Q: At the time you received Mr. Smith's letter asking you to further explain your denial, you knew he was *vulnerable and dependent* on your company. *[Rule 1]*

A: I didn't really know his situation.

Q: But you knew as a general principle *[pointing to chart]* that policyholders are particularly vulnerable and dependent on their insurance company?

A: Yes.

Q: And you knew he was claiming he couldn't work?

A: He was claiming that, yes.

Q: And you knew if that was true, he was entitled to his policy benefits?

A: Yes.

Q: And you knew if he couldn't work and you didn't pay his benefits, he might very well suffer hardship?

A: That could happen.

Q: When you told him you would not give him the IME report, was *that treating Mr. Smith's interests with equal regard to the company's interests? [Rule 2]*

A: It was company policy.

Q: Is that an example *of treating the insured's interest with equal regard to the company's interests?*

A: I don't know.

Q: Is that an example of *assisting him with the claim? [Rule 3]*

You have chosen these Rules because you believe you can show they were violated. Now is the time to do that. As the example above illustrates, you don't need to get the witness to *admit* the rule was violated. If you have structured your Rule correctly and ask good questions, the conclusion should be obvious.

Suppose you are also working with Rule 4 in appendix A:

Company must fairly, reasonably and promptly investigate the claim.

Q: Mr. Smith told you his doctor would support his disability and wanted to talk with you?

A: Yes.

Q: But you never called his doctor, did you?

A: His doctor could have called me.

Q: His doctor did not have a duty to fairly investigate this claim, did he?

A: No.

Q: You did, didn't you?

A: Yes.

Q: And you knew Mr. Smith was *vulnerable and dependent on you? [Rule 1]*

A: Yes.

Q: And you knew *it was part of your job to assist him with this claim? [Rule 3]*

A: Yes.

Q: You never called his doctor?

A: No.

Q: Is this an example of what Acme considers a *fair and reasonable investigation of his claim? [Rule 4]*

All you are doing is comparing the facts of the case to standards the witness has already adopted. This is what you have been working toward since you wrote your first draft Rule. Think again about what we discussed in chapter 13, "Finalizing the Rules of the Road," about looking at facts and then working backward to articulate standards that have been violated.

Appendix K, "Cross-Examination of School Bus Company Manager," comes from our bus stop case. He is being called in the plaintiff's case as an adverse witness. He was never deposed about the Rules of the Road. As you will see, because the Rules were carefully selected, he was not in a position to disagree with any of them. Notice what happens when he tries to resist. This is a good example of how the Rules allow you to keep the adverse witness fighting on your ground—ground you have prepared the jury to accept as critically important.

Intellectually Dishonest Witnesses

No matter how much we lawyers steep ourselves in whatever the case is about—be it neurosurgery or bridge design—a knowledgeable but dishonest expert witness can often run rings around us—at least, if we choose to let him define the issues.

With the Rules of the Road approach, *we* define the issues. Let the dishonest expert say child safety should not be the primary consideration in pupil transportation. Let him say a surgeon need not identify what he is cutting before he cuts it. And let him contradict the authoritative literature in his field. Using this literature to cross-examine defense experts is an essential part of the Rules technique.

Handling "Learned Treatises" at Trial

One of the most important weapons the plaintiff's lawyer has in establishing and enforcing Rules of the Road at trial is Fed. R. Evid 803(18) or its state counterpart. Read this rule until its substance is burned in your memory.[1] Here are the key features:

---

1. The full text of Fed. R. Evid. 803(18): "The following are not excluded by the hearsay rule, even though the declarant is available as a witness: . . . (18) To the extent called to the attention of an expert witness upon cross-examination or relied upon by the expert witness in direct examination, statements contained in published treatises, periodicals, or pamphlets on a subject of history, medicine, or other science or art, established as reliable authority by the testimony or admission of the witness or by other expert testimony or by judicial notice. If admitted, the statements may be read into evidence but may not be received as exhibits."

- "Statements" in learned treatises, literature, and so on.

- Established as "reliable authority." Remember, the entire treatise doesn't have to be established as reliable authority, just the statement you want to introduce. So a defense expert cannot run from conceding "reliable authority" by offering the truism that he doesn't agree with everything in the treatise. That's not your point. Of course, no book is infallible (aside from certain religious tomes beyond the scope of this book). A "reliable authority" is one that is generally highly regarded and looked to by experts in the field for answers.[2]

- Something can be established as "reliable authority" by one of three methods:

  1. Judicial notice.

  2. Your own expert's say-so on direct examination.

  3. The defense expert's concession on cross-examination.

As we discussed in chapter 17 under "Setting Up Evidence from Learned Treatises," part of your direct examination of any friendly expert should focus on identifying literature that supplies objective confirmation for your Rules. If your expert goes so far as to say she "relies on" these treatises, then they can be read into evidence while she is on the stand. But if you want to save your firepower for cross, just have the expert quickly identify the statements as reliable authority, without reading them into evidence, and move on without elaboration. You have laid the foundation for cross-examining the defense experts with the text, because your expert has established it as "reliable authority."

---

2. Two federal cases have interesting commentary on how wide the net can be cast to make a statement authoritative. Compare *Meschino v. North American Drager, Inc.*, 841 F.2d 429, 434 (1st Cir. 1988) with *Costantino v. David M. Herzog, M.D., P.C.*, 203 F.3d 164, 172 (2d Cir. 2000).

Once you have identified objective sources of rules through your own experts, you should come back to them when cross-examining defense witnesses. Here is one way we like to do it:

Q: Dr. ___, I want to show you a statement from Harrison's Principles of Internal Medicine, 14th edition. You agree Harrison's is a good book that has helpful knowledge for doctors?

[Two points here: You don't use the buzzword "reliable authority," which this witness has been trained to avoid like a third rail. You have already established through your expert that the relevant passage is "reliable authority"; this is a trap that helps you no matter which way the witness answers.]

A: I don't know what you mean by "good book."

Q: Well, a lot of people have used it over the years?

A: I don't know that.

Q: A lot of doctors have found it helpful over the years?

A: I don't use it myself, so I wouldn't know.

Q: Well, let's see here *[turning to copyright page]*. It says it was first published in 1937, right?

A: I'll take your word for it.

Q: And we know it's been updated and republished thirteen times, right? That's what it means by fourteenth edition, true?

A: Yes it's been through fourteen editions.

Q: And the editors are . . . *[here you go through a segue as long as you like, making the point that the editors and authors of individual chapters are tenured professors at leading medical schools.]*

Q: Are you familiar with the _____ Medical School? Do you know Dr. _____? Do you know Dr. _____? *[The witness will usually not know them, which won't improve the witness's stature in the eyes of the jury.]*

A: The publisher wouldn't keep putting out new editions of the book if doctors didn't buy it, would they?

A: I have no idea.

Q: Well, medical publishers are like any other publishers, they want to make money on the books they sell, true? If not enough doctors find the book helpful enough to buy it, the book will go out of print, won't it?

You get the idea. The same technique applies, in even greater measure, to professional journals, where you can read to the witness the list of persons on the editorial advisory board, note that the journal is sent to every member of the profession's specialty society, describe the peer-review process for screening articles, and make other points to shore up the journal's stature.[3]

Finally, after you have patiently built up the book or journal in the eyes of the jury and lowered the witness's stature at the same time, you bring out the passage your expert has already identified as reliable authority. At this point, you read the passage into evidence, while you show it on a poster board or overhead projector. (See discussion below about handling defense objections to showing the quotation visually.) After you read it, you ask:

Q: Did I read that correctly?

A: Yes you did.

---

3. Which takes us to a story about one of my (Pat Malone's) cases. I had a malpractice case against a surgeon in a country town of fifty thousand people. Knowing how conservative the town was, we did a series of focus groups. I was proud of what I thought was one unassailable fact in our case: that what the defendant did had been recommended against by an article and editorial published five years before in the *New England Journal of Medicine*. I figured everyone knew that the *New England Journal of Medicine*, which is quoted almost every week on the television news, is the nation's leading peer-reviewed medical journal. But one of the focus group jurors scoffed: "I don't care what some damned magazine says the doctor is supposed to do!" That taught me that jurors need painstaking education on the authoritativeness of our sources for our Rules of the Road.

You do *not* need to ask the witness if he disagrees with the passage. And you certainly do not want to ask him to explain why he disagrees. If you do that, you are elevating the dishonest expert to a stature equal to that of the book or journal.

If the witness volunteers, "I don't agree with that passage you just read," your next question is:

Q: Where is the treatise you brought to court that shows that this is wrong?

And here the whorish adverse expert is hoisted on his own petard, because no doubt he has already stated that he recognizes *no* treatises as authoritative.

The "Blocking Interrogatory" Technique

How do we know that he has already stated that no treatise is authoritative? *Because you have already asked him that in deposition and through interrogatories.*

You want to make sure to block the defense from introducing new treatises and other "authorities" at trial. Here is one technique. We'll use interrogatories as an example, but the technique is equally applicable to depositions.

First, your interrogatory seeks positive Rules of the Road material by simply asking factually what the defendant looked at or has in his possession.

For example:

> Identify [by author, edition, publication date, name of publication, and title] all treatises, literature, or other publications you reviewed concerning Mr. Rice's atrial myxoma while he was your patient. In addition, identify all treatises, literature, or other publications you reviewed concerning Mr. Rice before you were told about the diagnosis of atrial myxoma.

Then, you ask:

> Identify all medical literature that you regard as reliable authority supporting any contention by you that (A) your conduct concerning Mr. Rice conformed to all applicable standards of care and (B) your care did not contribute to his injuries.

For good measure, these questions need to be expressly addressed to experts as well. You can do this very simply in an interrogatory:

> Identify any "reliable authority" that any of your expert witnesses intend to refer to at trial in support of their testimony or in response to any of the plaintiff's contentions or opinions.

Notice the difference between the two kinds of literature-identifying interrogatories you use in the context of Rules of the Road:

- When you are looking to find new Rules, you ask simple factual questions: "What did you read? What do you own?"

- When you are looking to block the defense from last-minute offers of its own authorities, you use instead the language from the Rule—"reliable authority"—and seek anything the defense identifies as such.

Seldom will a defendant fail to sweepingly deny the existence of "reliable authority." This puts you in the perfect posture to run with your own authoritative literature and prevent the defense from putting in its own. All this can be done through depositions, as well, but interrogatories work well for "blocking" because you can show the judge a single sheet of paper where you asked the question and the other side said "none."

If you give proper attention to these two key setup details—(1) having your expert sprinkle the magic words "reliable authority" on the treatise, and (2) asking the interrogatory to block the defense from bringing in their own authorities at the last minute—you will never have to fear even the most glib dishonest expert.

Because you will be able to say:

> Ladies and gentlemen, which side brought you the authoritative textbooks that were written to teach industry standards? That weren't written just to win a lawsuit? That's what we did for the plaintiff.
>
> Which side brought you paid, so-called experts who could show you no support in standard textbooks for the excuses they made for the defense? That's what the defense did here.

There are a lot of ways to phrase this powerful idea. With the right setup, it can be a neutron bomb against the defense.

One final thought on treatises: some defense lawyers sputter an objection whenever you actually show the text of the treatise on a screen or poster board. "It can only be read! It can't be shown!" they cry. Their basis is an overly literal reading of the last sentence of Rule 803(18), which says, "If admitted, the statements may be read into evidence but may not be received as exhibits." The purpose of this sentence, as the advisory committee notes and evidence commentators make clear, is not to favor auditory learners over visual learners on the jury, but to prevent the jury from thumbing through lengthy tomes in the jury room without expert guidance about what is important for the case. So there is nothing wrong with showing the actual language to the jury, and, in fact, you will always enhance the impact of your Rules if you show them in writing from their original source material.

19

Closing Argument

You can use the Rules of the Road technique in a variety of ways in your closing argument. Remember, though, it is a tool, not a formula, which must be adapted to the unique circumstances of each case. Here are some ideas.

Jury Instructions: the Judge's Rules

Some lawyers treat jury instructions as a pesky nuisance or, at best, a routine bit of boredom that distracts from the fun part of trial: cross-examination and argument. We disagree. Jury instructions are the secret weapon of the plaintiff's lawyer. You already have heard us nag about writing a set of proposed jury instructions at the start of the case. Our intent was to get you to create a road map to guide your case from discovery and motions on through closing argument.

The eventual jury instructions that come from the judge's mouth can be the most important Rules of the Road that the jury will hear. If you've followed our advice, your own set of Rules on liability issues will dovetail nicely, and at times duplicate, the judge's rules. So how do you handle the judge's rules in your closing argument?

We like to put the key instructions on liability and damages on poster boards and use them to summarize the evidence in our closing. You don't need to enlarge all of them, but there are some boilerplate instructions many lawyers overlook that can help you mightily, and we discuss those shortly.

You can easily move back and forth from the judge's rules to your Rules. For example, when you discuss an instruction with an ambiguous standard, use your Rules to define that standard. You might say:

> In instruction number 12, the court tells you that for Mr. Smith to win, we must prove Acme "intentionally denied the claim *without a reasonable basis*." Because you have spent three weeks in this courtroom, watching and listening, you now know what is *reasonable* in the insurance industry.
>
> The defendant's own witnesses told you that it is well understood in the insurance industry that reasonable investigation means looking for and considering evidence that supports the claim, not just looking for evidence that supports denial. Yet, look what they did. They didn't talk to John's family, they didn't talk to his co-workers, they didn't even talk to his doctors. All they did is pick out three statements from his medical records and deny. If they had talked to his doctors, they would have known . . .
>
> The defendant's own witnesses told you it is well understood in the insurance industry that claim handling should not be an adversarial process. Yet, look what they did *[summarize evidence showing violation]* . . .
>
> You'd think, if they were interested in getting at the truth, they would have answered John's questions when he wrote and asked _____. If what they were doing was reasonable, why were they trying to hide this information from him?

Do they have a *reasonable basis* when they never contacted his family, friends, or the treating doctors? Do they have a reasonable basis when they refused to respond to his questions?

Your goal is to make your Rules fit with the judge's rules as a seamless garment, which then becomes the unchallenged authority by which the jury must decide. The more you work throughout the case on drafting and using jury instructions, at the same time as you draft and redraft your own Rules of the Road, the easier this will become.

Boilerplate Instructions to Enforce Rules

When talking about instructions with the jury, how many times do we skip over the "boilerplate" instructions that the judge gives in every case? How often, for example, do we leave it to the defense lawyer to talk about the "no sympathy" standard instruction? In our rush to focus on what looks really important—for example, the instructions that set out the elements we must prove—we may overlook some powerful Rules-enforcing material in the boilerplate instructions. Some examples follow.

All judges tell juries not to be influenced by sympathy, passion, or prejudice. You can tie this into your Rules, like this:

> In instruction seventeen, the court instructs you that your verdict should not be motivated by sympathy, passion, or prejudice. I hope we have done nothing in this trial to make you think we want you to decide this case based on sympathy. We have asked you to evaluate this case, not based on sympathy, but based on the most basic principles in this industry *[pointing to Rules of the Road]*. You know why these principles are important, you know why it was wrong to violate them, and we trust that you understand the human cost of their violation.

When the defense counsel argues, ask yourself if he is doing the same. Is he asking you to evaluate the case based on these basic principles—that all his witnesses agreed to? Or is he asking for your sympathy, [passion, or prejudice] when he argues _____?

A similar argument comes from the standard jury instruction on "equality of litigants,"[1] which is often given with the "no sympathy" instruction. We like to use this instruction in professional malpractice cases, where we often represent someone with little education and community standing compared to the multi-degreed defendant. Jurors often tend to give professionals the benefit of the doubt. This instruction lets you argue that the law does not allow that.

Other boilerplate instructions contain important truths that you can use to keep the jurors focused on the facts of the case and not their fantasies. For example, every jurisdiction tells jurors that they are to consider *only* the evidence admitted in the case, plus reasonable inferences from the evidence.[2] You can fit this instruction in with your discussion of the basic elements of your liability case to construct a strong argument about what the jury can and cannot consider. For example, in a malpractice case, you can say:

> The judge has instructed you that you cannot use sympathy to decide this case. She has told you that you must decide this case only on the evidence you've heard. She's also told you that you must decide whether the defendant is liable by considering only whether he failed to do what a reasonably prudent doctor would have done, and whether

---

1. "This case should be considered and decided by you as a dispute between persons of equal standing in the community, of equal worth, and holding the same or similar stations in life. All persons stand equal before the law and are to be treated as equals." O'Malley, Grenig & Lee, 3 Federal Jury Practice and Instructions, No. 103.11 (5th ed. 2000).
2. E.g., O'Malley, Grenig & Lee, 3 Federal Jury Practice and Instructions, No. 104.20 (5th ed. 2000).

that harmed the plaintiff. How do you put all those instructions together?

If someone says in the jury room, "I feel sorry for the doctor. It seemed like he was trying to do the best he could," you can tell that juror, "The judge told us not to use sympathy in deciding the case.[3] And the judge told us to focus not on how hard someone tried, but on what the professional standards required under those circumstances."

What if someone says, "I don't want to hurt the doctor's reputation or career"? You should look back at the instructions the judge gave you. Was there anything in the instructions about deciding this case on worries about reputation? And is there any evidence about that? No. You are required by your oath as jurors to decide this case based on the instructions the judge gave you and the evidence you heard. Not speculation about what might happen later after the verdict.[4]

Another key instruction in civil cases is the burden of proof. Often, lawyers rush through this instruction with a wave of their arms held out like the scales of justice. Talking to the jury about the meaning of "preponderance of the evidence" sounds too often like a concession that their case is so thin it barely squeaks past the 50/50 tipping point. And in some cases, especially where they have elicited raw evidence of dishonest conduct and potential perjury by the defendant's employees, coming back to the "more likely than not" standard seems to cheapen the moral weight of the case.

---

3. This technique, of imagining a dialogue in the jury room and arming plaintiff-sympathetic jurors with what they can say, is not for every lawyer or every closing. We offer it only as an example of what you can do with a Rules-oriented approach to closing argument.
4. RICK FRIEDMAN, RICK FRIEDMAN ON BECOMING A TRIAL LAWYER (Trial Guides 2008) 123.

On the other hand, some of the worst injustices we have seen in civil lawsuits have happened when juries apply an implicit "reasonable doubt" standard to erase a mountain of the plaintiff's evidence. We've even heard jurors say afterward: "Well, you had a lot of evidence, but we just had some doubts. We weren't convinced."

In a case that is close enough where the "more likely than not" standard can change the outcome, we believe the standard needs to be addressed by the plaintiff's counsel in a Rules-enforcing way. In many cases, this will mean that "more likely than not" needs to be part of the questioning of key witnesses and part of the closing-argument discussion, not just once, but on each of the key issues addressed in closing. We have no perfect formula for accomplishing this. But if you bear in mind the risks of sounding weak or cheapening your evidence, we believe you will find the right words for your case.

Damages Instructions and Rules of the Road

This is mostly a book about proving liability. But the concept of Rules of the Road can be critical in proving damages too. In personal injury cases, we always use the damages instructions extensively in closing argument. They are, after all, not only the judge's rules, but Rules the other side has agreed to as well. This is your best weapon for taming rebellious jurors who escaped your *voir dire* strikes and who want to strike a blow against awarding damages for "pain and suffering." The term "pain and suffering" itself has been so lampooned by tort reformers that it's best to avoid using it. We prefer to find language in the instructions that lets the jurors consider this important element of damages in a more natural, less legalistic framework. For example, one damages instruction tells the jury to consider "the effects that any physical injuries have on the overall physical and emotional well-being of the plaintiff."[5]

---

5. Standardized Civil Jury Instructions for the District of Columbia No. 13-1 (2002 ed.)

Much more can be said about damages that is beyond the scope of the Rules technique. The point here is that in closing argument, we can use the judge's instructions on damages as "Rules enforcers" to obtain fair consideration of our case, just as we use other instructions as "Rules enforcers." And, of course, we weave the judge's rules into our own Rules.

Your Own Rules in Closing Argument

Let's get back to considering how you can use your own Rules in closing, apart from how they fit into the jury instructions. There are basically three alternatives to consider.

Alternative 1: No Witness Has Disagreed with the Rules as Stated by the Plaintiff

This scenario is a cakewalk, right? Don't be so sure. An ever-present danger in trying cases is getting lured into the underbrush where complexity, confusion, and ambiguity flourish. The trees—the Rules of the Road—may stand as majestically as any redwood in a forest. Never mind that. The defense counsel has enlisted the plaintiff's counsel in a mad scramble through the pine needles looking for some microscopic point that the defense claims is a small gem in disguise, if we would only take the time to look for it.

It's noisy in that dry underbrush, isn't it? Overhead, the trees stand silent. Too bad the plaintiff's lawyer is not calling attention to these tall beauties. He mentioned them in his opening statement. Had a nice poster board listing them. What did it say? Hmm, hard to remember now, two weeks later, listening to the closing argument. If only . . .

Here's the hard lesson: don't let the defense define what the case is about, or every tiny dispute will become overblown and the key concessions and admissions will be lost. If your key Rules have stood unscathed through the trial, you must—you must!—point out those great big trees looming overhead, lest they got lost in the scramble through the underbrush. It may not take long, but it is an essential ingredient of your closing.

This isn't as easy and straightforward as you might think. The whole reason we wrote this book is because the defense so often is allowed to pick the issues it wants to put into controversy, and the entire trial becomes a fight over those issues: complexity, confusion, and ambiguity. That's what trials are about, right? What people disagree over, right?

No.

Trials are about proving that your story about what happened between the plaintiff and the defendant is true. The Rules of the Road tie you to the mast of your ship. They let you prove your story and avoid the adrenaline-pounding temptation of following those Sirens who sing so softly to lure the unwary plaintiff's lawyer to a certain death.

But the Rules of the Road are not the story. The story must stay front and center. You know the story:

- "Careless doctor in a rush to finish takes fatal shortcut."

- "Claims manager under pressure to meet improper financial goals denies valid claim."

- "Drug company hides evidence of risk from doctors to boost profits on its big new prescription medication."

The Rules of the Road are a tool. They help you stick to the story. This is not to say you always need to say much about them in closing. In some cases, it's enough to prop up the poster board of the Rules and leave it there as you argue the rest of the case. In others, they will take a more central role. Just remember, the story comes first.

Alternative 2: Not All Witnesses Agree with the Rules

If you've followed our ideas in this book, you will be able to show:

- The objective industry publications all favor the Rules as you stated them.

- The law, as recited by the judge in the jury instructions, reflects the Rules as you stated them.

- The defendant's own policies and procedures, and even some of the more honest defense witnesses, agree with the plaintiff's version of the Rules.

Never overlook visual ways to display the weight of this evidence. One simple technique: as you describe the evidence on your side of the case—books, manuals, pamphlets, deposition transcripts—pile it all up in a stack on your trial table as you mention each item one by one. Make another stack for the defense evidence. You should end up with a mountain opposed to a molehill.

So the fact that the defense can dredge up a witness or two to dispute the bedrock principles to which everyone else subscribes is merely testament to the power of organized money (Hugo Black's wonderful term; he was a plaintiff's lawyer, you know) to get people to say what organized money wants. But that sure doesn't make a mountain out of a molehill.

In this situation, there is another point you may wish to make with the jury. Our side says this is the Rule; their side says it is not. Our Rule results in the world's being a safer place; their rule results in its being a more dangerous place. "You, the jury, get to decide what sort of world we are going to live in."

Alternative 3: Rules Violations— Kinds and Their Significance

Here's where the red-sticker technique we discussed earlier flexes its muscle. What you want in closing is a tool to give the jury a quick overview of the evidence, without getting bogged down in too much complexity, confusion, and ambiguity. Nothing does this better than a graphic landscape. If you have marked key documents and testimony excerpts with red stickers and mounted all of this on poster boards, you can march through the evidence with speed and authority.

Ultimately, the point of the Rules of the Road technique is to show the jury that you have all the authority on your side. The defense is singing the Sirens' song and trying to distract from the main issues. The Rules of the Road help anchor the focus where it belongs.

In the appropriate case you might also want to remind the jury that these Rules are not traps for the unwary, but exist for the protection of everyone. They, of course, protect the public and the consumers of the defendant's products or services, but they also protect people or companies in the defendant's field or industry. If a _____ [drug company, doctor, garbage-collection company, insurance company, crane operator] is following these Rules, it is operating in the "safe zone." You can tell the jury, "A company that follows these rules can know that it is not only doing its best to keep its customers safe, but is also keeping itself safe. If these Rules had been followed, no one could criticize the defendant. These Rules provide a safe harbor for responsible companies."

20

FINAL THOUGHTS

Let's discuss some common issues that come up with the Rules of the Road approach.

USING THE RULES IN MIDSTREAM

This book is written as if you are taking a case from start to finish, using the Rules of the Road technique. What about your cases that are well under way? What if you are asked to try a case where discovery is already closed? The Rules technique can work in these situations as well.

The bus stop case was one in which Rick's firm did not get involved until after discovery closed. Fortunately, our co-counsel had done an excellent job of obtaining authoritative sources and conducting depositions. It was a relatively simple matter to prepare a set of Rules from these materials. Although the bus company manager had never been questioned about our Rules prior to trial, as you can see from his examination in appendix K, the Rules were still highly effective in his cross-examination.

Our point here is simple, but important: *start using the Rules technique now*. It is not appropriate for every case, but it will be of tremendous help in most.

If your expert has already been deposed or written a report, sit down with this material and extract some Rules. Then look at what he considers authoritative and extract some more. Then talk with him and see if you can't come up with more that are logically related or encompassed within what he has already stated.

If defense witnesses have already been deposed, read the depositions with an eye toward formulating Rules with which the witnesses will have to agree—either because the witnesses already have, or because the principles logically follow from what the witnesses have already said. Appendix D, "Bus Stop Safety Principles Annotated," is an example of an annotated Rules list, first prepared *after* the defense witnesses had been deposed.

Using the Rules with Co-counsel

The days of the Lone Ranger trial lawyer are quickly coming to an end. Scorched-earth defense strategies, judges' tolerance for excessive motion practice, and specialization all make those of us in the plaintiff's bar increasingly interdependent.

Whether working with other lawyers in your firm, or with co-counsel in a joint-venture arrangement, the Rules of the Road can help keep your entire team pulling in the same harness, in the same direction.

We suggest that you have one lawyer designated as the "keeper of the Rules," responsible for adding new Rules to the master annotated list. Others on the team can (and should) suggest Rules, but only the keeper can actually add or subtract Rules on the master list. This will keep the list from becoming a garbled mess.

Whether taking depositions, writing motions, or going to trial, each member of the team will have the master list as a resource. That should go a long way toward unifying your efforts.

USING THE RULES WITH OTHER ADVOCACY ADVICE

In learning how to do what we do, we've observed a paradox. The true *masters* of trial advocacy don't consider themselves masters at all. They are enthusiastic *students* of trial advocacy.

If you have read this far, you have an essential characteristic of a successful trial lawyer—the willingness to keep searching for ways to improve. As our gift for your perseverance, we give you our personal list of some of the brilliant books for trial lawyers. Each will improve your capacity as a lawyer fighting for justice for ordinary people. Here they are:

Anything by Gerry Spence. Let's face it, Spence is probably the most talented trial lawyer and trial teacher—ever. Only the most closed-minded person can read something Spence has written and not become a better trial lawyer for it.

Cross-Examination: Science and Techniques. 2nd ed. (LexisNexis 2004), by Larry Pozner and Roger Dodd. The definitive book on cross-examination. Any trial lawyer who has not read this book is derelict in the self-education process. *Caution:* Pozner and Dodd are, in our opinion, too dogmatic about their approach. Learn their techniques. When you have mastered them, do not be afraid to cast them aside when the occasion warrants it.

David Ball on Damages: The Essential Update, A Plaintiff's Attorney's Guide for Personal Injury and Wrongful Death Cases. Rev. ed. (National Institute of Trial Advocacy 2005), by David Ball. A book packed full of good ideas and wisdom for talking about damages. We don't always agree with one of Ball's central concepts—that the plaintiff's lawyer must spend a large percentage of trial time talking about damages—at least not as a blanket rule. Still, the best book out there addressing the vexing problem of how to talk to the jury about money.

Moe Levine on Advocacy (Trial Guides 2009), by Moe Levine. Moe Levine was recognized in his lifetime as one of the greatest personal injury lawyers who ever lived. This book collects his closing arguments. If you want to see Moe in action, watch the AAJ Press video from the Masterworks series, titled *Comparative Closing Arguments on Damages,* featuring Marvin E. Lewis and Moe Levine. It will give you chills.

Opening Statements (Callaghan 1980), by Alfred Julien There is no better book for teaching you how to do an opening statement. Read it carefully; it is like sitting at the feet of a master.

Recovering for Psychological Injuries. 2nd ed. (ATLA Press 1990), by William Barton. Don't let the title fool you. Great trial wisdom and insight jump off almost every page of this book—insight and wisdom applicable to any plaintiff's case. Trial Guides is working on a 3rd edition of this book, and will release it some time in 2010.

Reptile: The 2009 Manual of the Plaintiff's Revolution (Balloon Press 2009), by David Ball and Don Keenan. A brilliant book about what motivates jurors and how to access those motivations for your own case.

Winning Jury Trials: Trial Tactics and Sponsorship Strategies. 3rd ed. (National Institute for Trial Advocacy 2007), by Robert Klonoff and Paul Colby. This is one of the best trial strategy and tactics books written in the last twenty years. The authors have articulated ways of thinking about jury trials that talented and experienced trial lawyers have instinctively followed for years. They explain better than anyone how to think about presenting a case. *Caution:* Klonoff and Colby go further than many of us would advocate in their opposition to the "inoculation" strategy for handling bad facts.

We hope these books help you enjoy being a trial lawyer as much as they helped us. What we do is hard, and because of that, we need to help one another every way we can. Maybe we should be glad our work is so hard; if it were easy, anyone could do it.

APPENDICES

Appendix A

Annotated Rules of the Road: A Master List

Caution: this list was prepared during the course of several different types of cases. Many of the Rules on this list would not be applicable to a particular bad faith case. Many Rules that might be applicable to a particular case are not here. This list has two purposes: to illustrate how an annotated list should be put together and to stimulate your thinking as you put together your own lists.

1. **Business of insurance is highly specialized, with policyholders particularly vulnerable and dependent on their insurance company.**
   Authority: *Egan v. Mutual of Omaha Ins. Co.*, 598 P.2d 452, 457 (Cal. 1979) (discussing special nature of relationship between insurer and insured); *White v. Unigard Mutual Ins. Co.*, 730 P.2d 1014, 1019 (Idaho 1986) (same); *State Farm Fire & Casualty Co. v. Nicholson*, 777 P.2d 1152, 1154–56 (Alaska 1989).

2. **Company must treat its policyholder's interests with equal regard as it does its own interests. This is not an adversarial process.**
   Authority: *Egan v. Mutual of Omaha Ins. Co.*, 598 P.2d 452, 456 (Cal. 1979); Croskey, Kauffman, et al., Cal. Practice Guide: Insurance Litigation § 12:37 (The Rutter Group 1997).

Franklin Branch Claim Office Procedure Manual at p. 28: "Claims personnel are to assist policyholders and the claimants to the full extent of their authority in processing claims." *Nelson;* Barnes Dep. at 17:17–22 (same kinds of manuals and guidelines that apply to personal lines claims apply to commercial lines claims).

Deposition of Prince at 72:9–12, Gerry at 28:5–9, and Havlock 36:24–37:2 (all agreeing that investigation must be undertaken with utmost good faith to the insured).

Barnes Deposition at 31:12–16 (reasonable benefit of the doubt goes to the insured); Speers Deposition in *Park Nelson HOA v. Franklin Group, Inc.*, at 71:20–25 (same).

Speers Deposition in *Park Northridge HOA v. Franklin Group, Inc.* 55:2–25, 56:4–10 (insurer has obligation not to put its interests ahead of its insureds).

3. **Part of claim examiner's job is to assist the policyholder with the claim.**

Authority: Franklin Branch Claim Office Procedure Manual at p. 48: "Claims personnel are to assist policyholders and the claimants to the full extent of their authority in processing claims." (Ex. 13) see also id at I–3e (NAIC model reg. § 6D "Every insurer, upon receiving notification of a claim, shall promptly provide necessary claim forms, instructions and reasonable assistance so that first-party claimants can comply with the policy conditions and the insurer's reasonable requirements.") *Nelson;* Barnes Deposition at 17:17–22 (The same kinds of manuals and guidelines that apply to personal lines claims apply to commercial claims) (January 29, 1999).

Cal. Code of Regulations § 2695.4(a) (When additional benefits might reasonably be payable under an insured's policy upon receipt of additional proofs of claim, the insurer shall immediately communicate this fact to the insured and cooperate with and assist the insured in determining the extent of the insurer's additional liability.") § 2695.5(e)(2) ("Upon receiving notice of claim, every insurer, . . . , shall immediately . . . (2) provide to the claimant necessary claim forms, instructions, and reasonable assistance, including but not limited to, specifying the information the claimant must provide for proof of claim.")

4. **Company must create and implement reasonable standards for the prompt investigation of claims. The standards must be in writing.**
Authority: Cal. Ins. Code § 790.03(h)(3); 10 Cal. Code of Regulations § 2695.5(e)(3) (within 15 days of receiving notice of claim insurer must begin any necessary investigation); 10 Cal. Code of Regulations § 2695.6(a).

5. **Company must thoroughly investigate the claim.**
Authority: *Egan v. Mutual of Omaha Ins. Co.*, 598 P.2d 452, 456–57 (Cal. 1979); *Ainsworth v. Combined Ins. Co. of America*, 763 P.2d 673, 675 (Nev. 1988) (insurer has obligation to fairly and completely investigate claim); CAL. PRACTICE GUIDE: INSURANCE LITIGATION ¶ 12:848 (The Rutter Group 1997).

6. **Company must objectively investigate the claim.**
Authority: *Ainsworth v. Combined Ins. Co. of America*, 763 P.2d 673, 675 (Nev. 1988) (insurer has obligation to fairly and completely investigate claim); CAL. PRACTICE GUIDE: INSURANCE LITIGATION ¶ 12:866 (The Rutter Group 1997).

7. **An insurer has an obligation to recognize and promptly retain independent and qualified experts to assist in the fair, reasonable, objective, and prompt investigation of the claim.**
Authority: CAL. PRACTICE GUIDE: INSURANCE LITIGATION ¶ 12:888 (The Rutter Group 1997).

8. **An insurer must adopt and implement reasonable standards for the prompt evaluation of claims.**
Authority: 10 Cal. Code of Regulations § 2695.6(a) ("Every insurer shall adopt and communicate to all its claims agents written standards for the prompt investigation and *processing*

of claims.") (emphasis added). Note that the term "processing" is not defined in the regulations and will therefore either be defined by Franklin as simply moving paper or by us as the claims investigation and evaluation process leading to a claim decision.

9. **Company must objectively evaluate the claim.**
Authority: *Ainsworth v. Combined Ins. Co. of America*, 763 P.2d 673, 675 (Nev. 1988); CAL. PRACTICE GUIDE: INSURANCE LITIGATION ¶ 12:889 (The Rutter Group 1997).

10. **In evaluating a claim under a replacement-cost policy, it is not proper for an insurer to deduct depreciation from the value of the claim.**
Authority: 10 Cal. Code of Regulations §2695.9(a)(1).

11. **Failure to fairly and reasonably investigate a claim does not permit the company to deny the claim due to lack of information or one-sided information.**
Authority: *Mariscal v. Old Republic Life Ins. Co.*, 50 Cal. Rptr. 224, 227 (Cal. App. 1996); *Industrial Indemnity Co. of the Northwest, Inc. v. Kallevig*, 792 P.2d 520, 526 (Wash. 1990) (en banc); *Rawlings v. Apodaca*, 726 P.2d 565, 572 (Ariz. 1986) (fair debatability not raised where insurer failed to make adequate investigation), citing, *Farr v. Transamerica Occidental Life Ins. Co.*, 699 P.2d 376 (Ariz. App. 1984); *Deese v. State Farm Mutual Automobile Ins. Co.*, 838 P.2d 1265 (Ariz. 1992); 15A Couch, CYCLOPEDIA OF INSURANCE LAW, § 58:180 (2d rev. ed. 1983).

12. **An insurance company may not ignore evidence that supports coverage. If it does so, it acts unreasonably toward its insured and breaches the covenant of good faith and fair dealing.**
Authority: *Mariscal v. Old Republic Life Ins. Co.*, 50 Cal. Rptr. 2d 224, 227 (Cal. App. 1996).

13. **Company must fairly, reasonably, and promptly pay the claim if payment is warranted.**
    Authority: Cal. Ins. Code § 790.03(5), (12) (failing to attempt to effectuate prompt fair and equitable settlements when liability reasonably clear and failing to settle claim under one portion of policy in order to influence settlement under other portions); 10 Cal. Code of Regulations § 2695.1(a)(2) (purpose of regulations is to promote "the good faith, prompt, efficient, and equitable settlement of claims on a cost effective basis."); 10 Cal. Code of Regulations § 2695.5(e) (within 15 days of receiving notice of claim insurer must either pay or acknowledge receipt of notice and comply with other obligations including providing assistance to insured and beginning investigation); *Egan v. Mutual of Omaha Ins. Co.*, 598 P.2d 452, 456 (Cal. 1979) (insurer has an obligation not to impair the right of the insured to receive the benefit of the agreement); *Gruenberg v. Aetna Ins. Co.*, 510 P.2d 1032, 1038 (Cal. 1973) (insurer may not unreasonably withhold payment under the policy); Croskey, Kauffman, et al., CAL. PRACTICE GUIDE: INSURANCE LITIGATION ¶ 12:807 (The Rutter Group 1997).

14. **Company should pay the claim unless there is a good reason not to—denial should not be based on speculation.**
    Authority: *Industrial Indemnity Co. of the Northwest, Inc. v. Kallevig*, 792 P.2d 520, 526 (Wash. 1990) (en banc); *Rawlings v. Apodaca*, 726 P.2d 565, 572 (Ariz. 1986) (fair debatability not raised where insurer failed to make adequate investigation), citing, *Farr v. Transamerica Occidental Life Ins. Co.*, 699 P.2d 376 (Ariz. App. 1984); *Deese v. State Farm Mutual Automobile Ins. Co.*, 838 P.2d 1265 (Ariz. 1992); 15A Couch, CYCLOPEDIA OF INSURANCE LAW, § 58:180 (2d rev. ed. 1983).

15. **If denial, insurer must promptly give policyholder a reasonable explanation of the basis in the insurance policy in relation to the facts, policy provisions, or applicable law upon which it relies for denial of claim.**
    Authority: Cal. Ins. Code § 790.03(h)(13); 10 Cal. Code

of Regulations § 2695.7(b) (requiring acceptance or rejection within 40 days, requiring explanation for rejection, and requiring notice and explanation if additional time is needed to make a claim decision with specification of additional needed information).

16. **If offer is a compromise amount, must provide a reasonable explanation of the basis of that amount in the insurance policy in relation to the facts and law.**
Authority: Cal. Ins. Code § 790.03(h)(13).

17. **Cannot misrepresent facts or policy provisions. An insurer has an affirmative duty to disclose benefits and coverages that may apply to a claim.**
Authority: Cal. Ins. Code § 790.03(h)(1); 10 Cal. Code of Regulations § 2695.4(a); *United Fire Ins. Co. v. McClelland*, 105 Nev. 504, 515, 780 P.2d 193 (Nev. 1989) (insurer may not mislead or deceive its insured with respect to pertinent facts or insurance benefits).

18. **Insurer cannot condition the receipt of benefits under one provision of the policy on the waiver of claims either under another provision of the policy or that may otherwise exist against the insurer.**
Authority: Cal. Ins. Code § 790.03(h)(12); Croskey, Kauffman et al., CAL. PRACTICE GUIDE: INSURANCE LITIGATION ¶ 12: 926 (The Rutter Group 1997) (insurer has no right to bundle separate claims, and delay in settlement of some claims by bundling them with disputed claims may breach of the covenant of good faith and fair dealing.)

19. **Cannot discriminate in the claim-settlement practices based on the claimant's race, gender, income, religion, sexual orientation, national origin, or physical disability or the territory of the property or person insured.**
Authority: 10 Cal. Code of Regulations § 2695.7(a).

20. **Cannot attempt to settle a claim for an unreasonably low amount.**
Authority: 10 Cal. Code of Regulations § 2695.7(g).

21. **An insurer must communicate with its insured to keep it apprised of the status of its claim.**
Authority: Croskey, Kauffman et al., CAL. PRACTICE GUIDE: INSURANCE LITIGATION ¶¶ 12:953–56 (The Rutter Group 1997); 10 Cal. Code of Regulations §§ 2695.4(a); 2695.5(b); 2695.7(b)(1), (c)(1).

22. **Upon receiving any documentation submitted to the insurer that provides any evidence of the claim and supports the magnitude or the amount of the claimed loss shall within forty (40) days, accept or deny the claim, in whole or in part.**
Authority: 10 Cal. Code of Regulations §§ 2695.2(s); 2695.7(b).

23. **Where an insurer denies or rejects a first-party claim in whole or in part, it shall do so in writing and shall provide to the claimant a statement listing all bases for such rejection or denial and the factual and legal bases for each reason given for such rejection or denial that is then within the insurer's knowledge. Where an insurer's denial of a first-party claim, in whole or in part, is based on a specific policy provision, condition, or exclusion, the written denial shall include reference thereto and provide an explanation of the application of the provision, condition, or exclusion to the claim.**
Authority: 10 Cal. Code of Regulations § 2695.7(b)(1).

24. **If more than forty (40) days is required to determine whether a claim should be accepted and/or denied in whole or in part, insurer shall provide the claimant, within that initial forty-day period, with written notice of the need for additional time. This written notice shall specify any additional information the insurer requires in order to make a determination and shall state any continuing reasons for the insurer's inability to make a determination. Thereafter, the written notice shall be provided every thirty (30) calendar days**

until a determination is made or notice of legal action is served. If the determination cannot be made until some future event occurs, then the insurer shall comply with this continuing-notice requirement by advising the claimant of the situation and providing an estimate as to when the determination can be made.
Authority: 10 Cal. Code of Regulations § 2695.7(c)(1).

25. **Where there are undisputed amounts due under one provision of a policy, an insurer may not withhold payment of those amounts because there are disputes with respect to liability or amounts due under other provisions of the policy.**
Authority: 10 Cal. Code of Regulations § 2695.7(h).

26. **It is improper for an insurer to tie, in any manner, claim-personnel compensation to claim decisions or payments to its insureds.**
Authority: Cal. Ins. Code § 816.

27. **An insurer has a duty to disclose all significant facts to its insured.**
Authority: *Albert H. Wohlers and Co. v. Bartgis*, 114 Nev. 1249, 969 P.2d 949 (Nev. 1998).

28. **An insurer's unreasonable interpretation of its contract may amount to bad faith.**
Authority: *Albert H. Wohlers and Co. v. Bartgis*, 114 Nev. 1249, 969 P.2d 949 (Nev. 1998).

29. **An insurer may not rely on an ambiguous contract as the sole basis for claim denial.**
Authority: *Ainsworth v. Combined Ins. Co. of America*, 763 P.2d 673, 676 (Nev. 1988).

30. **An insurer may not deny disability benefits on the basis that the insured is still able to do the functions of his occupation where common prudence would require that the insured not work in order to protect his health.**

Authority: *Massachusetts Casualty Ins. Co. v. Rief*, 176 2d 777, 780 (Md. 1962); *Besh v. Mutual Benefit Health & Accident Ass'n*, 8 N.W.2d 91, 94 (Mich. 1943); *Benefit Ass'n of Railway Employees v. Secrest*, 39 S.W.2d 682 (Ky. Ct. App. 1931); *Doyle v. New Jersey Fidelity & Plate Glass Ins. Co.*, 182 S.W. 944 (Ky. Ct. App. 1916); *Hohn v. Interstate Casualty Co.*, 72 N.W. 1105 (Mich. 1897); *Young v. Travelers' Ins. Co.*, 13 896, 897 (Me. 1888); *Fohl v. Metropolitan Life Ins. Co.* (1942) 54 Cal. App. 2d 368, 381; *Wright v. Prudential Insurance Co. of America* (1935) 27 Cal. App. 2d 195, 212; *Joyce v. United Ins. Co. of America* (1962) 202 Cal. App. 2d 654, 664–665; *Lasser v. Reliance Standard Life Insurance Co.* (D. N.J. 2001) __F.3d __ 2001 WL 672579; *Honeysucker v. Bowen* (N.D. Ill. 1986) 649 F. Supp 1155; *Stark v. Weinberger*, 497 F.2d 1092, 1098–99 (7th Cir. 1974); *Oppenheim v. Finch*, 495 F.2d 396, 398 (4th Cir. 1974); *Stillwell v. Sullivan*, 1992 WL 401971, *6 (D. Kan., Dec. 30, 1992). *Metropolitan Life Ins. Co. v. Lambert*, 128 So. 750 (Miss. 1930) (If, in order to effect cure, prudence required that insured cease attempting to work, he was "totally disabled" within policy.); *Mutual Life Ins. Co. of New York v. Dowdle*, 71 S.W.2d 691 (Ark. 1934) (As regards question whether insured was totally and permanently disabled under policy, law does not require one to perform duties at peril of life or health, or if performance entails pain and suffering which persons of ordinary fortitude would be unwilling to endure.) *Equitable Life Assur. Soc. of U.S. v. Watts*, 160 So. 713 (Al, 1935) Where work is accompanied by suffering and aggravation of chronic disease and medical advice favors rest, fact that employee has strength to work and does work occasionally will not bar recovery on group policy covering "total permanent disability."); *Wiener v. Mutual Life Ins. Co. of New York*, 179 S.W.2d 39 (Mo. 1944) (An insured is "disabled" within meaning of disability provision of life policy if he is not able to work without running risk of increasing his disability or shortening his life); *John Hancock Mut. Life Ins. Co.*

v. Cooper, 386 S.W.2d 208 (Tex. Civ. App. 1965) (Controlling issue in case involving total disability is whether ordinary prudent person in exercise of ordinary care would refrain from working under same or similar circumstances, and whether it would be physically possible for insurance claimant to work is not an ultimate issue, but is merely evidentiary); *Prudential Ins. Co. of America v. Girton*, 12 N.E.2d 379 (Ind. App. 1938) (One is "totally disabled," within permanent total disability clause of insurance policy, if it is impossible for him to work without hazarding his health or risking his life.); *Rezendes v. Prudential Ins. Co. of America*, 189 N.E. 826 (Mass. 1934) (Insured is suffering "total and permanent disability" within disability provisions of life insurance policy, if his condition is such that he is unable to work without running risk of increasing his disability or of shortening his life).

Appendix B

Sample Insurance Bad Faith Rules of the Road

The following Rules of the Road are samples from three different types of insurance bad faith cases: a commercial property case and two disability cases.

Commercial Property Claim

1. Must treat its policyholders' interests with equal regard as it does its own interests. This is not an adversarial or competitive process.
2. Insurance company should assist the policyholder with the claim.
3. Insurance company must disclose to its insured all benefits, coverages, and time limits that may apply to the claim.
4. Insurance company must conduct a full, fair, and prompt investigation of the claim at its own expense.
5. Insurance company must fully, fairly, and promptly evaluate and adjust the claim.
6. Company must pay all amounts not in dispute within thirty days.

7. Company may not deny a claim or part of a claim based upon insufficient information, speculation, or biased information.

8. If full or partial denial, must give written explanation, pointing to facts and policy provisions.

9. Company may not misrepresent facts or policy provisions.

10. Company may not make unreasonably low settlement offers.

11. Company must give claimant written update on status of claim every thirty days, including a description of what is needed to finalize the claim.

Disability Case 1

1. Business of insurance is highly specialized, with policyholders particularly vulnerable and dependent on their insurance company.

2. Company should pay the claim unless there is a good reason not to.

3. Company must fairly, reasonably, and promptly investigate the claim.

4. Company must fairly, reasonably, and promptly evaluate the claim.

5. Company must fairly, reasonably, and promptly pay the claim if payment is warranted.

6. Company must treat its policyholders' interests with equal regard as it does its own interests. This is not an adversarial process.

7. Failure to fairly and reasonably investigate a claim does not permit the company to deny the claim due to lack of information or one-sided information.

8. It is not appropriate to use biased consultants to assist in investigation or evaluation.

Disability Case 2

1. Company has a duty to deal fairly and in good faith with its policyholders.

2. Company must treat its policyholders' interests with equal regard as it does its own interests. This is not an adversarial process.

3. Company has a duty to act reasonably and fairly in interpreting and applying its policy provisions.

4. Claims decisions should be made without regard to effect on company profitability.

5. Company must fairly, reasonably, and fully investigate the claim.

6. Company must fairly, reasonably, and promptly evaluate the claim.

7. It is not appropriate to use biased consultants to assist in investigation or evaluation.

8. Failure to fairly and reasonably investigate a claim does not permit the company to deny the claim due to lack of information or one-sided information.

9. Denial of claim should never be based upon speculation.

10. Documents should not be destroyed to hide the company's policies or claims handling from its policyholders.

Appendix C

Bus Stop Safety Principles

This set of safety principles was developed for the bus stop case discussed in detail in chapter 1, "Defining the Problem."

1. Child safety is always the primary consideration in any decision concerning pupil transportation.
2. Defendants had the duty and responsibility to select safe waiting areas for the children to wait for the bus.
3. Neither the child nor the parent has the duty, responsibility, or right to select the location of a designated waiting area.
4. If there is more than one reasonable and practical place to locate a waiting area, the one safest for the child should be designated.
5. Because factors affecting the safety of a waiting area can change at any time, its location must be continually re-evaluated.
6. A child's designated waiting area should be located on the same side of the arterial road as the child's home, unless it would be unsafe to do so.
7. Children should be trained not to cross the arterial road until after the bus arrives and driver gives signal.

8. The bus company should take appropriate action to correct unsafe loading and unloading behavior observed on the route.

Appendix D

Bus Stop Safety Principles Annotated

1. **Child safety is always the primary consideration in any decision concerning pupil transportation.**

2. **Defendants had the duty and responsibility to select safe waiting areas for the children to wait for the bus.**
   Court's order; Ex. 51, p. 13 (Contract VII [A] and [D]); District Transportation Manual (Ex. 55, p. 10); Responses to RFA, 8 & 9.

3. **Neither the child nor the parent has the duty, responsibility, or right to select the location of a designated waiting area.**
   Carey dep. at 82; Requests for Admission 11–13; Nabors dep. 24.

4. **If there is more than one reasonable and practical place to locate a waiting area, the one safest for the child should be designated.**

5. **Because factors affecting the safety of a waiting area can change at any time, its location must be continually reevaluated.**
   Deering dep. at 36–38; Lay dep. at 35.

6. **A child's designated waiting area should be located on the same side of the arterial road as the child's home, unless it would be unsafe to do so.**

School Bus Safety Curriculum Guide (Ex. 37, p. 2); Alaska School Bus Driver's Manual (Ex. 48, p.10).

Jamie Fields: Was told by Shellbus not to have children cross the road until bus arrived. (13)

This was taught to her in her initial bus driver training. (14)

Was taught that if children crossed the road ahead of time, she should advise dispatch or the manager. (14)

One of the things drivers were taught (and are taught) was that students are supposed to wait on their own side of the road until driver signals them to cross. (David James 42–43)

If driver became aware that students were crossing the road before the bus arrived, would expect driver to tell them to stay on their own side of the road. (Jane Simon 59)

David Turner: Absent exceptional or unusual circumstances, students who are coming from the left side of the road should wait on their own side of the road until the bus arrives. (33–34)

Industry practice is for students to wait on their own side of the road until driver signals them to cross. (37, 38–39)

"Basic school bus procedure, students should wait on their side of the road." (58)

Sam Shepherd, Alaska District Manager: Generally considered safer for children to cross road under the bus' protection. (44)

If bus stop was across the street, then children are told to wait for the bus' protection before crossing. (54)

We endeavor to have the children wait on own side of the road until the bus arrives before crossing the road. (55)

7. **Children should be trained not to cross the arterial road until after the bus arrives and driver gives signal.**
School Bus Safety Curriculum Guide (Ex. 37, p. 2); Alaska School Bus Driver's Manual (Ex. 48, p.10)

National Association of State Directors of Pupil Transportation position paper on "Transporting the Nation's School Children." Not an exhibit: Says: "Stopping traffic in areas where children get on and off school buses, and are often crossing the street has proven to be beneficial in protecting students who must cross the street to reach the bus or go home. Stopping traffic creates a safer environment for young children who are not as adept as adults in negotiating their way through traffic."

Alaska School Bus Driver Training Manual: Diagram on "How Students Cross the Road Safely" (1) Stay (2) Wait (3) Check (4) Cross (5) Walk. (p. 35a)

Alaska School Bus Driver Training Manual: "Drivers of school buses have full responsibility for the safety of students while they are boarding the bus, on the bus, leaving the bus, and *crossing the road*." (appendix A) (emphasis added)

Jamie Fields: Was told by Shellbus not to have children cross the road until bus arrived. (13)

This was taught to her in her initial bus driver training. (14)

Was taught that if children crossed the road ahead of time, she should advise dispatch or the manager. (14)

Jane Simon: If driver became aware that students were crossing the road before the bus arrived, would expect driver to tell them to stay on their own side of the road. (59)

David James: One of the things drivers were taught (and are taught) was that students are supposed to wait on their own side of the road until driver signals them to cross. (42–43)

Ex. 52: National Standards for School Transportation, page 276, appendix E: "Pupil shall cross the road or street in front of bus only after bus has come to a complete stop and upon direction of the driver." Page 278—"Here's how to cross the road safely."

George Ballard: Absent exceptional or unusual circumstances, students who are coming from the left side of the road should wait on their own side of the road until the bus arrives. (33–34)

Industry practice is for students to wait on their own side of the road until driver signals them to cross. (37, 38–39)

"Basic school bus procedure, students should wait on their side of the road." (58)

Sara Hall: On the School Bus Safety Committee: approved curriculum guide. "Absolute rule" that students were not to cross road before bus arrived. They got in trouble if they crossed before bus arrived. (6–7) Not a topic of any disagreement on the Committee. (7)

Ex. 65: Letter dated 8/15/99: Admission of Ballard and David George.

8. **The bus company should take appropriate action to correct unsafe loading and unloading behavior observed on the route.**

Shellbus employee handbook, Northwest Region: "Your responsibility to the student does not end at the door. Safeguard the children outside your bus by being watchful of their actions. Correct them when noticing improper loading and/or unloading procedures." (Ex. 20, p.18)

Alaska School Bus Driver Training Manual: "Drivers of school buses have full responsibility for the safety of students while they are boarding the bus, on the bus, leaving the bus, and *crossing the road*." (Ex. 24, p. A-5) (emphasis added)

Appendix E

Proposed Jury Instructions in a Disability Bad Faith Case[1]

INSTRUCTION NO. ___

Every contract imposes upon each party a duty of good faith and fair dealing in its performance or its enforcement.

An insurance company which intentionally deals in bad faith with its insured by refusing unreasonably to pay the insured for a valid claim, or settle a valid claim, covered by the policy may be found liable for damages which legally result from such conduct. Bad faith does not mean bad judgment or negligence, but means having a dishonest purpose through some motive of self-interest or ill will, or having malicious or hostile feelings toward its insureds, or acting with reckless indifference to the rights of its insureds.

If you find it more likely than not that Aetna unreasonably refused to pay Mr. Fredricks's long-term disability claim, then

---

1. All of the proposed instructions from the case are not included, only those directly addressing bad faith liability issues.

your verdict must be for the plaintiff. Otherwise, your verdict must be for the defendant.

Authority: *State Farm Fire & Casualty v. Nicholson*, 777 P.2d 1152, 1154 n.3 (Alaska 1989).

• • •

INSTRUCTION NO. ___

An insurer's obligation of good faith and fair dealing includes giving at least as much consideration to the insured's interest as to its own. To meet the obligation of good faith and fair dealing the insurer must fully inquire into possible bases that might support the insured's claim. It may not in good faith deny payments to its insured without thoroughly investigating the foundation for its denial.

Authority: *Egan v. Mutual of Omaha Ins. Co.*, 598 P.2d 452, 456, 457 (Cal. 1979).

• • •

INSTRUCTION NO. ___

In evaluating the reasonableness of Aetna's conduct in this case, you may consider several legal principles that apply to insurance companies doing business in Alaska. These principles are outlined in instructions ___–___.

• • •

INSTRUCTION NO. ___

The Alaska Administrative Code provides that any person transacting a business of insurance who participates in the investigation, adjustment, negotiation, or settlement of a claim under any type of insurance must document each action taken on a claim. The documentation must contain all notes, work papers, documents, and similar material. The documentation must be in sufficient detail that relevant events, the dates of those events, and all persons participating in those events can be identified. The documentation may include legible copies of originals and may be stored in the form of microfilm or electronic media.

If you find that the defendant violated this law, you may consider this in deciding whether or not it breached its duty of good faith and fair dealing in this case.

Authority: 3 AAC 26.030; *State Farm Mutual Automobile Ins. Co. v. Weiford*, 831 P.2d 1261, 1269 & n.6 (Alaska 1992).

• • •

INSTRUCTION NO. ___

Alaska Statute 21.36.125 provides that an insurance company may not commit or engage in with such frequency as to indicate a practice any of the followings acts or practices:

1. Misrepresent facts or policy provisions relating to coverage of an insurance policy.

2. Fail to acknowledge and act promptly upon communications regarding a claim arising under an insurance policy.

3. Fail to adopt and implement reasonable standards for prompt investigation of claims.

4. Refuse to pay a claim without a reasonable investigation of all of the available information and an explanation of the basis for denial.

5. Fail to affirm or deny coverage of claims within a reasonable time of completion of proof-of-loss statements.

6. Fail to promptly provide a reasonable explanation of the basis in the insurance policy in relation to the facts or applicable law for denial of a claim.

If you find the defendant violated this law, you may consider this in deciding whether or not it breached its duty of good faith and fair dealing in this case.

Authority: S. 21.36.125(1–5, 14); *State Farm Mutual Automobile Ins. Co. v. Weiford*, 831 P.2d 1264, 1269 & n.6 (Alaska 1992).

• • •

INSTRUCTION NO. ___

The Alaska Administrative Code also regulates the conduct of those engaged in the business of insurance. It states:

Any person transacting a business of insurance who participates in the investigation, adjustment, negotiation, or settlement of a claim shall promptly undertake the investigation of a claim after notification of the claim is received, and shall complete the investigation within 30 working days, unless the investigation cannot reasonably be completed using due diligence.

If you find that defendant violated this law, you may consider this in deciding whether or not it breached its duty of good faith and fair dealing in this case.

Authority: 3 AAC 26.050(a); *State Farm Mutual Automobile Ins. Co. v. Weiford*, 831 P.2d 1264, 1269 & n.6 (Alaska 1992).

• • •

INSTRUCTION NO. ___

The Alaska Administrative Code which regulates the business of insurance also requires any person conducting the business of insurance to assist a claimant in making a claim under their insurance policy.

The regulations require an insurer, upon receiving notice of a claim to provide the necessary claim forms, instructions and assistance so that a claimant is able to comply with all reasonable requirements.

Authority: 3 AAC 26.040(a)(3); *Ace v. Aetna Life Ins. Co.*, 139 F.3d 1241 (9th Cir. 1997); Slip Op. 96–35183 at 4455 n.19 (May 7, 1998).

• • •

INSTRUCTION NO. ___

Alaska law requires an insurer to give a claimant a reasonably detailed written explanation of the facts, policy provisions, and applicable law upon which it relies for the denial of a claim. If you find that Aetna breached these requirements, you may consider this as evidence of bad faith.

Authority: *Ace v. Aetna Life Ins. Co.*, 139 F.3d 1241 (9th Cir. 1997), Slip Op. 96–35183 at 4455 n.18 (May 7, 1998); AS 21.36.125(1), (14); 3 AAC 26.070 (a)(1).

• • •

INSTRUCTION NO. ___

The Alaska Administrative Code provides that any persons transacting a business of insurance who participates in the investigation, adjustment, negotiation, or settlement of a claim shall fully disclose to a first-party claimant all relevant benefits and other provisions of coverage under which a claim may be covered.

A first-party claim means a person asserting a right to payment under his or her own coverage. In this case the parties agree that Mr. Fredricks was a first-party claimant.

If you find that the defendant violated this law, you may consider this in deciding whether or not it breached its duty of good faith and fair dealing in this case.

Authority: 3 AAC 26.060(1); *State Farm Mutual Automobile Ins. Co. v. Weiford*, 831 P.2d 1264, 1269 & n.6 (Alaska 1992); 3 AAC 26.300(5); *State Farm Fire & Casualty Co. v. Nicholson*, 777 P.2d 1152, 1154 (Alaska 1989) (defining a first-party claim as "when an insured seeks coverage for losses he or she incurred.")

• • •

INSTRUCTION NO. ___

If an insurer believes there are ambiguities regarding a claimant's medical status which make it unclear whether a claim for long-term disability benefits qualifies for payment, the insurer has the right to conduct an independent medical examination, to clarify this issue.

Authority: *Ace v. Aetna Life Ins. Co.*, 139 F.3d 1241 (9th Cir. 1997), Slip Op. 96–35183 at 4455 n. 15 (May 7, 1998).

• • •

INSTRUCTION NO. ___

An insurer does not act in bad faith when it challenges a claim which is "fairly debatable," or where it is acting under an honest mistake of the facts concerning the nature of the claim. A refusal to pay a claim based on a defense that the claim itself is "fairly debatable" is valid only where it is proven that the insurer, after giving equal consideration to the insured's interests as to its own interests, had a legitimate question over the existence of coverage or the amount due.

Authority: *White v. Unigard Mutual Ins. Co.*, 730 P.2d 1014 (Idaho 1986); *Rawlings v. Apodaca*, 726 P.2d 565, 572 (Ariz. 1986); *Deese v. State Farm Mutual Automobile Ins. Co.*, 838 P.2d 1265 (Ariz. 1992).

• • •

INSTRUCTION NO. ___

Whether a claim is fairly debatable is judged as of the time the decision to deny or delay payment is made.

Authority: *Buzzard v. Farmers Ins. Co., Inc.*, 824 P.2d 1105, 1109 (Okl. 1991) ("The knowledge and belief of the insurer during the time period the claim is being reviewed is the focus of a bad faith claim."); *State Farm Fire and Casualty Company v. Balmer*, 891 F.2d 874, 876 (11th Cir. 1990) ("Whether the insurer had such an arguable basis for denial is judged as of the time the decision to deny is made."); *Aetna Life Ins. Co. v. Lavoie*, 505 So.2d 1050, 1053 (Al. 1987) ("The decision of the insurance company to deny a claim under an insurance policy must be judged by what was before it at the time the decision was made." [citations omitted]); *Austero v. National Casualty Co. of Detroit Mich.*, 148 Cal. Rptr. 653, 673 (Cal. App. 1978) ("The reasonable or unreasonable action by the company must be measured as of the time it was confronted with a factual situation to which it was called upon to respond."); *Paulson v. State Farm Mutual Automobile Ins. Co.*, 867 F.Supp. 911, 918 (C.D. Cal. 1994).

• • •

INSTRUCTION NO. ___

An ambiguity in the insurance policy does not make a claim "fairly debatable." An insurance company has a good faith obligation to construe an ambiguous policy provision in a way that favors its insured.

Authority: *Grace v. Insurance Company of North America*, 944 P.2d 460 (Alaska 1997); *State Farm Fire and Casualty Company v. Bongen*, 925 P.2d 1042, 1047 (Alaska 1996) (ambiguities are interpreted in favor of insured); *Bering Strait School District v. RLI Insurance Company*, 873 P.2d 1292, 1295 (Alaska 1994) (where a clause in an insurance policy is ambiguous, the court accepts the interpretation most favoring the insured); *Erickson v. Nationwide Mutual Ins. Co.*, 543 P.2d 841, 845 (Idaho 1978) (causation language of insurance policy had to be construed in light most favorable to insured; the court is not to "sanction a construction of the insurer's language that will defeat the very purpose or object of coverage."); *Ferrel v. Allstate Ins. Co.*, 682 P.2d 649 (Idaho App. 1984) (if language of policy can be construed in more than one way, construction favorable to insured must be adopted); *Rawlings v. Apodaca*, 726 P.2d 565, 572 (Ariz. 1986), citing, *Sparks v. Republic National Life Ins. Co.*, 647 P.2d 1127, 1137, *cert. denied*, 459 U.S. 1070 (1982).

• • •

INSTRUCTION NO. ___

A claim is not fairly debatable if an insurer has failed to make a reasonable investigation, or acts based on suspicion or conjecture.

Authority: *Industrial Indemnity Co. of the Northwest, Inc. v. Kallevig*, 792 P.2d 520, 526 (Wash. 1990) (en banc); *Rawlings v. Apodaca*, 726 P.2d 565, 572 (Ariz. 1986) (fair debatability not raised where insurer failed to make adequate investigation), citing, *Farr v. Transamerica Occidental Life Ins. Co.*, 699 P.2d 376 (Ariz. App. 1984); *Deese v. State Farm Mutual Automobile Ins. Co.*, 838 P.2d 1265 (Ariz. 1992); 15A Couch, CYCLOPEDIA OF INSURANCE LAW, § 58:180 (2d rev. ed. 1983).

• • •

INSTRUCTION NO. ___

In conducting a reasonable investigation an insurer may not just focus on those facts that justify denial of the claim. An insurer that ignores evidence available to it that supports payment of the claim acts unreasonably.

Authority: *Mariscal v. Old Republic Life Ins. Co.*, 50 Cal. Rptr. 2d 224, 227 (Cal. App. 1996).

• • •

INSTRUCTION NO. ___

In conducting a reasonable investigation of a claim under disability coverages the obligation of good faith and fair dealing requires the insurer to obtain all available medical information relevant to the claim. When there is a question or questions as to whether coverage exists based on the medical condition of the insured, or how that condition relates to employability, and an insurer has failed to consult with the claimant's treating doctor, it has not conducted a reasonable investigation.

Authority: S. 21.36.125(4) (Investigation must be based upon "all available information"); *Ace v. Aetna Life Ins. Co.*, 139 F.3d 1241 (9th Cir. 1997), Slip Op. 96–35813 at 4455, 4459–60 (9th Cir. May 7, 1998) (bad faith and liability for punitive damages established in part by the insurer's "failing to investigate the claim and to seek or request supporting information alleged to be missing."); *Aetna Life Ins. Co. v. LaVoie*, 505 So.2d 1050, 1052–53 (Al. 1987) (health coverage); *Bankers Life & Casualty Co. v. Crenshaw*, 483 So.2d 254, 270, 272 (Miss. 1985) (disability coverage); *Mariscal v. Old Republic Life Ins. Co.*, 50 Cal. Rptr. 224, 227 (Cal. App. 1996); *McCormick v. Sentinel Life Ins. Co.*, 200 Cal. Rptr. 732, 742 (Cal. App. 1984).

• • •

INSTRUCTION NO. ___

The fact that an insurer ultimately pays the benefits due under the contract does not relieve it from liability for bad faith if, in its handling of the claim, it breached its obligation of good faith and fair dealing.

Authority: *State Farm Mutual Automobile Ins. Co. v. Weiford*, 831 P.2d 1264 (Alaska 1992) (insurer held liable for bad faith claims handling, despite having paid claim); *Rawlings v. Apodaca*, 726 P.2d 565, 571 (Ariz. 1986); *Deese v. State Farm Mutual Automobile Ins. Co.*, 838 P.2d 1265 (Ariz. 1992) (fact that insurer ultimately paid MPC coverage claim did not relieve it of potential liability for bad faith based on its use of improper claim review practices).

• • •

INSTRUCTION NO. ___

In conducting a proper investigation in a disability case the obligation of good faith and fair dealing requires an insurer to obtain all available medical information relevant to the claim.

Authority: *Bankers Life & Casualty Co. v. Crenshaw*, 483 So.2d 254, 270, 272 (Miss. 1985); *Aetna Life Ins. Co. v. LaVoie*, 505 So.2d 1050, 1052–53 (Al. 1987). See also *Ace v. Aetna Life Ins. Co.*, J94–018 Civ. (JWS) at Trial Ex. 54 at 8a guideline 11, Trial Ex. 69 (Doc. No. 501388, 501390, Aetna internal documents regarding fact that claims handlers should obtain medical documents themselves rather than have outside vendors get the documents at the first instance.)

• • •

INSTRUCTION NO. ___

An insurance company under a group policy may not balance the rights of its individual insured on a particular claim against either the rights of all the group members or its stockholders. An insurer's conduct is judged based on whether, given the circumstances, the insurer unreasonably withheld or delayed benefits due under a policy. An insurer acts unreasonably if it places the rights of its other group members or stockholders at large above the rights of its individual insured who is presenting a claim.

Authority: *McCormick v. Sentinel Life Ins. Co.*, 200 Cal. Rptr. 732, 739 (Cal. App. 1984).

• • •

INSTRUCTION NO. ___

An insurance policy is strictly construed against the insurance company. If a term is not part of the insurance contract it may not be read into the contract by the insurer.

Authority: *Linscott v. Rainier National Life Ins. Co.*, 100 Idaho 854, 860, 606 P.2d 958 (Idaho 1980); *Ace v. Aetna Life Ins. Co.*, 139 F.3d 1241 (9th Cir. 1997), Slip. Op. 96–35813 at 4456 (May 7, 1998) (bad faith and punitive damages warranted in part by finding that insurer denied claim based on an "undefined requirement" not a term of the policy).

• • •

INSTRUCTION NO. ___

For a long period of time the law has recognized the following principles and imposed them on insurers:

First, insurance policies are to be construed or interpreted most liberally in favor of the insured.

Second, any reasonable doubts an insurance company may have concerning an obligation under an insurance policy must be resolved in favor of the insured.

Accordingly, if you find that Aetna resolved or attempted to resolve ambiguities in the terms or its obligations under the contract in favor of itself rather than its insured you may consider that as evidence of bad faith.

Authority: *Grace v. Insurance Company of North America*, 944 P.2d 460 (Alaska 1997); *State Farm Fire and Casualty Company v. Bongen*, 925 P.2d 1042, 1047 (Alaska 1996) (ambiguities are interpreted in favor of insured); *Bering Strait School District v. RLI Insurance Company*, 873 P.2d 1292, 1295 (Alaska 1994) (where a clause in an insurance policy is ambiguous, the court accepts the interpretation most favoring the insured); *Abbie Uriguen Oldsmobile Buick, Inc. v. United States Fire Ins. Co.*, 95 Idaho 501, 511 P.2d 783 (Idaho 1973); *Moss v. Mid-American Fire & Marine Ins. Co.*, 103 Idaho 298, 647 P.2d 754 (Idaho 1982); *Shields v. Hiram C. Gardner, Inc.*, 92 Idaho 423, 444 P.2d 38 (Idaho 1968).

• • •

INSTRUCTION NO. ____

In determining whether a claimant is totally disabled under the terms of an insurance policy, an insurer must take into account the real-world employment marketplace. An insurer cannot reasonably rely on an unsupported assumption that one who has a serious disability is able to compete for work on an equal basis with the nondisabled, even assuming the skills of the disabled worker are otherwise equal. The law recognizes that in evaluating an insured's claim for long-term disability benefits the insurer's duty of good faith and fair dealing requires it to consider her actual employment prospects.

Authority: *Moore v. American United Life Ins. Co.*, 197 Cal. Rptr. 878, 890, 891 (Cal. App. 1984).

• • •

INSTRUCTION NO. ____

If an insurer denies liability and compels an insured to bring suit, the rights of the parties are fixed as of that time for it is assumed that the insurer then has sound reasons based upon the terms of the policy for denying the claim. An insurer cannot rely on reasons created or discovered after suit is filed to justify its prior conduct.

Authority: *American Paint Service v. Home Insurance Co. of N.Y.*, 246 F.2d 91, 94 (3rd Cir. 1957); *Ichthys, Inc. v. Guarantee Ins. Co.*, 57 Cal. Rptr. 734 (Cal. App. 1967).

Appendix F

Direct Examination of Plaintiff's Insurance Expert in a Bad Faith Case

Paraphrases of the Rules of the Road are in **bold** type.

Direct Examination Continued by Mr. Friedman

Q: Mr. Prater, when we ended yesterday we were talking about whether or not there were certain claims handling standards or principles that were well accepted in the industry and that you considered applicable to this case?

A: Yes.

Q: Could you tell the jury what some of those principles are?

A: Sure. One of the principles is that **an insurance company is supposed to treat its insured's interests at least equal with its own. It's not supposed to be an adversarial process** when you're dealing with what we call a first-party claim where you pay an insurance premium to your own company for your homeowner's or auto policy, and something happens. You don't pay the premium expecting to have to get into an adversarial relationship, and insurance company claims handlers are trained with first-party claims to try and not be adversarial, and to give the insured's interest at least as much consideration as they give themselves.

Q: Now, how about as that applies to financial issues? Suppose there's a claim that's come in, and the insurance company knows that it can make some money if it shaves something off or denies something—you know, I guess what I'm trying to do is ask you to address the issue of finances, or doesn't the company have a right to look after its own financial interest?

A: Well, in the claims department when it comes time to paying the claim, as I mentioned yesterday, it is their responsibility to pay the claim fully and fairly and completely. And **if, for example, an insured doesn't recognize they are entitled to something that they may be entitled to, it's an insurance company's obligation to point it out to them and to say, look, here's something else you're entitled to.**

Q: Even if that's going to cost them more money?

A: Yeah, absolutely.

Q: Other principles or standards that you considered well accepted in the industry and applicable to this case?

A: Yes. **An insurance company cannot deny a claim or refuse payment on a claim without first conducting a full, a fair, a thorough investigation of the facts and circumstances.** And I always train the people at CSE, and I talk about it in lectures, that the mind-set of a claims handler when they're handling a claim should be, Let's look for reasons to pay covered claims that are honestly made. In other words, the focus should be not hold on to the money. It's not their money. It's not the claims handler's money. It belongs potentially to the policyholders if they have a covered claim. So the focus of an investigation should always be, Let's look for reasons to pay covered claims that are honestly made. Let's investigate it fully and fairly, and you cannot deny or terminate a claim or cut off benefits unless you've done that.

Q: We'll talk more later about investigation and what's encompassed in a claims investigation, but generally speaking, and let's talk about disability claims now, what are the sorts of things that a company ordinarily does to investigate a disability claim?

A: Well, ordinarily they would gather records, medical records. They would gather statements from the insured. They would gather information about the insured's actual occupation because with disability policies like this one, it's very important to understand what the insured's actual occupation is because with these kinds of policies you're always looking at what the insured's occupation is and whether or not because of sickness or injury they are unable to do that occupation or the material and substantial duties of that occupation with reasonable continuity. So typically you're gathering information from doctors. You're gathering information from the insured. You're gathering information from the workplace, and potentially other sources as well depending on what you learn through that investigation.

Q: And how do you, how far—well, I'll get to that later. Let me ask you, are there other standards that you thought were applicable to this case?

A: Yes. **When you're investigating a claim and you've gathered information, you have to fairly and objectively evaluate it. You can't just focus on facts that would support denying a claim.** You are supposed to be evenhanded and fair. And remember that, you know, somebody paid premium in exchange for the promise, and you've got to give the equal consideration, and then you can't ignore facts that support coverage. You need to go out and look for facts to support coverage, and when you see it, you have to objectively and fairly evaluate it.

Q: Let me just ask now before we go through the other standards, are the standards that you're talking about today, are they standards that are Professor Prater's standards or are these well accepted in the industry?

A: No, these are not my standards. These are concepts that are well known and understood by claims handlers around the

United States. These are basic elementary claims handling standards that people are trained in.

Q: And, in fact, were some of the claims handlers in this case asked about many or most of these standards?

A: Yes, many of the people in their depositions that worked on this claim were asked if they agreed with these standards, these concepts, and they all unanimously basically agreed.

Q: Other standards you felt applicable to this case?

A: **Insurance companies should pay claims unless there's a good reason not to. They shouldn't deny claims based on speculation** because in the world of insurance sometimes there's no certainty. It's a gray area. Nobody knows for sure exactly what happened if you're not there. So if you gather facts and you gather information and you get suspicions or hunches. And sometimes insurance company people get false information submitted, you know, false claims and inflated claims, but you can't think everybody is a fraud just because you get some of those. You have to kind of keep an open mind, and it's a challenging thing for a claims handler because sometimes they get exaggerated burglary claims and those kinds of things, but we train claims handlers that you can't speculate. You know, you're supposed to objectively and fairly evaluate and try not to let your bias come into it, and evaluate the facts that you gather fairly and not kind of speculate or I think that the person, you know, this is a phony. You know, that they didn't have this nice camera, they had a better camera than they claimed or something, I don't believe the person. You know, things like that speculating about whether the camera was stolen was the one they reported or not, so that's part of it.

Q: Who has the obligation as between the person who has the insurance policy and the insurance company, who has the obligation to gather the facts and make this evaluation?

A: It's clearly the insurance company's obligation to do the investigation and gather the information. Insureds don't have to read insurance company's minds. Insurance people know what they need, and they have to ask for it. The insured doesn't have to wonder about what a company wants. If the company wants or needs something or should gather it, they know what they need, and it's their obligation affirmatively to go out and seek it and gather it.

Q: Are there other principles that you found applicable to this case?

A: Yes. **Insurance companies when they're evaluating claims are not permitted to use predictable or biased experts.** They are not supposed to use people that they then in turn say they relied on in connection with handling a claim that are biased in favor of the insurance company or that will say what the insurance company wants them to say to give the insurance company a basis to deny a claim or withhold benefits for example. So when you are using outside experts to assist you in evaluating a claim, you're supposed to use people that are objective and fair and not trying to influence them in any way and let the chips fall where they may.

Q: Are there biased experts out there willing to be hired if somebody wants to hire them?

A: Yes, there's a lot of biased experts that assist insurance companies with claims handling, doctors, biomechanical people, people that cater—you know, market themselves to insurance companies and infuse their ideas into the claims handling process. So if an insurance company relies on a biased or predictable expert that they hire hundreds of times to say a claim isn't payable, that kind of thing is really looked down upon in the insurance industry. You are not supposed to do it. It happens, but it's not supposed to happen.

Q: Other standards or principles?

A: **An insurance company has a duty to assist an insured with a claim** because, you know, insurance policies are written with complex phraseology that's written by the insurance company, and a lot of times people don't understand what they are entitled to or understand what the insurance company needs. And so it's an insurance company's obligation to assist the insured in any way necessary to help the insured receive everything they are entitled to. **They have to point out other kinds of coverages that the insured might not know about**, or if something is needed or necessary, they have to assist the insured in obtaining it if they can't get it themselves, those kinds of things.

Q: Other standards?

A: **An insurance company cannot misrepresent important facts or insurance policy provisions to their insureds.** This is a universal well-known concept that's embodied in the Unfair Claims Practices Provisions and Regulations that exist in Nevada and in every state, but you cannot misrepresent pertinent facts or policy provisions relating to coverages at issue, which means you can't lie basically about the policy coverages or what's required to get your money, or those kinds of things. You have to tell the truth, and you have to, as the expert in the insurance policy, interpret it fairly, and handle the claim in relation to the actual insurance policy, not in relation to extraneous things that don't apply.

Q: Other standards?

A: **An insurance company may not use the claims department as a profit center.**

Q: What does that mean?

A: Well, we talked a little bit about that yesterday that the claims department's obligation is to basically keep the promise. And as I said yesterday, sometimes you win and sometimes you lose. It's a gambling business. You design a product. Some products are very profitable, some products are not, but if the product is not profitable, and you have to pay claims, you have to pay claims. And that's the way it is, and you shouldn't use your claims people, put any pressure on your claims people, train them in any way to teach them techniques or methods that would assist the company in meeting its financial objectives. The claims department is to look at the policy contract at issue, interpret the policy reasonably and fairly, give everything the policy promises without regard to if it costs the company extra money. You're not supposed to try and figure out ways in the claims department to chisel, or hold back, or not pay everything that's due. It's not fair, it's not right.

Q: Is it appropriate for a company to give a claims department goals for terminating or denying claims?

A: Absolutely not.

Q: Is there any reputable person in the insurance industry that you are aware of who would say that that is appropriate?

A: No.

Q: Other standards?

A: **Other standards would be the insurance company knows that it has to keep a total claims file that—**

Q: Would you—

A: **—reflects everything.**

Q: Excuse me. Would you describe what a claims file is?

A: Yes, a claims file is a written record, if you will, of what happened in connection with the handling of the claim from the point the claim is made throughout the entire handling of the claim. You have to document the claims file as a claims person so that there's continuity in claims handling. For example, if another claims handler picks up the claims file, they know what went on. It also has to contain all important documents, notes, work papers, everything so that the department of insurance, or the insured, or the insured's lawyers can look at the file and see how it was handled from beginning to end, and see who did what and what decisions were made and why. It's supposed to tell a story. We say in the business the claims file is supposed to tell the story of the claim, and it's very important that the claims file tell the whole story and that **documents not be destroyed** or documents not be withheld or pulled out of the file.

Q: Is there another saying in the insurance industry, something to the effect that if it's not in the claims file, it didn't happen?

A: That's true. We often tell our claims people in training that if it's not in the claims file, it didn't happen. It's hard to come later and say, well, something happened. If it's not recorded in the claims file, there's no evidence to support the concept that it happened. Sometimes the claims people make mistakes, but for the most part we expect claims files to fully document the activity on the claim.

Q: And these obligations or standards that you've talked about, do they end at some particular point in time?

A: No, the obligations in connection with handling the claim continue. It's a continuous obligation throughout the life of the claim, and it even survives litigation. Even if there's a lawsuit like in this case that's filed, the insurance company has a continuing obligation to act fairly and in good faith. And if in the course of the investigation post-litigation, they find facts to support the claim, they're supposed to say, okay, we've got further support, we're going to do the right thing, we're going to pay the claim. We teach claims handlers that there's a continuing obligation of good faith and fair dealing.

Q: So let's take a hypothetical example. If a disability claim comes in, it's paid for a while, then it's terminated, they stop payment, and the insured—so the claim is closed, it's not a live claim anymore, if you will, but the insured then sends in more paper, is there—more material to review saying, you know, please reconsider—

A: Right.

Q: —is there still an obligation on the part of the insurance company to follow all the standards you've just discussed?

A: Yes.

Q: They still have—if new material comes in, for example, they have an obligation to investigate that new material?

A: They do.

Q: All right, and all the other standards you discussed would also apply as they now evaluate this new material that came in?

A: They would.

Q: All right. Overall what is the purpose of these kinds of standards in the insurance industry, the overarching principle or goal?

A: To make sure that insurance companies act fairly and in good faith. In every insurance contract there's implied in it, this implied promise if you will. It's not written in the policy that the insurance company is not going to do anything to deprive their insured of their right to receive the benefits, and insurance companies are typically big institutions, and they're dealing with oftentimes little individuals, and they have much more power obviously, and they control the checkbook.

And it's a very special relationship that exists between an insurance company and an insured. So if and when that claim arises, you know, the insured has the right to expect in exchange for that regular premium payment they make, they have the right to expect that the insurance company is not going to use its power to do things improperly, but rather that they are going to be fair and that they are going to look at it from the insured's point of view as well as their own and deliver on the promise made in the policy that's at issue.

Q: Have you been involved in other cases involving Provident, Paul Revere, or Unum Provident?

A: I have.

Q: And can you give us an idea of how many internal company documents you've reviewed?

Appendix G

Direct Examination of Plaintiff's Bus Stop Expert[1]

Paraphrases of the Rules of the Road are in **bold** type.

Direct Examination Continued

Q: Now you've been in the pupil transportation business for over 30 years?

A: Yes.

Q: Turning to the issue of safety, are there basic principles of school bus safety that are applicable to your analysis of this case?

A: Yes.

Q: And can you tell us what they are?

A: Yes, I can, as far as overall. Number one, I think we talked about **safety from the standpoint is—has to always be the primary concern** that drives this industry.

MR. FRIEDMAN: Your Honor, I wonder if I could have Mr. Beasley write some of this on the board?

THE COURT: Sure.

---

[1] This transcript is edited for illustrative purposes. Nothing is added, but some material is redacted to aid your analysis.

MR. FRIEDMAN: Let's just turn the mic.

Q: All right. And you said that always needs to be the primary concern. I suppose the reasons for that are obvious.

A: Well, absolutely. It's the driving force of the industry. You can have efficiency, you can have economy, and certainly you need both. But there's no more important factor than overall safety. I think that's certainly an industry—appreciation of everyone in this industry. I think, you'll find this is a very caring, sharing, industry. And—but paramount to everything, safety drives the total operation.

Q: All right. Now with respect to this case, is there another basic principle that you think is applicable?

A: Well—repeat—repeat the question.

Q: With regard to the case we're talking about here, is there another principle, basic principle, that you believe is applicable?

A: Sure. **I feel that the defendants had the responsibility and duty to select a safe waiting area for youngsters in this particular case.**

Q: For them—you say a waiting area—

A: A waiting area whereby they can wait safely away from the road until the bus arrives and be directed to the boarding area.

Q: If you'd write that on the board, then I'm going to ask you a couple questions about that. Can you tell us what Exhibit 51 is?

A: Kenai Peninsula Borough School District transportation contract.

Q: And this is between who and who?

A: That's Shellbus Contract Services and the Kenai District.

Q: All right. Probably the easiest thing would be for you to sit down for just a minute.

MR. FRIEDMAN: Your Honor, I move for admission of Exhibit 51?

MR. GILLIGAN: There's no objection.

THE COURT: 51 will be admitted.

[Plaintiff's Exhibit 51 admitted.]

Q: Now, if you'd turn to page 20 of the contract.

THE COURT: Mr. Friedman, we're going to have to move that mic around again.

MR. FRIEDMAN: I'm sorry.

THE COURT: In under two months we'll be in the new millennium, but for now, we're still in the last one.

Q: The contractor in this case is Shellbus, is that right?

A: That's correct.

Q: Okay. And referring you to paragraph E on page 20, would you read that out loud please?

A: "The contractor will assure that each driver and attendant adheres to all applicable rules and regulations of the District which have been made known to the driver. The contractor will assure that each driver is provided with a copy of the District's transportation handbook."

Q: And would you also look at page 24. Under regulatory compliance, could you read the last sentence in that paragraph?

A: "The contractor shall comply with all applicable statutes of the State of Alaska, policies and regulations of the Kenai Peninsula Borough School District, and applicable provisions of chapter 27, Regulations of the Alaska Department of Education."

Q: And because we don't have it enlarged—well, let me ask you this, is there a District transportation handbook?

A: Yes.

Q: Are you familiar with that?

A: I am.

Q: Let me hand you what's been marked as Exhibit 55 and ask you if you can identify that.

A: That is the Kenai Peninsula Borough School District Transportation Manual.

Q: That's the manual referred to in this contract?

A: That's correct.

MR. FRIEDMAN: Your Honor, I move admission of Exhibit 55.

MR. GILLIGAN: No objection.

THE COURT: 55 will be admitted.

[Plaintiff's Exhibit 55 admitted.]

Q: Now before we get to the transportation manuals specifically, if you'd turn to page 13 of the contract. Paragraph A, who was given the responsibility for determining the composition of routes and stops.

A: "Transportation routes will be approved by the District, subject to the State Department of Education approval. The contractor, with the approval of the associate superintendent, planning, operations and technology, will determine the composition of routes and stops at the beginning of each school year and provide a list and copy of all routes with stops to the District by August 1."

Q: So the contractor determines the composition of routes and stops and submits those to the school district each year, under this contract.

A: That's correct.

Q: All right. And if you'd go to paragraph D of the contract.

A: "The contractor shall establish the route stops, parenthesis, student pickup points, subject to their approval of the district. The route stops shall be in a safe, convenient location for students."

Q: Now let me ask you about that. Ordinarily, when a school district contracts out the job of establishing route stops, safe pickup points, that sort of thing, does the school district ordinarily have the expertise to make judgments about the safety of the stops?

A: Generally, no.

Q: And who do they rely upon to tell them what's safe and what isn't?

A: It would be the contractor.

Q: Let's go, then, to the transportation manual that's referred to in the contract. And if you would turn to page 10, under loading and unloading, it says, "loading and unloading of students on public streets presents conditions more critical to safety than exist at any other time while students are being transported to and from schools." First of all, do you agree with that?

A: I do, yes.

Q: Can you give us a sense of how dangerous the loading, unloading process is for schoolchildren?

A: Let's—the most dangerous part of a school's—of a child's day is the loading and unloading, basically, in and around school transportation. That's the most dangerous part of a school day for a young child.

Q: It then says, "it is imperative that drivers perform certain procedures in order to protect students from death or injury. The driver must, one, designate a safe area for students to stand and wait for the bus." Is that right?

A: That's correct.

Q: Do you have an opinion as to whether it's appropriate to have a delega—well, first, let me ask you this. **In the industry, is it always the driver who is given the responsibility of designating a safe place to wait for the bus?**

A: Yes, generally speaking. The vast majority of cases it would have to be the driver.

Q: All right. And can you tell us why that is?

A: A properly trained driver would be the one on the scene that's going over that route multiple times a day. Two, four, whatever. A properly trained driver would know what's best for youngsters as it relates to boarding areas along any school bus route. In my judgment, there's not a better person in the industry that would be capable of knowing the surroundings of a particular route, than the school bus driver.

Q: Now, in the industry, are there ever any quality controls on that to make sure the driver is exercising his judgment appropriately?

A: Oh, sure.

Q: What sort of quality controls do you see?

A: Well, number one, you can't overtrain a driver. Number two, you would want quality checks from route investigators, route supervisors, transportation administrators, that would cross-check this to make sure that waiting areas were appropriately placed.

Q: All right. I'd like to get back to—well, let me ask you a kind of conclusory question, then. In this situation, that is, Route 66 on East End Road in Homer in the 96–97 school year, in your opinion, **who was responsible for selecting a safe area for the students to stand and wait for the bus?**

A: **The contractor.** Ultimately the driver should have established, based on the transportation manual, that safe waiting area.

Q: And who was responsible, in your view, for making sure the driver was adequately trained to do that?

A: Contractor.

Q: How important is that?

A: Well, I think I prefaced that by saying you cannot overtrain a driver. I think training is—would come to me, under safety as far as the driving force of this industry. I would never put it above safety, but I'd certainly put training right up with it.

Q: In your opinion, who was responsible for making sure the driver—for supervising his decision, for checking the quality of his decisions with regard to waiting areas?

A: It would be the contractor.

Q: Are there other principles of school bus safety or transportation safety that you feel are applicable to this concept of a waiting area?

A: Well, certainly, yes.

Q: Okay. Do—what—**do the parents have a responsibility to select a waiting area for their children to wait for the bus?**

A: **No.**

Q: Why not?

A: You would have mass confusion if you allowed parents to select a waiting area. You would have some parents—in fact, most parents would probably want it at their driveway. You would have some parents that would not want the stop anywhere near their driveway. So you would have almost hysteria in—if you allowed parents to place the waiting area for their children. It's just—will not work. You've got to have uniformity in that.

Q: Is that a particularly controversial stand that you're taking on that principle?

A: No.

Q: Are there districts that allow or—districts or contractors that have the parents select the waiting areas?

A: No. You would—you would not find that.

Q: Do children—**are children ever given the responsibility in selecting the waiting area?**

A: I would certainly hope not, no.

Q: I'd like to hand you what's been marked as Exhibit 77. Can you tell us what that is?

A: Responses to plaintiff's first request for admissions, directed to defendant, Kenai Peninsula Borough.

Q: Have you been hired as an expert in other cases involving school bus safety?

A: I have.

Q: Are you familiar with what a request for admission is?

A: Basically, yes.

Q: Can you tell the jury, basically, what it is?

MR. FRIEDMAN: Or actually, Your Honor, I wonder if you could just instruct the jury what it is. That'd probably be more accurate.

[Court instructs on requests for admissions.]

MR. FRIEDMAN: Thanks, Your Honor. So admission six and seven are admitted then, Your Honor?

THE COURT: Well, if they're offered.

MR. FRIEDMAN: They are offered.

THE COURT: Mr. Gilligan?

MR. GILLIGAN: We don't deny that we admitted what we admitted, so, yes.

THE COURT: Okay.

MR. GILLIGAN: No objection.

THE COURT: Exhibit 77, as redacted, which now relates to request for admission six and seven, are—or is admitted.

[Plaintiff's Exhibit 77 admitted.]

Direct Examination Continued by Mr. Friedman

Q: Mr. Beasley, these admissions—first one says, please admit that Anne had no legal duty to select a designated waiting place. And it's admitted. Putting aside the question of legal duty, in terms of industry custom or practice, **is there any duty or responsibility placed upon children to select safe waiting areas?**

A: No.

Q: And there is a question about the parents in this case, Margaret Steven's legal duty, is there—putting aside the legal duty, is there any responsibility by industry custom or practice, to put the responsibility of—well that's a bad question, let me start over. Under industry custom or practice, is there any responsibility ordinarily placed upon parents to select a safe waiting area for their children to wait for the bus?

A: Yes. Parents, yes.

Q: What is that duty?

A: Parents have, certainly, a responsibility as it relates to their young children. **It is not a parent's responsibility to select the waiting area as it relates to where they board the bus.**

Q: And that's for the reasons we discussed earlier?

A: That's correct.

Q: All right. If there's a choice in waiting areas, whether it's the contractor or the district that is responsible for the waiting area. Selecting a waiting area. If there's a choice in the industry between waiting areas, is there any principle that comes into play as to what that—how that choice should be made?

A: Yes, sure.

Q: Can you tell us what that is?

A: I think it—he's back to number one. It has to be the safest choice. **The safest waiting area.**

Q: Is that a controversial concept in this industry?

A: Not—not at all.

Q: Once a waiting area is selected, is that the end of the contractor's responsibility in terms of safety evaluation? Excuse me.

A: No.

Q: Why is that?

A: Waiting areas change, they need to be monitored. Many things can change a waiting area. **You want to continually look at waiting areas to make sure they're continually safe for young children.**

Q: What sort of things can change?

A: Overhanging foliage, vehicles blocking good site distance around waiting areas, configurations of the road, construction. Many things can—this particular month, a waiting area may be safe. Six months from now, a waiting area may need some corrections.

Q: What—well, before I get to that, let me hand you Exhibit 52. Can you tell us what this book is?

A: Yes. That's the 1995 National Standards for School Transportation.

Q: And how do those standards get created?

A: This is a consensus of every state. The state director of school transportation approves up to seven delegates from every state to attend this particular meeting. It's held every five years. And not only do you have participation from every state director appointing up to seven local directors, you have sponsorship of this—of this particular document from the National Association of Pupil Transportation, the National Contractor's Association, the National Safety Counsel, and the National Highway Traffic Safety Administration is also involved in this document.

Q: All right. And are these standards required—well, let me ask that a different way. Are these standards laws, as that term is generally understood?

A: No, they're not laws, they're best practices in the industry.

Q: All right.

MR. FRIEDMAN: Your Honor, I'd move for admission of Exhibit 52?

MR. GILLIGAN: No objection.

THE COURT: 52 will be admitted.

[Plaintiff's Exhibit 52 admitted.]

Q: And turning to page 106 of the Standards, do the standards address—

MR. GILLIGAN: Sorry, what page? 102?

MR. FRIEDMAN: 106.

MR. GILLIGAN: 106, thanks.

Q: Do the standards address the question of whether or not waiting areas should be reevaluated for bus stops?

A: Yes.

Q: Now do these standards talk about—excuse me—the issue of reevaluating bus stops or bus waiting areas?

A: Yes.

Q: Okay. It talks in this paragraph about—excuse me—sort of in the middle of the paragraph, "stops should be established only after thorough investigation has revealed the location to most desirable in the area." I think it starts about here.

A: Uh-huh *[affirmative]*.

Q: Do you agree with that?

A: Definitely. Yes.

Q: At the very bottom of the paragraph, it says additional precautions—I need you to stand back a little bit, Mr. Beasley—

A: Sorry.

Q: —because some of the jurors over there—additional precautions should include, but may not be limited to the following. It says, "determine the location and destination of all pupils to be transported." Do you agree with that as one of the factors that ought to be taken into account as these surveys are being conducted?

A: Yes.

Q: If, while these surveys are being conducted, it's determined that the route doesn't need to be changed, but that there's a problem with a stop or a waiting area, is there an industry practice in how to deal with that?

A: Yes.

Q: What's that practice?

A: That would be for communication to the driver to take appropriate action to make sure the students were told to wait in a safe area.

Q: Do you have an opinion as to whether, **within the school bus industry, reevaluation of the safety of waiting areas and bus stops is considered a regular reasonable practice?**

A: Very reasonable, yes.

Q: Would—let me ask you the flip side of it. Within the industry, would it be reasonable not to reevaluate the safety of bus stops and waiting areas?

A: No, I think you have to do that.

Q: Is there any principle or standard in the industry with regard to which side of the road a bus should be lo—a bus stop waiting area should be located on?

A: Yes.

Q: And what is that standard?

A: **The residence side of the highway.**

Q: By residence, you mean the child's residence?

A: That's correct.

Q: And what's the reason for that?

A: Not having the young child cross the road. The hazard of crossing the road. Again, we said earlier, that's the most dangerous part of a student's day. Having a child cross the road without the protection of an adult, and especially a school bus with a eight-light warning system, the stop arm, and the caution color. But the adult, primarily, to supervise that.

Q: All right. What—most people are probably familiar with it, but can you describe for us what a controlled crossing is?

A: Controlled crossing is where a driver arrives, directs the student from the waiting area after they have made sure there's no approaching cars from either direction. And they control that crossing by use of the alternately flashing lights and the stop sign, and then direct the youngster from the waiting area to cross the road, with a signal, and board the bus.

Q: Is it common for people in the industry to try to educate students in that regard? That is, to stay on their own side of the road until the bus arrives.

A: Yes.

Q: And are there educational programs in various states designed to reach the children in the schools and educate them about this principle?

A: Yes.

Q: I'd like to hand you what's been marked Exhibit 37 and you can sit down for a minute if you like.

A: That's the school bus safety curriculum guide.

Q: And what is your understanding as to what this curriculum guide is? Who is it guiding?

A: The curriculum guide was prepared primarily for teachers to instruct youngsters by the Alaska School Bus Safety Committee.

Q: All right. And it's sponsored by—if you turn two pages in?

A: Sponsored by the Alaska School Bus Safety Committee and the Department of Education, State of Alaska.

Q: All right.

MR. FRIEDMAN: Your Honor, I move for admission for Exhibit 37.

MR. GILLIGAN: There's no objection.

THE COURT: 37 will be admitted.

[Plaintiff's Exhibit 37 admitted.]

Q: If you'd turn to numeral page two in that. Sorry, I guess that'd gotten over here. What does it say with regard to how and when children should cross the road?

A: "Always stay on your side of the roadway. Never cross the road before the bus arrives."

Q: Let me ask you, Mr. Beasley, have you seen other curriculum guides, teaching materials for students in various states?

A: Oh, I have, yes.

Q: Do you have an opinion as to how the Alaska teaching materials stack up with regard—and compare to other states?

A: I would rate the Alaska School Bus Safety Committee curriculum guide one of the top ones I've—I've ever seen. It's very good.

Q: Okay. **Do you think it's appropriate to teach children that they should stay on their side of the roadway and never cross the road before the bus arrives?**

A: Yes, I do.

Q: Should the students be getting that message from other sources besides just their teacher in the classroom?

A: Yes.

Q: Who else should be beating that into their heads, if you will?

A: **The school bus driver.**

Q: And why is that?

A: School bus drivers, the real role model that they see, first in the morning and last in the afternoon, it can certainly have an impression on young children. But the school bus driver has a great opportunity to impart that information over and over and over again.

Q: What if the school bus driver is telling them something else? What if the school bus driver is telling students, cross the road and be across the road from your residence before I arrive. Is that appropriate in your view?

A: If a school bus driver was doing that, no, it's certainly not appropriate.

Q: How does that stack up in—compared to industry practice?

A: It would be very reckless, as far as I'm concerned, if the school bus driver was saying that.

Q: I'd like to hand you what's been marked Plaintiff's Exhibit 48 and ask if you can identify that.

A: Alaska School Bus Driver's Manual.

Q: Can you tell us what that is? I mean what a driver's manual is?

A: Well, a driver's manual is as much information as you can impart to a driver on rules, regulations, standards, that are appropriate for driving a bus. A lot of times in a manual you'll see the different parts of the bus. Inspection techniques for daily inspections, but primarily it's a road map, if you will, for a driver to receive instructions.

Q: And this particular manual is dated 1987, is that correct?

A: August 1987.

Q: How does the—are—do other states have driver's manuals?

A: Yes.

Q: And do the Alaska driver's manual materials stack up or compare to those of other states?

A: I thought they were excellent.

MR. FRIEDMAN: I'm sorry, I can't remember if I moved for admission of 48 or not?

THE COURT: I don't think so.

MR. GILLIGAN: No objection.

THE COURT: It's admitted.

[Plaintiff's Exhibit 48 admitted.]

Q: Would you turn to page 10? It says, **"drivers of school buses have full responsibility for the safety of students while** they are boarding the bus, on the bus, leaving the bus, and crossing the road." Do you agree with that?

A: I do, yes.

Q: Then in paragraph three, it says down at the bottom, "**students should not cross the road until signaled to do so by the bus driver.**" Do you agree with that?

A: Definitely, yes.

Q: Can the bus driver signal the students to cross before the bus driver arrives at the waiting area?

A: No.

Q: You've read the depositions of many employees of Shellbus—the driver, the regional manager, and pretty much everyone in between?

A: I have.

Q: Including the training director, what they call the Driver Development supervisor?

A: Yes.

Q: How many different Shellbus employee or manager's depositions have you read?

A: Thirteen or fourteen.

Q: Do any of those people disagree that **a child's designated waiting area should be located on the same side of the road as the child's home?**

A: No.

Q: Unless there's a reas—a safety reason not to do so?

A: No. They do not disagree.

Q: Let me step back for a minute, Mr. Beasley. We've seen the curriculum guide that tells the students not to cross the road until the bus arrives. We've seen the national standards that talk about that same concept and illustrated how—with the chart. Are there other materials in the industry that communicate the same message, either to children, teachers, or other people in the industry?

A: Yes.

Q: Now Exhibit 20—well, is there an understanding in the industry as to whether or not bus drivers or other contractor personnel have an **obligation to correct any unsafe behavior they see on the part of the children?**

A: Well, that's general practice in the industry. When I said earlier it's a very caring, sharing industry, yes, there's an obligation. If a driver knows or sees anything that would enhance safety for a student, yes, they have that responsibility.

Q: All right. And looking at Exhibit 20, page 18, does Shellbus recognize that responsibility? And does Shellbus recognize its responsibility to correct unsafe behavior, particularly loading and unloading behavior on the part of children?

A: Yes, I think so.

Q: Would you read that portion, the last two sentences of section one?

A: "Your responsibility to the student does not end at the door."

Q: You—

A: "Safeguard the children outside your bus by being watchful of their actions. Correct them when noticing improper loading and/or unloading procedures."

Q: In light of your review of all the material you've seen in this case, do you have an opinion as to whether these eight principles you've talked to us about today were followed with respect to the Pavik bus stop?

A: I don't think they were, no.

Q: Why not?

A: The waiting area was on the wrong side of the road. The children were instructed that they were to be at the mailboxes. The overall location of that was extremely dangerous, in my judgment, for youngsters that lived on the north side of the road, especially when you consider the slight hill, the curve, and more importantly, the darkness in that area.

Q: All right. Do you have an opinion as to whether designating the waiting area on the south side by the mailboxes, for the children who lived on the north side, was consistent with careful and reasonable industry practice?

A: It was not.

Q: Okay. Can you give us an idea of how far outside of industry practice this was?

A: I think that was off the page of what I would expect industry practices to be. It wasn't within the loop. I think it was as far as you can get.

Q: You happy about having to say that?

A: No.

Q: Do you have an understanding as to how long children on the north side had been told they needed to be on the south side before the bus arrived?

A: It's my understanding over ten years. Between ten and fourteen years.

Q: Do you have an understanding as to whether the bus driver was trained to understand that it was his job to designate a safe waiting area?

A: I think management knew. No one imparted that, in my judgment, to the driver. I don't think he was ever told, based on his testimony.

Q: Do you have an opinion as to where that lies with regard to industry practice or standards?

A: I think the contractor should certainly have trained him and told him that.

Q: And do you have an opinion or can you tell us again—you're the expert in this field, how outside reasonable industry practice is that?

A: Well, that's a school bus driver's responsibility, certainly he should have been told. And I think that the fact that he wasn't—I think you were lucky in fourteen years that this didn't occur prior to that—

Appendix H

Discovery Requests
Obtaining Rules of the Road and Impeachment Material

This tracks and expands on Fed. R. Civ. P. 26(a)(2).

Expert Interrogatory

1. With respect to any expert witness you expect to call at trial, please:

   a. Give a complete statement of all opinions to be expressed and the basis and reasons therefore.

   b. Identify the data or other information considered by the witness in forming the opinions.

   c. Describe and produce any exhibits to be used as a summary of or support for the opinions.

   d. State the qualifications of the witness, including a list of all publications authored by the witness within the preceding ten years (please produce a current curriculum vitae if available).

   e. Describe the compensation to be paid for the study and testimony.

   f. Provide a listing (by jurisdiction, caption, and case number if available) of any other cases in which the witness has testified as an expert at trial or by deposition within the preceding four years, indicating the side or party for whom the witness testified and the attorney representing such party.

g. State the number of cases on which the witness has previously consulted with the counsel or firm retaining that expert in this case, and identify the case/s if the testimony occurred within the last four years.

h. State the number of cases in which the witness has previously testified in deposition, hearing, or trial on behalf of a party represented by the counsel or firm retaining that expert in this case, and identify the case/s if the testimony occurred within the last four years.

i. Provide a listing of any medical, professional, or technical literature that the witness has read in connection with this case.

j. Provide a listing of the books in the witness's possession or control that relate to the subject matter of the witness' testimony.

k. Provide a listing of the professional journals to which the witness has subscribed during the past four years.

l. State whether the expert knows the party or parties on whose behalf the expert is testifying, and describe any personal, professional, or social relationship between the expert and such party.

Document Request

Document request for experts (and for individual defendants sued in malpractice cases):

Please produce the following documents pursuant to Fed. R. Civ. P. 34. The above definitions and instructions apply.

3. All documents provided to any expert witness whom you expect to call at trial, including records, reports, literature, memoranda, or any other documents prepared by you or your attorney.

8. All records of attendance at continuing medical education courses for you for the previous five years.

10. Your most recent curriculum vitae.

13. Any literature file maintained by you of articles, treatises, pamphlets, and the like concerning any subjects related to this litigation, including but not limited to stroke, transient ischemic attack and/or cardiac myxoma.

14. Any articles, treatises, books, speeches, or other writings, whether published or unpublished, that you have written or delivered on the topic of stroke, transient ischemic attack and/or cardiac myxoma.

15. Transcripts of any testimony you have given in any case as an expert witness on any topic.

17. All transcripts of testimony, whether by deposition or in court, given by you in any case in which you were a defendant concerning any issues relevant to this case.

18. All medical literature, articles, treatises, pamphlets, videotapes, educational materials of any kind, or instructions used or relied upon by you in your treatment of John Doe.

19. As to each expert witness whom you expect to call at trial:

    a. All documents provided to such expert in connection with this case, including records, reports, literature, memoranda, or any other documents.

    b. Any records, reports, notes, memoranda, bills, correspondence, or any other documents prepared by any expert witness in connection with this case.

c. Copies of any manuscripts, drafts, galleys, outlines, slides, and the like, concerning any oral or written presentations made by the expert on any subject relevant to this case which are not in the public domain.

d. Transcripts of any deposition or trial testimony in the expert's possession or control on any subject relevant to this case.

e. A current c.v. for each such expert.

f. Any exhibits prepared by or with the assistance of the expert which are intended to illustrate aspects of the expert's testimony.

Appendix I

Bad Faith Case Opening Statement

Comments by Rick Friedman

The purpose of this appendix is to illustrate the use of the Rules of the Road technique in a bad faith case. For that reason, only excerpts pertinent to the Rules technique are provided.

I do feel strongly that in insurance bad faith cases, there is an important concept that must be communicated to the jury before you get to the Rules of the Road. The concept is that *insurance is not like any other business*. This is important because many jurors (and judges) believe hardball business tactics are completely appropriate. They expect an insurance company to play fast and loose to save money. They believe that is the American way of business: something to be accepted, if not applauded.

You must quickly teach the jurors and judges that *insurance is not like any other business*.

There are many ways to do this. My preferred method is to draw a diagram like this:

I then explain that insurance is not like any other business because the company is selling a promise, nothing tangible. I explain that the

Figure I-1

activities of an insurance company can be divided into four major functions: Actuarial, Marketing, Underwriting, and Claims.

The actuarial department is concerned with what price to put on the promises to be sold; marketing, with how to get people to buy the promise; underwriting, with whether the company wants to sell this particular promise to this particular person. All three of these functions are properly concerned with company profitability.

When a claim is made, however, it is time to deliver the promise. The promise should be delivered, regardless of the effect on company profitability. At the point a claim is made, *insurance is not like any other business*. It is time to treat the customer's interest with equal regard as to the company's. That is what the insured has been paying for.

The diagram above is drawn while the principal functions of an insurance company are being discussed, as in the following example.

Opening Statement by Mr. Friedman

Good afternoon. Unum Provident Corporation is the largest disability-insurance carrier in the country, and before this case is over, the eight of you are going to know more about how Unum Provident does business than any other eight people in Nevada, and with that knowledge will come a responsibility. A responsibility not just to judge how Mr. Merrick was treated by this insurance company, but the responsibility to pass judgment on corporate conduct that affected literally tens of thousands of people, tens of thousands of disabled people.

To be able to exercise your judgment responsibly, you are going to need to learn some things about insurance because the business of insurance is not like any other business. If you think about it, when you buy a car, you give someone or some corporation money and you get a car in return. When you give an insurance company money, premium money, what you get back is a promise. The promise is, if this bad thing happens, if my house burns down, if I'm in a car wreck, the insurance company will pay according to the terms of the contract.

But what the corporation is selling, this promise, really involves four major functions, and this is one way to think about it. One way to think about it is product design or actuarial. These are the people in the insurance company who decide what sort of promise do we want to sell and how do we price it so that we can make money on this promise. For example, if it's car insurance, do we want to sell to people who have drunk driving convictions? Do we want to sell to people who have perfect driving records? Do we want to sell to the people in between? The actuarial product development people decide this is the sort of promise we want to sell, and this is how we want to price it to make sure we make a fair profit.

Now, there's also the marketing function. The marketing department is in charge of selling the promise. How do we get people interested in buying this type of insurance? Do we use sales people? Do we take out ads, so forth, and so forth? Marketing is designed to get people interested in buying the insurance.

Underwriting is the part of the company that decides, do we want to sell this particular promise to this particular person?

So if it's house insurance, for example, and you've got a really old house, they may decide in your particular case they don't want to sell you house insurance. So underwriting looks at the individual person who is applying for insurance and decides whether the company is going to sell to that person, enter into a contract with that person.

Now, all three of these functions are properly concerned with profitability. How do we make money as an insurance company? And every one of them is very concerned with how to make money. The last function is the claims department. Now, not every promise that they sell results in a claim, of course. There's all sorts of people who have driven for thirty or forty years and never had an insurance claim on their car insurance, for example.

So now it's time to deliver on the promise. A claim has been made, and what you're going to hear in this case is that when it comes to paying claims, it is now no longer proper for the insurance company to be concerned with profitability. Now, let me tell you what I mean by that. It doesn't mean you pay a fake claim or a fraudulent claim, and it doesn't mean you don't look, you know, if someone is claiming $25,000 to repair her roof, you don't look and see if maybe it can be done for $23,000.

But they are not supposed to be concerned with profitability. What they are supposed to be concerned with is fairness. They can sell it for an unfair price if they want. They can market it in various ways if they want. They can unfairly deny someone underwriting, but when it comes to claims, they have a special obligation recognized in the insurance industry to not be concerned with their own self-interest, their own money, but to now be fair, to deliver on the promise, whatever that promise is.

Well, this case really begins with Provident Life Insurance Company in the mid-1980s, and some of you may remember that in the mid-1980s the stock market was doing very well, interest rates were very high. Insurance companies were hungry for premium dollars. If they could get premium dollars, they could invest it and make a lot of money, and that's what they were interested in doing. And the disability-insurance companies—there were sixteen to eighteen of them in this country—decided that disability insurance was a very good place to put their emphasis.

[The opening statement continues with a discussion of the institutional history of the bad-claim practices adopted by the defendant. Then it is time to talk about the Rules of the Road.]

*[In the following excerpt, the Rules are introduced and discussed. Depending on your case, you may want to spend more or less time discussing the sources of the Rules and the reasons for them. In this excerpt, I have placed in **bold** type the part of the transcript that constitutes the actual Rule shown on the chart, or a close paraphrasing of the Rule.]*

Now, because the business of insurance is not like other businesses, there are certain principles or standards that are accepted in the insurance industry as to how you handle claims. And basically if you think of a disability claim, somebody files and says, "I meet the standards under the contract to qualify as disabled." And in the case of an own-occupation policy, it's "I can't do my own occupation. Here's my physician certifying to that fact."

"Here is my—here's my problem," whatever it is, "please pay me the monthly benefit."

Now, if the insurance company accepts that claim and pays, they pay every month until the person gets better, or dies, or the company decides to terminate the claim for some other reason. If they deny the claim, of course, they never pay. So how do they decide whether to pay and how do they decide to terminate once they do pay or start paying? There are rules about that that are really not controversial in the insurance industry.

[Rules of the Road shown to jury.]

It's well recognized that the company **must treat its policyholder's interests with equal regard as it does its own interests,** but the claims handling, the handling of claims, is not supposed to be an adversarial process. It can be free-market competition when it comes to these first three functions, but when you get to the claims part of the promise, it is, "we are going to take care of you, we're going to treat you fairly, we're going to give you what you're entitled to." It's not an adversarial process anymore.

And so **the insurance company may not deny or terminate a claim without fairly, reasonably, and fully investigating and evaluating it,** and to say, "we don't want to pay it, sorry," well, there are whole standards that have grown up about what a reasonable fair investigation is, and you'll be hearing a lot about that in this trial. When investigating a claim, **an insurance company may not focus on only those facts which would defeat coverage while ignoring those facts which would support coverage.**

In other words, it's supposed to be a fair and impartial inquiry. Is this person entitled to benefits or not? It is not a search for reasons to deny the claim. **The company should pay unless there's a good reason not to. The denial or termination should never be based on speculation. The company may not use predictable or biased experts. An insurance company has a duty to assist the insureds with a claim.**

If there is something missing—if you file a claim, and there's some critical piece of information missing—it's the claims handler's job to say, "I can't rule on this claim until you get me X." So they're supposed to help, direct, help insureds make their claims.

An insurance company may not misrepresent facts or policy provisions. An insurance company may not use the claims department as a profit center. Claims decisions should be made without regard to company profitability.

So even if you've got six hundred thousand claims or policies out there and the claims are coming in every month and it's affecting your profitability, you can't say, well, we're just not going to pay because it's costing too much money. The claims department is supposed to be sort of like a judge, fair and unbiased, calling it like it sees it. If fulfilling the promises made by the other parts of the company means that the company is losing money, that's not the claims department's responsibility.

A document should not be destroyed to hide the company's policies for claims handling, and these obligations are continuing. It's not like a one-time thing. A claim can be denied—and you'll hear testimony about this—a claim can be denied and frequently someone will submit more information. Well, those obligations continue. The company can't just say, well, we've denied it once, so we're not going to look at it again.

They have a continuing obligation to their policyholder to evaluate new information and be fair about it. If those standards are followed, it results in fairness regardless of the decision, but if these standards aren't followed, it's a huge potential for unfairness.

[The opening then returns to the "story" of the case. In this particular opening, I did not specifically address these standards again in the opening. The list of Rules stayed before the jury, however, and it was clear as particular facts were discussed that the jury was comparing the facts to the Rules.]

Appendix J

Bus Stop Case Opening Statement

Opening Statement by Mr. Friedman

MR. FRIEDMAN: Thank you, Your Honor. Many of you have heard rumors about this case or opinions about this case. And over the next three weeks you're going to hear evidence about this case. By the time we're done, you're going to know more about this case, what happened here, than anyone else on the Peninsula. And you will be the only people empowered to pass judgment on the people here.

By the time this case is over, you're going to know more about certain bus stop safety principles than anyone on the Peninsula. And when it's time to pass judgment, you're going to be making a judgment with enormous consequences. Not only for the parties involved, but for children throughout the state of Alaska. Some school districts have their own school buses they use to transport students to and from school. Other districts choose to go outside their own employee force and hire experts in student transportation. It saves the district having to develop its own expertise in the area, it saves their having to invest in the materials, the school buses. And there are a lot of companies that are in the business of transporting students to and from school. It's a big business. And the biggest corporation in this business, in this industry, is Shellbus.

For a long time, the Homer—or the Kenai Peninsula School District—has contracted out. They've gone outside. They've asked for experts to help them provide safe transportation to the students. They decided not to do it themselves. And what these outside companies like Shellbus sell is essentially three things. They sell the buses, which they own; they sell the personnel, the drivers who operate the buses; and they sell safety, expertise. And you'll see some of their promotional literature in the course of this trial, and you'll see that's one of their big selling points. We are the experts in the field. We know how to safely get your children to and from the school. You can trust us to apply our expertise to see that your children are safe.

In this situation, in this case, the Kenai School District hired Shellbus. It relied upon those promises, those promises of safety.

What you will learn during the course of this trial is that there are certain very basic principles of school bus safety. We all have experienced some experience with school buses. What you'll learn is it is a profession. It is a profession that demands the highest standards of conscientiousness, of attention, because what they're dealing with is so important. These basic principles of school bus safety will, when you read them or hear about them, seem pretty simple and straightforward and commonsensical. But to understand this case, you need to understand those principles. The first principle you'll hear about is that **child safety is always the primary consideration in any decision concerning pupil transportation.** And you're not going to hear a single witness or see a single document that contradicts that. That will be noncontroversial. Everyone will agree with that. **Defendants have the duty and responsibility to select safe waiting areas for the children to wait for the bus.** Now, that may not seem quite so obvious. It might seem as though maybe that's the parents' responsibility or maybe it's the child's responsibility. But, in fact, the judge will tell you at the end of the trial that that's not the case.

And the reason he will—or one of the reasons—is there was a contract between Shellbus and the School District. And in that contract, the School District, which had the responsibility for selecting safe waiting areas, delegated that responsibility to Shellbus.

Shellbus agreed to perform that duty. Select the bus routes, select the bus stops, subject to the District's approval, and also select safe waiting areas for the children to wait. That's crucial in this case because that wasn't followed. So that's where we're headed as we talk about some of the things that happened in this case. **Neither the child nor the parent has the duty, responsibility, or right to select the location of a designated waiting area.** And again, that may not seem, at first glance, like it makes sense. But if you think about it, it really does because if each parent or child were to have the right to select where the child was going to wait, there'd be no way to keep track. It would be chaotic. And the parent could change his or her mind, the child could change his or her mind, parents might disagree about where was the safest or the most sensible place for a waiting area. So in the school bus industry, a basic principle is that **it's not the parent or the child who decides on the waiting area;** it's either the District, or in this case, when the District contracts out that responsibility, it's whoever they contracted out to. In this case, Shellbus.

If there's more than one reasonable and practical place to locate a waiting area, the one safest for the child should be designated. Again, I don't think you'll hear much dispute about that. You've got two alternatives; you're going to go back to your primary consideration and do the one that's safest. If you're not selecting the safest one, you'd better have an awfully good reason.

Because the factors affecting the safety of a waiting area can change at any time, its location must be continually reevaluated. And essentially what that means is, people move, road conditions change, new buildings get put up, old buildings get torn down, lighting changes, signage changes, traffic patterns change, it's not a static situation. And what that means in practical terms is, you've got to always be looking. Always paying attention to whether or not the waiting area that you designated continues to be the safe waiting area. The right place to tell the children to wait.

A child's designated waiting area should be located on the same side of the road as the child's home, unless it would be unsafe to do so. Again, this is critical to the decisions you will have to make. Because in this case, this principle wasn't followed either. And what was required of the children at this bus stop is that they cross the road. We'll talk more about that in a little bit.

But this principle, that a child's designated waiting area should be located on the same side of the road as the child's home, isn't controversial either.

Except, perhaps, in this courtroom. Some of you may know that in a lawsuit, each side can do what's called take a deposition. We can go to someone like Mr. Ashton, the safety expert for Shellbus, and we can ask him questions under oath. And we can find out what witnesses have to say before the trial even starts. And in this case, that's one of the things Mr. Westerburg did. And what he learned in questioning the Alaska Shellbus people is that they all agreed with number six: **a child's designated waiting area should be located on the same side of the road as the child's home.** That's bus stop safety 101, if you will.

It's one of the most basic, well-understood principles in this industry. Now parents might not know it. Some of you may not have known it, even though you may have operated under that rule when you went to your own bus stops or when your children went to their bus stops. That's why we were asking those questions: did your children have to cross the road; did you have to cross the road? And what we're talking about here is arterial roads, major roads. Not the little subdivision roads with the gravel, the backwoods farm roads. What we're talking about are the relatively major arterial roads that have some traffic to them and have some danger. Mr. Westerburg asked the Shellbus people from Alaska if they agreed with that principle.

Every one of them said yes. Children should be told to wait on their own side of the road. They're supposed to wait on their own side of the road until the bus comes and the lights go on, the stop sign goes out, the driver, an adult, sitting six feet or more above the road, can look down the road in both directions, make sure the traffic is stopped, and then wave the children across. That's the protection, the lights—the flashing lights, the stop sign, the adult supervision, and the traffic, understanding that it needs to stop, it goes from being an uncontrolled situation to a controlled stop.

Every one of these people will tell you in this trial that that's the way it's supposed to be. The most basic of principles of bus stop safety. And the only people you're going to hear who disagree with this are a couple of guys the defense have hired from down south. Two of them work for Shellbus. Actually three guys, two of them work for Shellbus, who will tell you, no, that's not the way it's supposed to be. The children—it's not enough to just designate the waiting area on the correct side of the road; the other thing you need to do is train the children not to cross the road until after the bus arrives and the driver gives the signal. And you're going to see a lot of paperwork, manuals, training manuals, in this case, what I've blown up is a page out of—the State of Alaska publishes a curriculum guide to be given to students to tell them, to train them, on how to cross the road or how to get on the bus, if you will. And again, one of the basic principles, always stay on your side of the roadway. Never cross the road before the bus arrives. If the system is working, the children are taught that, the bus drivers are taught that, the parents are taught that, and everybody's on the same page, setting up a system that's as safe as it can possibly be. And if the kids aren't doing it, **the bus company should take appropriate action to correct unsafe loading and unloading behavior observed on the route.** They're the experts. They're the ones operating these big buses. They're the ones getting paid to look after the safety of this transportation system.

And again, every one of their witnesses will tell you that it's the bus driver's responsibility if he—it comes to his attention that something unsafe is going on, to try to correct it, either by telling the children, telling the school so they can tell the parents, or by changing whatever's going on in Shellbus's system. Those are the basic principles of bus stop safety that you're going to be hearing an awful lot about in this case. And the reason you're going to hear a lot about them is because they weren't followed.

There was one bus stop in Homer, out East End Road at approximately Mile 9, where these principles weren't followed. It was on what's called Route 66 or what Shellbus calls Route 66. A bus run that runs the kids out East End Road, out to McNeil Canyon School. It's not a particularly desirable route for the bus drivers. Because of the way the road is, it's busy . . .

Appendix K

Cross-Examination of School Bus Company Manager

Here is the exam of a manager of the bus company in our bus stop case. He is being called in the plaintiff's case as an adverse witness. He was never deposed about the Rules of the Road. As you will see, because the Rules were carefully selected, he was not in a position to disagree with any of them. Notice what happens when he tries to resist. Rules of the Road are in **bold** type.

Cross-Examination by Mr. Friedman

Q: Mr. Hendricks, how many years have you been in the school bus industry in one capacity or another?

A: Approximately twenty-five.

Q: Would you agree that child safety is always the primary consideration in any decision concerning pupil transportation?

A: Are you asking me if that's—that's my opinion?

Q: Yes.

A: Yes.

Q: If that's supposed to be in the industry.

A: I would not say necessarily in the industry.

Q: There are people who don't honor that principle?

A: There are other constraints other than child safety.

Q: And I'm not suggesting that there aren't, but would you agree that that should be at the top of everybody's mind as—

A: I agree.

Q: —they make decisions?

A: Yes, I agree.

[Now, we turn to our source, before asking him about the next Rule.]

Q: If you would turn to Exhibit 51, which if they're—they're in numerical order there. *[Pause]* Okay. Have you found it?

A: Not yet . . . I found it.

Q: All right. If you'd turn to page 13. Exhibit 51 is the contract between Shellbus and the School District? Is that right?

A: At that time, yes.

Q: All right. And if you'd turn to page 13 of the contract, one of the things that Shellbus undertook to do under the contract was to establish the route stops subject to the approval of the District?

A: That is item D, yes.

Q: All right. And furthermore, Shellbus agreed that the route stops would be in a safe, convenient location for students?

A: Correct.

Q: And, in essence, what Shellbus is promising to do there is to exercise its expertise to **ensure that the stops are in safe, convenient locations?**

A: As best we can, correct.

Q: Okay. Under the contract, Shellbus was also required to have its personnel follow the rules and regulations of the School District's transportation manual. Is that correct?

A: That's correct.

Q: And that should be in that book that you have there, as well, a little bit further on, Exhibit 55. And if you look at Roman numeral V, the transportation manual provided that **Shellbus would designate safe areas for the students to stand to wait for the bus?**

A: That's correct.

Q: Okay. And Shellbus understood that certain actions and duties were necessary to protect students from death and injury?

A: That's correct.

Q: And Shellbus agreed under the contract to exercise its safety expertise and designate a safe area for students to stand and wait for the bus?

A: That's correct.

Q: And you would agree, wouldn't you, that **Shellbus did have the duty and responsibility to select safe waiting areas for the children to wait for the bus?**

[The court had ruled that Shellbus had that duty, so this was one instance where using the word "duty" was permissible.]

A: With approval from the School District, yes.

Q: Okay. And that is an important responsibility, isn't it?

A: That's correct.

Q: Something that Shellbus takes seriously?

A: Yes.

Q: Do you know whether, before Anne Lawrence's accident, Shellbus ever designated a place for the students at the Travers bus stop to wait for the bus?

A: No, I do not know that Shellbus did that.

[He has now agreed to the Rule, as well as the violation. The next two questions are aimed at emphasizing the negligence of the violation.]

Q: Does Shellbus have any manuals on bus routing or bus stop selection to assist its personnel in performing their contractual duties to select safe bus stops and safe waiting areas?

A: Not that I know of.

Q: Does Shellbus have any guidelines or published material that a Shellbus person can use in fulfilling Shellbus's contractual duty to designate safe bus stops and safe waiting areas?

A: I would say we do not. We rely primarily on local information.

• • •

Q: At the beginning of each year when you're doing the route sheets for the School District, you would exercise your expertise in determining whether it's a safe waiting area?

A: That's correct.

Q: And the contract imposes that obligation on you?

A: Correct.

Q: Okay. And the contract does not put that obligation on the School District, correct?

A: I don't know that that contract does, no.

Q: All right. And likewise the contract **does not put that responsibility on the parents?**

A: Correct.

Q: **Or the child—children?**

A: Correct.

Q: And as between the School District, the parents, the children, and Shellbus, Shellbus understands that it is the entity with the most expertise on pupil safety, doesn't it?

A: In general?

Q: In general.

A: In general, yes.

Q: Would you agree, then, that at least in Homer during the time period we're talking about, **neither the child nor the parent had the duty or responsibility or right to select the location of a designated waiting area?**

A: I don't know that I would agree with that. At the beginning of the school year, we have students who, for instance, may not have been at a designated stop from a prior year, will come out to the road. In that case, we pick the students up where they're at and transporting them, and then they get into the system and it's determined whether a new stop is needed or whether they're directed to an existing stop.

Q: Uh-huh. And—**that decision as to where they're directed to wait for the bus rests with Shellbus and the School District, doesn't it?**

A: Correct.

Q: And the School District, as we heard this morning, relies upon Shellbus's expertise as to where that safe place is?

A: As well as their own information as well, too.

Q: Sure. But it's not the parent or the child who has the decision-making authority as to where the waiting area is going to be?

A: That's correct.

Q: *[Pause]* Now, would you agree that the **factors affecting the safety of a waiting area can change at any time?**

A: Correct.

Q: You can have students moving in or out of the area, for example?

A: It could have different weather conditions, different road conditions.

Q: Traffic patterns changing?

A: Traffic patterns, correct.

Q: Vegetation growing up or being cut down, the road being resurfaced or changed somehow?

A: Yes.

Q: All sorts of things. Therefore, **would you agree that the safety of a bus stop or waiting area ought to be continually reevaluated, that—well, let me just stop there, that it ought to be continually reevaluated?**

A: I suppose.

Q: **Would you agree that if there is more than one reasonable and practical place to locate a waiting area, the one safest for the child should be designated?**

A: Yes.

• • •

Q: As I understand it, Mr. Hendricks, you served on the school bus safety committee?

A: That's correct.

Q: Do you still serve on it?

A: I do.

Q: Okay. One of the things the committee tries to do is encourage uniform and safe people-transportation practices?

A: That's correct.

Q: One of the things the committee did to encourage those reasonable and safe transportation practices was to issue the curriculum guide?

A: That's correct.

Q: And you're familiar with that?

A: I am.

Q: Okay. We can find that at Exhibit 37 in that book that you have. Will you turn to page 2 in the curriculum guide, Arabic numeral 2?

[Remember, he was not deposed on these Rules before trial. Here, we are showing him the source first, to make sure he knows he must agree with our Rule.]

Q: Up at the very top, **one of the things that the curriculum guide told the teachers to teach the children was to never cross the road until after the bus arrives?**

A: Correct.

Q: And that is because that was considered the best and safest practice by the committee in terms of how to handle students who lived on the opposite side of the road from where the bus would be boarding?

A: That's correct.

Q: That gave the students the flashing lights, the stop sign, an adult six feet above the road who can look, observe, and stop traffic and so on, right?

A: That's correct.

Q: Okay. Would you agree, then, that **a child's designated waiting area should be located on the same side of the road as the child's home unless it would be unsafe to do so**?

A: Correct.

Q: And if a driver became aware that a—well, let me ask it this way: If a driver became aware that a waiting area was requiring a child to cross the road—in other words, if the child lived on the opposite side of the road from the waiting area—**you would expect the driver to correct the child, wouldn't you?**

A: If they saw them cross the road prior to getting there or they may question the child how they got to that stop.

Q: However they get the information, if they know the child lives, let's say, on the west side of the road and is crossing before the bus arrives, you would expect the driver to tell the child no, wait on the other side of the road?

A: Not necessarily. The parent crossed the child prior to getting there or if the parent came down, for instance, in their vehicle on their way to work and dropped the child off, in those cases the driver would have no knowledge.

Q: Okay. And that is my question: If the driver knows—

A: If the driver knows.

Q: —that the students are crossing ahead of time—

A: If they know.

Q: Okay. You would expect them to correct the child and put them on the other side?

A: If it wasn't under a parent crossing.

Q: Right. And let me ask you this: If we have a situation where a group of children lives on one side of the road, the waiting area is on the other side of the road, would you agree as you did earlier the designated waiting area for that child should be on the same side of the road as where he lives?

And that is because parents can't always take children across the road?

A: Or don't always.

Q: Or don't always.

A: Choose not to, correct.

Q: Okay. And so as a matter of safe school bus industry practice, the waiting area for those children should be on their own side of the road. But if a parent wants to take them across to another safe area, another waiting area, that's okay?

A: If you have a real simplified situation as you just mentioned, correct.

Q: Okay. And I take it **you agree that children should be trained not to cross the road until after the bus arrives and gives the signal?**

A: Correct.

Q: Okay. And Shellbus, when it goes to a district and says we can help you with your transportation system, one of the things it says it will do is provide those constant reminders?

A: Correct.

Q: You would agree that **the contractor, in this case Shellbus, should take appropriate action to correct unsafe loading or unloading behavior that it becomes aware of?**

A: Correct.

Q: Are you familiar through your work at Shellbus, through your own education, with industry outside of Alaska?

A: Yes.

Q: This idea of having children wait—have their waiting areas be on their own side of the road until the bus arrives—isn't unique to Alaska, is it?

A: No, it is not.

Q: It is in the national standards, for example?

A: Correct.

Q: It is incorporated in the Alaska Driver's Manual, for example?

A: Correct.

Q: Would it be fair to say that **this is standard and accepted industry practice, that waiting areas should be on the children's own side of the road?**

A: Where all practical and safe, yes.

Q: Okay. And that standard is put in place to protect the safety of children?

A: Correct.

Q: It would be irresponsible for Shellbus to be instructing students to cross the road before the bus arrives as a general practice?

A: Yes.

Q: It would be irresponsible for any legitimate pupil-transportation contractor to be instructing children to cross the road before the bus arrives as a general practice?

A: I would say as a general practice, but you may have situations in the Lower 48 where maybe that's a school-district instruction or a state instruction. I can't speak to that.

Q: Understood. But as a general safety—you know, from a safety perspective in the industry, in your view that's not how that should be done?

A: That's correct.

Q: *[Pause]* Children are also taught—as reflected in the national standards, the curriculum guide, the bus stop training manual, children are also taught in this industry that they should obey the directions of the bus driver, aren't they?

A: That's correct.

Q: And it is important that children get the same directions from the bus driver that they're getting from the schools?

A: I would say so, to have a consistent message.

Q: And it's understood in this industry that if children are not getting a consistent message, you've got a safety problem on your hands?

A: You may have a safety problem, yes.

Q: Now, after you learned of Anne Lawrence's accident, you made an attempt to learn what had happened, correct?

A: Correct.

Q: And after learning what happened, you issued no directives or orders to the Shellbus branches under your control to do anything differently. Is that correct?

[Objection and discussion with counsel and court.]

Direct Examination Continued by Mr. Friedman

Q: Mr. Hendricks, after the accident, you issued no directives or orders to Shellbus branches as a result of the accident, is that fair to say?

A: Correct.

Q: And there were no changes in Shellbus's policy as a result of the accident?

A: Correct.

[A long "cross-examination" by the defense followed, concluding with the following exchange.]

DEFENSE COUNSEL: Do you agree with the following proposition: that the School District or school bus contractor cannot assume the duty of safety for a school child before the bus gets to the bus stop, and the child steps from the unpaved to the paved portion of the road to start the boarding process?

A: That's correct.

Q: Why?

A: We have no control over what happens prior to that point. We're not in the area; we don't have knowledge; we don't—we can't—we're not there to see. You know, if you were going to expand that responsibility to us, we would have to have people in the vicinity of the bus stops to monitor what's going on. And, I mean, you'd have to add a lot of staff people to do that. As a practical matter—I mean, we'd be glad to do it if somebody wants to pay for those services. But, you know, it's—it's not in any of the contracts; it's not a requirement.

And as a practical matter, I don't think it's something that—that the public would want to pay for.

DEFENSE COUNSEL: Okay. That's all I've got for Mr. Hendricks.

Redirect Examination by Mr. Friedman

Q: Well, actually, Mr. Hendricks, you did assume that responsibility by contract, didn't you? Let me ask the question this way. Before the student ever leaves his home, if Shellbus has followed its contractual obligation, it has designated a safe place for the student to wait, isn't that right?

A: That's correct.

Q: So long before the bus ever leaves the bus barn, or the student ever leaves the house, **Shellbus has a responsibility to designate a safe waiting spot?**

A: To designate the safe waiting spot, yes.

Q: And you do have control of that waiting spot before the student ever leaves the house?

A: No, we do not.

Q: You don't—

A: How could we? We're not there.

Q: You have control because you set it up. You con—

A: Of the location. But we don't have control what happens at that location.

Q: That's right. Once the dangerous situation has been set up, you don't have control how—as to how people react to it?

A: Or how the student gets there or anything.

Q: That's right. But it is your responsibility to set up those bus stops and those waiting areas safely?

A: To designate the—to designate the waiting area, correct.

Q: And that's a responsibility you did get paid for under the contract?

A: To designate those waiting areas, yes.

Q: Safe waiting areas?

A: Yes.

Q: And as we've discussed, **safe waiting areas means on the child's side of the street?**

A: Where at all possible, yes.

Q: And if it's possible, and you designate a waiting area across the street from the child's residence, then you've breached your contractual duty that you assumed under the contract, isn't that right?

A: Repeat the question?

Q: If it's possible to set up a safe waiting area on the child's side of the road, and you failed to do that, then you failed to do what you promised to do in the contract, isn't that right?

A: I'm not sure what the answer is to that.

MR. FRIEDMAN: Thank you. I don't have any other questions.

Appendix L

Response to Motion *In Limine*

Plaintiffs, Reginald Sparks and Christine Sparks, by and through their attorneys, Leventhal, Brown & Puga, P.C., hereby respond to Defendants Louis Barnes, D.O. and Boulder Orthopedic and Fracture Clinic, Inc.'s Motion *In Limine* To Preclude Mention of Improper Standard of Care as follows:

Summary

Defendants' motion is in effect asking the Court to grant a motion for summary judgment on Plaintiffs' claim of negligence against Defendant Dr. Barnes. Defendants are asking the Court to preclude the Plaintiffs from presenting expert evidence establishing what governs or mandates what a reasonably careful physician would do under the circumstances in this case as required under Colorado law. In addition, Defendants want to preclude Plaintiffs' counsel from arguing that the well-accepted medical literature, community standards, and principles establish rules that a reasonably careful physician must follow under these circumstances. In the alternative, Defendants argue that they should be entitled to simultaneously interrupt Plaintiffs' opening statement, direct examination, and closing argument and present evidence of what they believe governs or mandates what a reasonably careful physician would do under the same circumstances. Defendants' motion is baseless, unfounded and wholly unsupported by legal authority.

Background

This is a medical negligence action which was originally tried in December of 2008. During the trial, after Plaintiffs presented their case, a mistrial was declared. This case is now set for trial beginning October 27, 2009.

During the first trial, Plaintiffs' counsel presented expert testimony establishing what well-accepted standards or rules govern what a reasonably careful physician should do under the same circumstances pursuant to C.J.I.—Civ. 15:3. Plaintiffs' experts testified that a reasonably careful physician under the same circumstances would order objective testing to rule out a blood clot and that Dr. Barnes's failure to order objective testing such as an ultrasound was negligent and below the standard of care.

Plaintiffs' experts testified that they reviewed the well-accepted medical literature in the community, including Defendants' endorsed medical literature, applicable to the diagnosis of a blood clot. Plaintiffs' experts testified that the well-accepted rules govern what a reasonably careful physician must do under the same circumstances at the same time. Plaintiffs' experts testified that the rule required a reasonably careful physician to order objective testing to rule out a blood clot before sending Reginald Sparks home. Plaintiffs' experts testified that this well-accepted medical rule governs what a reasonably careful physician must do under these circumstances at the same time; and that a violation of this rule was negligent.

Defendants failed to object to the use of the word "rule" during the first trial, and therefore waived any objection. Furthermore, Defendants had and will have a full and ample opportunity to present their own opening statement, cross-examine Plaintiffs' experts, and present their own experts to establish what a reasonably careful physician was required to do under the same circumstances.

Defendants are now moving *in limine* to preclude Plaintiffs from presenting what well-accepted rule governs what a reasonably careful physician should do under these same circumstances. Defendants also want to preclude counsel for Plaintiffs from arguing that there are well-accepted standards and rules that govern what a reasonably careful physician is mandated or required to do under the circumstances.

Defendants are in effect moving for Summary Judgment on Plaintiffs' claim of negligence against Dr. Barnes and asking the Court to tie the hands and cover the mouths of Plaintiffs' counsel and their experts. Specifically, Defendants want to pick the words that Plaintiffs may use and move to preclude Plaintiffs from using the words "the rule." In the alternative, Defendants are requesting to interrupt Plaintiffs' opening statement, direct examination, and closing argument and contemporaneously present evidence of other parts of literature referring to the rule.

Defendants' motion is improper and without basis. The motion seeks to exclude expert evidence without citing a single legal authority in support. Granting such a motion at this point in the litigation would prejudice the Plaintiffs by requiring the Plaintiffs to rework their entire case, including developing a new theme and legal theory, redoing trial exhibits, and changing expert testimony and reports.

Argument

Plaintiffs' counsel advised the jury in her opening statements that Plaintiffs' experts would all testify about what the "rule" was in this case that governed how a reasonably careful physician must act under the facts and circumstances in this case. Plaintiffs' experts all testified about what the rule was that governed Dr. Barnes's care and treatment and how Dr. Barnes broke the rule. Defendants made no objections during the first trial to the use of the word "rule." In fact, Defendants' own experts relied on literature that contained the rule consistent with Plaintiffs' literature and expert testimony.

Because Defendants failed to assert objections to the use of the word "rule" throughout discovery and during the first trial, they have waived their objections.

A. Use of the word "rule" by Plaintiffs' Experts Is Probative and Admissible

Relevant evidence means evidence having any tendency to make the existence of any fact that is of consequence to the determination of the action more probable or less probable than it would be without the evidence. C.R.E. 401. All relevant evidence is admissible, except as otherwise provided by the Constitution of the United States, the Constitution of the State of Colorado, by these rules, or by other rules prescribed by the Supreme Court, or by the statutes of the State of Colorado. C.R.E. 402.

In a medical negligence case, the jury must determine what a reasonably careful physician would have done in the same circumstances at the same time. C.J.I.—Civ. 4th 15:3. The jury instruction itself does not use or define "standard of care" so the Court must look to the applicable case law. Under Colorado law, the standard of care that governs what a reasonably careful physician should do under the circumstances is established by expert testimony.

In a medical malpractice case, the burden is on the plaintiff to establish a *prima facie* case of negligence. *Melville v. Southward*, 791 P.2d 383 (Colo. 1990). The standard of care in a medical malpractice action is measured by whether a reasonably careful physician would have acted in the same manner as did the defendant in treating and caring for the plaintiff. *Id.*, at 384.

Because the applicable standard of care in a medical malpractice action is not within the common knowledge and experience of ordinary people, "the standard *must* be established by expert testimony." *United Blood Services v. Quintana,* 827 P.2d 509, 520 (Colo. 1992). (emphasis added); *Wallbank v. Sothenberg,* 74 P.3d 413, 416 (Colo. App. 2003); see also *Spoor v. Serota,* 852 P.2d 1292, 1296 (Colo. App. 1992) (a jury is to be guided in its determination of the standard of care solely by expert testimony.); *Clayton v. Hepp,* 504 P.2d 1117, 1118 (Colo. App. 1972) (the standard of care must be based upon the testimony of experts.).

The applicable standard of care in a medical malpractice action is best viewed as a mixed question of law and fact. "It is a question of fact to the extent that [it] . . . must be established by expert testimony." *State Bd. Of Med. Exam'rs v. McCroskey,* 880 P.2d 1188, 1194 (Colo. 1994); *Quintana,* 827 P.2d at 520. Accordingly, the jury is to determine the applicable standard based solely upon the testimony of expert witnesses. *Spoor,* 852 P.2d at 1296.

To be distinguished from the legal standard of care applicable to a medical malpractice action is the admissibility of expert opinion testimony. *Melville, supra.* C.R.E. 702 governs the admissibility of expert testimony and states as follows:

> If scientific, technical, or other specialized knowledge will assist the trier of fact to understand the evidence or to determine a fact in issue, a witness qualified as an expert by knowledge, skill, experience, training, or education, may testify thereto in the form of an opinion or otherwise.

As a prerequisite to admitting expert testimony, a trial court must make the following two preliminary determinations: first, the court must decide if the expert testimony will assist the trier of fact in understanding the evidence or in determining a fact in issue; and second, the court must determine whether the witness is properly qualified by knowledge, skill, experience, training, or education, to offer an opinion on the issue in question. See M. Graham, *Handbook of Federal Evidence,* § 702.1, at 604–05 (1986). The text of C.R.E. 702 is an implicit acknowledgment that the primary consideration in determining a witness' qualifications is the witness' actual "knowledge, skill, experience, training, or education," rather than the particular title attributed to the witness. *Melville, supra.*

Colorado Rule of Evidence 702 states that an expert may testify in the form of opinion or otherwise if such testimony will help the trier of fact determine a fact in issue. C.R.E. 702 (2009). Further, any qualified expert can present evidence with respect to the applicable standard of care. *Smith v. Hoffman,* 656 P.2d 1327, 1329 (Colo. App. 1982).

In the case at hand, Plaintiffs' experts have testified that they reviewed the well-accepted medical literature in the community, including Defendants' endorsed medical literature, applicable to the diagnosis of a blood clot. Plaintiffs' experts testified that the well-accepted rules govern what a reasonably careful physician must do under the same circumstances at the same time. Plaintiffs' experts testified that the rule required a reasonably careful physician to order objective testing to rule out a blood clot before sending Reginald Sparks home. Plaintiffs' experts testified that this well-accepted medical rule governs what a reasonably careful physician must do under these circumstances at the same time; and that a violation of this rule was negligent.

Black's Law Dictionary defines "rule" as "generally, an established and authoritative *standard* or principle; a general norm mandating or guiding conduct or action in a given type of situation"; and defines "standard" as "a measure or *rule* applicable in legal cases such as the 'standard of care' in tort actions." Black's Law Dictionary (8th Ed. 2004) (emphasis added).

The Colorado Supreme Court has adopted a liberal standard for admissibility of expert testimony, which is balanced against "vigorous cross-examination, presentation of contrary evidence, and careful instruction on the burden of proof." *People v. Shreck*, 22 P.3d 68, 78 (Colo. 2001).

Defendants will have the opportunity, in opening and closing arguments, direct and cross-examination, and submission of proposed jury instructions to the Court, to dispute that a rule exists and to explain how physicians make decisions about when objective testing is indicated. See *Farmland Mut. Ins. Cos. v. Chief Indus., Inc.*, 170 P.3d 832, 838 (Colo. App. 2007) (defendant's contention that plaintiff's expert testified to an improper standard of care has no merit, since defendant had the opportunity to cross-examine the expert and incorporate its own understanding of the applicable standard into jury instructions submitted to the court.).

Colorado Rule of Evidence 403 Analysis

Defendants do not dispute that evidence of a "rule" in medicine is relevant. Instead, Defendants seek to exclude the words "the rule" on the basis that it is unfairly prejudicial and misleading without citing any legal authority to support this contention.

Defendants argue to the Court that it is their theory of the case that there is no hard and fast "rule" that physicians must follow, and instead, physicians use a variety of scientific and intellectual processes including differential diagnosis and risk-benefit analysis. Therefore, they are asking the Court to preclude Plaintiffs' experts from testifying that there is a rule in this case that governs how a reasonably careful physician must act in providing care and treatment. The only legal authority Defendants cite in support of their motion is that such evidence is unduly prejudicial, confusing, and misleading under C.R.E. 403.

Colorado Rule of Evidence 403 states "evidence may be excluded if its probative value is substantially outweighed by the danger of unfair prejudice, confusion of the issues, or misleading the jury, or by considerations of undue delay, waste of time, or needless presentation of cumulative evidence." C.R.E. 403.

"Rule 403 provides that the trial judge may exclude evidence that is excessively prejudicial. Accordingly, if the evidence arouses the jury's emotional sympathies, evokes a sense of horror, or appeals to an instinct to punish, the evidence may be unfairly prejudicial under Rule 403. Usually, although not always, unfairly prejudicial evidence appeals to the jury's emotions rather than intellect." Best, Hardaway, et. al., *Colorado Evidence: 2009–2010 Courtroom Manual,* p. 47.

The Colorado Supreme Court ruled that the trial court properly admitted evidence related to the Occupational Safety and Health (OSH) regulations in a negligence action as nonconclusive evidence of the standard of care in the industry although the statute bars the use of OSH regulations to establish a negligence *per se* claim. The Colorado Supreme Court ruled such evidence was relevant to show whether the defendants complied with the industry standard regarding full protection and the probative value outweighed any prejudice. *Scott v. Matlack, Inc.,* 39 P.3d 1160 (Colo. 2002).

The use of the word "rule" is not prejudicial let alone excessively prejudicial and clearly does not have a tendency to suggest a decision on an improper basis. In fact, the definition of "rule" bears a striking similarity to the jury instruction which describes how the standard of care should be determined. Use of the word "rule" in the medical profession is practically universal and appears frequently in the literature relied on by experts in this case.

The word "rule" is not inflammatory, unfairly prejudicial, or misleading. It is a generally accepted term used by medical professionals. Any potential prejudice that may exist can be easily overcome by Defendants in their arguments and through examination of experts.

Preclusion of Expert Evidence Is Drastic and Unfairly Prejudicial

If the Court granted Defendants' motion and precluded Plaintiffs' experts from testifying about the well-established rule applicable to this case, Plaintiffs would be severely prejudiced and forced to rework the presentation of their entire case just weeks before trial. Plaintiffs would have to develop a new trial theme and strategy, prepare new exhibits, and present different expert testimony.

If granted, the motion would effectively preclude large portions of Plaintiffs' experts' testimony. Under such circumstances, the Court should consider the standards set forth in *Shreck* and the subsequent case law. Notably, Defendants have not filed a motion challenging the qualifications of Plaintiffs' experts or the reliability of their opinions.

Granting of Defendants' motion would also hinder Plaintiffs' counsel's ability to present Plaintiffs' case. The rules governing conduct of counsel in opening and closing arguments are well settled. Wide latitude must be allowed in an attorney advocating his client's cause. *Spears Free Clinic & Hosp. for Poor Children v. Maier,* 261 P.2d 489, 492 (Colo. 1953); *see* e.g., *Adams Exp. Co. v. Aldridge,* 77 P. 6 10 (Colo. App. 1904) (in personal injury case, where attorney argued "some of you, many of you, are married men and have families. How much would you take to have your wife run down in the public street, her leg broken, and her body covered with cruel bruises? How much would you take to have wife run down in the public street and subjected to the curious gaze of the gaping crowd? How much would you take to have your wife knocked from her bicycle, rolled in the dirt in the public street, and humiliated and made the spectacle of a crowd on the public street?" Court stated "we are not prepared to say that by the language quoted the bounds of propriety were overstepped.")

Statement or argument may be improper where counsel uses language calculated to arouse the jury's sympathy or prejudice, engages in personal attacks on the opposing party or counsel, or refers to evidence not in the record. Here, the language "the rule" refers to the standard of care for diagnosing blood clots, which is common to the medical profession. Use of "the rule" does not misstate the facts nor does it overstep the bounds of propriety.

Preclusion of establishing the applicable rule would be unduly prejudicial to the Plaintiffs in this case. Such preclusion would allow the Defendants to dictate Plaintiffs' trial strategy and theme and the content of Plaintiffs' experts' testimony. This preclusion is not warranted when Defendants could easily overcome any potential prejudice through cross-examination and presentation of evidence.

Colorado Rule of Evidence 106 Is Inapplicable to Expert Evidence

In their motion, Defendants argue in the alternative that if Plaintiffs are allowed to present expert evidence that there is a "rule" based upon the well-accepted standards in the community and medical literature, that C.R.E. 106 precluded Plaintiffs from relying upon select pieces of medical literature without contemporaneously introducing all portions of medical literature that Defendants believe is relevant to the standard of care.

Defendants' arguments are creative but ludicrous and baseless. Defendants fail to cite any authority in support of their argument that C.R.E. 106 applies to any expert opinion testimony or evidence.

Colorado Rule of Evidence 106 states "When a writing or recorded statement or part thereof is introduced by a party, an adverse party may require him at that time to introduce any other part or any other writing or recorded statement which ought in fairness to be considered contemporaneously with it."

Colorado Rule of Evidence 106 is not applicable to the introduction of expert testimony establishing the rule governing what a reasonably careful physician should do under certain circumstances. Defendants have the ability on cross-examination to introduce or bring to the expert's attention any other portion of the applicable medical literature that would discredit the applicable medical rule. Requiring introduction of other parts of the literature during direct exam would cause undue delay in the trial and unduly burden the Plaintiffs. Defendants can overcome any potential misleading impression through cross-examination of Plaintiffs' experts and through their own experts.

The Colorado Court of Appeals has ruled that permitting the opponent to introduce any or all of a transcript on cross-examination when the prosecutor introduced a partial transcript of a co-defendants' statement satisfied the requirements of C.R.E. 106.

The medical literature relied on by the parties in this case is extensive. There are 49 pieces of medical literature marked as trial exhibits by Plaintiffs and Defendants in this case. Requiring Plaintiffs to introduce other parts of the literature when referencing "the rule" would by unduly burdensome on the Plaintiffs, especially when "the rule" appears throughout Defendants' own medical literature. It would also cause undue delay and waste of judicial resources.

Defendants will have an opportunity to overcome any alleged potential misleading impression when they cross-examine Plaintiffs' experts about the content of any literature upon which they rely and can have their experts explain the context in which the literature was written.

WHEREFORE, Plaintiffs request the Court deny Defendants' Motion *in Limine* to Preclude Mention of the Improper Standard of Care.

Respectfully submitted this 6th day of October, 2009.

LEVENTHAL, BROWN & PUGA, P.C.

A duly signed original by Hollynd Hoskins is available at the law offices of Leventhal, Brown & Puga, P.C.

> Hollynd Hoskins,
> #21890
> *ATTORNEY FOR PLAINTIFF*

Appendix M

Samples of Rules in Different Types of Cases

Since the first edition of this book, we have talked about the Rules approach with talented plaintiff's attorneys all over the United States (and Canada too). Many of them have generously shared the lists of "rules" they have constructed for their cases. We have also held brainstorming sessions at continuing-education conferences—where we've seen proof that creative minds working together can quickly develop Rules that cut through the fog that seems to shroud a case contemplated in solitude.

In this appendix, we have gathered samples of Rules from a variety of cases, to show the reader how the technique applies to all sorts of liability cases, and to help jump-start the reader's own creative process. Bear in mind as you read that each case has some unique feature, and while Rules can be adapted for other cases, this should not be treated like a form book with copy-and-paste. A good set of rules for one fact pattern could be a disaster with a slightly different fact pattern.

With the benefit of hindsight, little knowledge of the facts, and no responsibility to any client, we offer comments in italics on improving some Rules that were sent to us. The point is not to show that any set of rules is right or wrong, but to get you thinking of ways to improve your own Rules.

In some of these examples, we also show a set of basic principles that can give rise to Rules for that case.

Rules for an Unnecessary Surgery Case

Our client lost use of one hand when a nerve was destroyed in the surgeon's effort to open up an artery feeding the arm. The arm worked fine, but in taking blood pressure one day, nurses could not get a pressure reading in that arm because it was fed by collateral circulation deep in the arm rather than through the normal path of the brachial artery. The patient was referred to a thoracic surgeon, who sold the client on the idea of preventing future consequences from the lack of flow from the brachial artery. He used a cut-down procedure, cutting into the shoulder and into the bundle of nerves and blood vessels feeding the arm, rather than a safer approach from inside the artery (snaking up a tube from the groin to the area of blockage). Rules we developed for the case included:

1. First, do no harm (Hippocratic Oath).
   [This is a good rhetorical principle but really doesn't tell the jury what a doctor should specifically do or not do. It does not make a good Rule. A doctor can do harm, without being legally or morally responsible for the harm.]

2. "Physicians should not provide, prescribe, or seek compensation for medical services that they know are unnecessary." AMA—Code of Medical Ethics Opinion 2.19 Unnecessary Medical Services (updated 2003).
   [This language from the AMA is powerful. It can be simplified to:]

   A surgeon should not perform a surgery he knows is unnecessary.

3. "Treatments which have no medical indication and offer no possible benefit to the patient should not be used." AMA—Code of Medical Ethics Opinion 8.20 (1) Invalid Medical Treatment (1998).
   [This AMA citation supports the earlier Rule. Two Rules on this subject are probably not necessary. If you wanted to draft a Rule that incorporated both AMA opinions, you could write:]

A surgeon should not perform a surgery he knows offers no benefit to the patient.

4. Surgical treatment should not be offered to treat patients without symptoms or disability when what is being treated is unlikely to cause any harm.
[Good Rule. Maybe the most important Rule in the case.]

5. A doctor must discuss with the patient the risks and benefits of surgery and obtain the patient's informed consent.
[This could be made more specific in some cases, by identifying the actual risks, such as:]
   Before performing a _____ surgery, doctor must discuss the risks of _____ and _____ with the patient and obtain his consent.
[Remember, the more specific you can make the Rule, the more powerful it will likely be.]

6. Part of the informed-consent discussion with the patient should include informing the patient that other surgeons have significantly more experience with the procedure.[1]
[If you can get an instruction to this effect, this is a great Rule. Otherwise, the defense is unlikely to agree to it.]

7. When a doctor has a choice of surgical treatments, the treatment option with the lower risks should be offered.
[If this wasn't done, this makes a great Rule.]

After focusing our tentative list of Rules with several mock juries, we developed a revised list focusing more on the surgeon's failure to use the safest technique. See appendix N, "Rules in a Surgical Malpractice Case" for this list, and the introduction of these Rules by the plaintiff's expert witness at trial.

---

1. This is a developing area of the law. An earlier case of ours established the principle in Maryland that a surgeon has a duty to inform the patient of his lack of experience and the availability of other more-qualified surgeons. See *Goldberg v. Boone*, 393 Md. 242, 900 A.2d 749 (2006).

Travel Insurance Failure to Disclose Benefits

A couple bought a Blue Cross Blue Shield policy to cover any medical needs on their Caribbean trip. When the wife fell in a hole and suffered several displaced fractures of her leg, her husband called the insurance company to ask about coverage. He never inquired specifically about the possibility of the insurer paying for an air ambulance to bring her back for quicker, more definitive fracture treatment, and the customer service agent never volunteered that the policy they bought in fact covered that. She suffered worsened physical and psychological injuries from the delay in treatment.

Principles

- Insurance policyholders are not expected to carry around the policy with them.
- An insurer has "customer service" reps to give service to customers.
- When someone has an emergency, he cannot be expected to know all the right questions to ask his insurer.
- Claims handlers are the experts on the policy; policyholder is not.
- Policyholders are often vulnerable and dependent on their insurance company when it comes time to make a claim.

Rules

- Claims handler must assist the policyholder with the claim.
- Claims handler must disclose to policyholder any benefits that might be applicable.
- Claims handler must do everything possible to see policyholder receives all benefits due under the policy.

Medical Malpractice: Poor Handoff from Generalist to Specialist

Many malpractice cases stem from garbled communications in the referral process from generalist to specialist. Multiple opportunities for fumbled handoffs occur in the transition back and forth of one patient among several doctors. This occurs so commonly that the ethics code of the American College of Physicians, a "generalist" society, specifically addresses the ongoing responsibility of the generalist for a patient she has referred, unless and until there has been an explicit takeover by the specialist.[2]

In one case, an optometrist who saw a thirteen-year-old girl identified suspicious "cupping" of the optic discs and referred the family to an ophthalmologist. No sense of urgency was conveyed by the referral form faxed to the specialist's office, and six months went by before an appointment was obtained, at which point permanent damage had been done.

Our Rules were focused in part on helping the jury see how commonly this applied to any medical-referral situation, so that they could see the relevance to their own health care. We wrote:

Principles

- Part of a generalist's job is to refer patients to appropriate specialists.
- Part of a generalist's job is to educate the patient and the specialist about the reason for the referral.
- When _____ is suspected, immediate evaluation by a specialist is required.

---

2. American College of Physicians, "American College of Physicians Ethics Manual. Third Edition," Annals of Internal Medicine 117.11 (Dec. 1, 1992): 956. Ethics codes frequently can be goldmines for Rules of professional behavior. Of course, if the defendant does not agree to the Rule, the plaintiff's expert must testify it is part of the standard of care.

Rules

- When _____ is suspected, the generalist must make a referral to a specialist.

- When a generalist thinks a patient needs to be seen urgently by a specialist, the generalist must explain this to the patient.

- When a generalist thinks a patient needs to be seen urgently by a specialist, the generalist must explain to the specialist why there is a need for an immediate evaluation.

Landowner's Duty for His Animals

Two cows escaped from a fenced field because the gate had been installed with the hinge pins facing in such a way that the animals could easily lift the gate off its hinges by rubbing against the gate. The cows wandered onto a highway, and a passing motorcyclist was killed when he hit one of the cows.

Rules

- A landowner must keep his large animals off the highway.[3]

- If a fence is needed to control livestock, it must be constructed so animals cannot open it.

- When a landowner has a choice of constructing a gate that an animal can open versus constructing it so the animal cannot open it, at no extra cost, the landowner should build it so the animal cannot open the gate.

Jet Ski/Personal Watercraft Products Case

Until the last few years, all jet-propelled personal watercraft—Jet Skis in layman's terms—had a peculiar characteristic, called "off-throttle steering loss." When confronted with an unexpected

---

3. NB: Most jurisdictions have statutes that govern landowner duties, and they often reflect in any particular jurisdiction how much influence ranchers have on the state legislature.

obstacle, the normal reaction of the operator was to turn off the throttle and turn the handlebars to the side. In other words, the operator tried to slow down and turn away from the obstacle. In fact, these craft have virtually no steering if the throttle is off, and have no brakes. So the normal human reaction of going off-throttle and turning the handlebars means the craft will keep going straight, possibly striking the very obstacle the operator is trying to avoid.

Principles

- Personal watercraft can cause injury or death to riders. *[Or, while riding a personal watercraft, rider can suffer injury or death.]*

- Personal watercraft can cause injury or death to other members of the public.

- The safety of the consumer and the public should be the primary consideration in any decision concerning the design and manufacture of a personal watercraft.

- A manufacturer should never expose a consumer to unnecessary risk of harm.

- Compliance with government regulations and standards cannot be relied upon to achieve an optimally safe outcome.

- Safe design and manufacture of personal watercraft requires recognizing that emergency situations involving sudden stops or turns arise every day in the operation of personal watercraft.

Rules

1. Safe design and manufacture of personal watercraft requires a written safety policy.

2. Safe design and manufacture of personal watercraft requires specific assigned safety responsibilities for employees who design and build the product.

3. Before designing a product, the manufacturer must review similar existing products, their features and their safety history.

4. Before putting a product on the market, the manufacturer must make sure it performs as safely as an ordinary consumer would expect.

5. The potential hazards of a product must be identified in the design phase and reduced as much as possible:

    a. Eliminate

    b. Guard or backup

    c. Warn

6. Hazards identified and efforts to minimize them must be documented.

7. Before putting a product on the market, the product must be evaluated and tested for any safety issues or hazards that may exist when used by intended users under real-world conditions.

8. If a manufacturer learns that a product does not perform as safely as an ordinary consumer would expect, it must either change the product, or change the ordinary consumer's expectations.

9. If the manufacturer has a method for changing the product or the consumer's expectations to make use of the product safer, that method should be tested to see if it is effective.

10. Any "solutions" to safety issues presented by a product's performance characteristics must be tested and evaluated to determine if they are effective.

11. Postproduction safety review of a product must be undertaken by a manufacturer's engineers with all available data as to private or government studies, injuries, or deaths.

12. If, after putting a product on the market, a manufacturer learns that it is not performing as safely as an ordinary consumer would expect, manufacturer must either change the product or change the ordinary consumer's expectations.

13. Documents reflecting accidents, injuries, or death should not be hidden or destroyed.

Rules and Principles for High School Football

These principles and rules were prepared by Rick and Sacramento lawyer Randy Harvey, a former high school football coach, as part of a CLE demonstration.

Principles

1. Football can be dangerous.
2. Student safety is the most important consideration in the sport of football.
3. Licensed staff are responsible for student welfare in football activities.

Rules

1. Coaches and athletic trainers must be trained in the dangers of football.
2. Training must include the dangers of ill-fitting helmets.
3. Coaches and athletic trainers must be trained annually on helmet fit and maintenance.
4. Coaches and athletic trainers should properly fit the student's helmet.
5. Student safety equipment must be maintained according to NOCAE standards.
6. Coaches and athletic trainers are responsible to inspect player helmets to ensure they are functioning properly.

7. Coaches and athletic trainers must check helmets weekly during the season.
8. Helmets should be used no more than five years.
9. Coaches and athletic trainers must teach players to inspect their helmets before every use and identify improper fit.
10. Coaches and athletic trainers must routinely and consistently train, monitor, and enforce safe contact.
11. Coaches and athletic trainers must know and monitor for signs of a concussion.
12. Coaches and athletic trainers must not allow a student to reenter the game when they see indications that a student has had a concussion.

Appendix N

Rules in a Surgical Malpractice Case

In the "unnecessary surgery" case described in appendix M, we learned from focus groups that the plaintiff's strongest claim was not in the lack of need for the surgery (because the patient's condition, a blocked major artery feeding the arm, sounded ominous at first blush to a lay audience), but in the surgeon's failure to use the accepted technique for unblocking the artery. Lay people were also critical of the plaintiff for failing to obtain a second opinion before consenting to the surgery. Accordingly, we revised the Rules for the case to emphasize the unwise choice of technique, which was driven, we contended, by the surgeon's lack of experience with the accepted techniques. We also placed the unnecessary surgery issue into an informed consent claim: failure to advise the patient of the lack of urgency so that the patient would have the time to obtain a second opinion.

Here are the Rules used at trial, followed by an excerpt from the trial transcript with the introduction to the rules by the plaintiff's expert vascular surgeon.

Rules

A vascular surgeon should always:

1. Give the patient the safest option that does the job.

2. Avoid cutting near nerves if the surgeon doesn't have to.

3. Ask for help if the surgeon lacks experience.

4. Tell the patient the important facts so the patient can make intelligent decisions.

5. Put the patient's interests ahead of the surgeon's interests.

A simple PowerPoint slide listing these rules was used in opening statement, closing argument, and the direct examination of the plaintiff's expert.

Direct Examination by Mr. Malone (excerpt)

THE COURT: The Court is going to accept the witness as an expert in vascular surgery. And, Mr. Malone, you may continue.

MR. MALONE: All right. Thank you, Your Honor.

Q: Now, I want to start, Dr. Lee, with some of the general safety rules for vascular surgery or standards of care, that you have given me a list of, that you thought applied to this case. Do you recall that?

A: Yes.

Q: I would like to run through them generally and say—and talk about their—about why they exist, and then bring them down to this case. And let me just show you on the board what we have here. "A surgeon should always give the patient the safest option that does the job."

MR. QUINN: Your Honor, can I object? May we approach?

THE COURT: You may.

MR. QUINN: When I took this man's deposition, I asked him: What are your opinions in this case? He gave me four breaches of the standard of care. I have never heard out of this man's mouth, or in his deposition, anything about giving the patient the safest option, or the other things that were used in opening. So at this point, I'm objecting to that. The opinions that I understand that are coming are: There was no indications for this surgery, the axilla approach was wrong—

MR. MALONE: That's what we're talking about right here.

MR. QUINN: What?

MR. MALONE: That's what we're talking about, right here, is that the axilla approach was wrong, he didn't give the patient the safest choice.

MR. QUINN: Well, can I finish?

MR. MALONE: I'm sorry.

MR. QUINN: I did not object that surgery, the axilla approach was wrong—Dr. Johnson did not provide appropriate informed consent, and Dr. Johnson was not an expert to do this procedure. Nowhere was I told anything about, a surgeon always has to tell the patient what the safest option is. All right? I think I was entitled to know that, and I'm prepared to cross this gentleman on those four things that I was told. So I'm objecting to this.

THE COURT: Okay. Counsel?

MR. MALONE: It's a—he testified in his deposition that the man used the wrong approach because it wasn't the safest approach. And so this is just the generalized statement of why you give the patient the safest approach. It's the standard of care, which he had testified this was particular violation of that.

THE COURT: The Court's going to overrule your objection for the following reasons. Based upon his deposition, you may cross-examine as to whether or not he, you know, had rethought this and come up with some new theories regarding this that was not there at the time of the deposition. But the Court doesn't find that this is a basis not to allow any of the general statements.

MR. QUINN: But we are here—

MR. MALONE: Can I add one thing?

MR. QUINN: Sure. Go ahead.

MR. MALONE: On our supplemental certificate that we filed in March, you know, at the end of discovery, we said one of the items of what the standard of care was, said the standard of care required Dr. Johnson to use a surgical technique that did not elevate the risk of nerve injury; and that, again, is just like this.

THE COURT: I understand. Overruled.

MR. QUINN: Well, I just want this record to be clear: There's a reason for discovery, and it's not so that a witness can come in and all of a sudden say I now have these five—

THE COURT: Nor do they have to, word for word, repeat what was—

MR. QUINN: I agree with that. I agree with that. But this is a discovery violation, in that I asked this man what his opinions were relative to this case. And now I'm hearing—or I'm getting these general rules of standard of care and—

MR. MALONE: No. No.

MR. QUINN: Well, then they're not relevant. What's relevant for this case is how Dr. Johnson breached the standard of care.

MR. MALONE: But you have to define the standard of care.

THE COURT: Hold on. And move on.

MR. MALONE: Now, before we come down to this case, let's go through these one at a time and just talk in general about why the use of the safety rules, or, quote, "standards of care" that apply in your field of vascular surgery—and by the way, is this across the country, big hospitals, small hospitals, wherever?

A: Yes.

MR. QUINN: Your Honor, for the record, I object and would like a standing objection so I don't have to keep—

THE COURT: You have a standing objection.

MR. QUINN: Thank you.

THE COURT: However, you don't have a standing objection to leading. The Court will grant the objection based upon the leading question.

MR. QUINN: All right.

Q: "A surgeon should always give the patient the safest option that does the job." What does that mean?

A: Well, what I mean by that is, is that if there are several options for treatment, you want to provide the treatment that accomplishes the goal, whatever it might be. And not just in vascular surgery, it might be in general surgery.

MR. QUINN: Objection. Move to strike that. We're talking vascular.

THE COURT: Doctor, if you'll stay focused on—

THE WITNESS: Yes.

THE COURT: —otherwise, I'm going to open up a huge area that's beyond what we need.

THE WITNESS: Yes. There may be three treatment options. You want to pick the—or recommend the option that will—and what I mean by "get the job done," that opens up the artery or improves the flow, and it minimizes at the same time any risk, damage, to adjacent nerves, heart attack, or whatever it might be. In other words, it minimizes the complications.

Q: And is this an accepted standard or rule that applies in other parts of the body, other than the subclavian artery for vascular work?

MR. QUINN: Objection.

THE COURT: Overruled.

THE WITNESS: Yes, in any vascular procedure.

Q: Just give us an example to—so that we can have some context here.

A: Well, for instance, there's a newer technique for fixing aneurysms where you don't have to open up the abdomen. When you do—when you do it the open way, where you have to make this, you know, the large incisions to do the bypass, it potentially can cause damage to the ureter, one of the tubes that drains the kidney. It could also cause nerve damage that could lead to impotence. So that's one of the advantages of the lesser approach—or the less-invasive approach that we do now, which is endovascular aneurysm repair, where we just make small incisions in the groin area and can put the graft in, that doesn't run the risk of damaging the ureter or these pelvic nerves.

Q: That approach in the groin is the same that we're going to be talking about later on, or—

A: This is a bit different because—

Q: Okay.

A: —it requires open surgical—open incisions, not just punctures in the skin.

Q: But it's the same area of the body we're talking about as your access port?

A: Yes. It is the same area.

Q: Let me just put down the next one here. "Avoid cutting next to the nerves if the surgeon doesn't have to." Explain that, just in general.

A: Well, it just goes along the same, I guess, line of thinking as the first point, that you want to min—you want to get the job done but you want to minimize any damage, any complications. So if you can do a procedure where there are not adjacent nerves or veins that potentially could be cut, that would be the better approach, to minimize any complications or damage to adjacent structures.

Q: And the third one here is: "Ask for help if the surgeon lacks experience." Tell us about that.

A: Well, the best example I could—it just means that if you're not qualified or haven't done a certain procedure, but you have a patient that needs that procedure, then it's common in our practice, we get one of our associates and we do the procedure together. You get somebody else who's more experienced, and either send the patient to them or you do the procedure together. And an example of that vascular procedure is carotid stenting, where you put a balloon and dilate the carotid artery and then put in the stent, and that's—

Q: And that's the artery that runs up to the brain in the front of the neck?

A: Correct.

Q: Okay.

A: I don't have privileges to do carotid stenting. I haven't—I'm in a phase of my training where one of my partners is credentialed, so if I have a patient that needs a carotid stent, then I do the procedure with him and then that counts towards my training. And once I've done twenty-five procedures like that with him, then I would be considered qualified to do it. So it's just an example of where, if you're not qualified, you would seek the help of somebody else who is.

Q: Is that kind of like mentoring?

A: It is. I mean, that's generally what it's considered, where—that you do a series of procedures with somebody who is qualified and they serve as your mentor. There are other terms for it, but that's as good as any of them.

Q: Are there guidelines in the field of vascular surgery for how much mentoring a surgeon should have before he starts working by himself on a particular type of surgery?

A: Yes.

Q: And tell us those, briefly.

A: They're on the—the Society for Vascular Surgery has—there's a website, and they have adopted a position paper where several societies, including the Society For Vascular Surgery, got together and said we really need to have standards of who's—these are newer procedures, a lot of these percutaneous procedures with angioplasty and stent placement. And so initially, as they came about, people were putting them in, doing these procedures, but there were no real guidelines for training. And so these societies got together and said, well, we've got to establish, you know, what—who should be doing them, if they've got the right amount of training to do these procedures, and so they established some guidelines for that. So for—we have a vascular fellowship in vascular fellowships now, as the residents—as the fellows come through that are being trained, to do these procedures, they have to do 100 arteriograms, fifty of which have to be done as the primary operator, and then they have to have done fifty peripheral procedures, meaning an angioplasty and stent—stent placement. And also, I think it's between five and ten endovascular aneurysm repairs.

Q: And these were effective as of about 2004 roughly?

A: Yes. That—

MR. QUINN: Objection.

THE COURT: Sustained.

Q: Do you know when they were published?

A: That particular paper was published in 2004.

Q: Now, let's go finish our list here just on the general stuff. "Telling the patient the important facts so that the patient can make an intelligent decision." The surgeon should always do that. Tell us what that means in vascular surgery.

A: That means explaining what the condition is that they have so that they can understand it and then what the treatment options are. So you know, treatment options may be; one, you don't need to have anything done; two, we can do surgery; three, you can have angioplasty, just as an example. Or for a dialysis patient, I might say, well, we can create a fistula here, or we could put a graft in up here, and I explain the pros and cons of each of those and what the risks and the benefits are. And then generally, then I would say I think for you the best option is this one. So I try to help them with that decision, and I explain why I to help them with that decision, and I explain why I think for that—for them, that that particular procedure is the right one.

Q: And then we've got one more here on our general list, "The surgeon should always put the patient's interests first." Would you tell us about that one?

A: Well, I think that that goes without saying, in that you always—you're there for the patients. That's why we do the proced—you know, that's why we're there, to do surgery or not do surgery, or whatever treatments there are. The patient always comes first.

Q: Now, let's talk specifically about this case and what Dr. Johnson did to Mr. Forrest.

INDEX

A

A&E Prods. Group, L.P. v. Mainetti USA Inc., 75n3
Abbie Uriguen Oldsmobile Buick, Inc. v. United States Fire Ins. Co., 224
Ace v. Aetna Casualty & Surety Co., 5n2, 42n8, 215, 216, 217, 221, 222, 223
Adams Exp. Co. v. Aldridge, 298
Administrative code provisions, 40–41, 42n8, 42n9
    avoiding "implied cause of action" and, 41–44, 41n7
    defense arguments and plaintiff's countering, 43
    "negligence *per se*" and "evidence of negligence," 42
Aetna Life Ins. Co. v. Lavoie, 218, 221, 222
Ainsworth v. Combined Ins. Co. of America, 131, 132, 135, 193, 194, 198
Albert H. Wohlers and Co. v. Bartgis, 131, 198
Alexander v. FBI, 76n5
Amadeo v. Principal Mutual Life Ins. Co., 136
Ambiguity. *See* complexity, confusion, and ambiguity
American Paint Service v. Home Insurance Co. of N.Y., 225
Anderson, John, 110
Austero v. National Casualty Co. of Detroit Mich., 218
Automobile accident cases, 121–25, 121n1, 124n3
    ambiguous liability standards, 11–12, *12*

Automobile accident cases (continued)
    breach of contract approach, 125
    Bus Stop Case Opening Statement, 266–71
    Bus Stop Safety Principles, 205–6
    Bus Stop Safety Principles Annotated, 207–10
    "child dart-out" case, 124
    common jury instructions, 43
    common plaintiff errors, 122–23
    Cross-Examination of School Bus Company Manager, 273–85
    damages, 124–25, 124n3
    Direct Examination of Plaintiff's Bus Stop Expert, 237–56
    emphasizing the differences approach, 124
    polarizing the case approach, 124–25
    sample Rules for landowner's duty for his animals, 308, 308n3
    school bus stop case, 11–12, *12*, 45–46, 53–54, 53n2, 74, 74n1, 185

B

Ball, David, 29n4, 124n3, 151n1, 153, 187, 188
Bankers life & Casualty Co. v. Crenshaw, 221, 222
Barton, William, 188
Benefit Ass'n of Railway Employees v. Secrest, 199

324   *Rules of the Road*

Bering Strait School District v. RLI Insurance Co., 219, 224
Besh v. Mutual Benefit Health & Accident Ass'n, 199
Best Place Inc. v. Penn American Ins. Co., 134
Black, Hugo, 183
Black Horse Lane Assoc. v. Dow Chem. Corp., 79n6
Black's Law Dictionary, 294
"Blocking interrogatory" technique, 172–74
Buzzard v. Farmers Ins. Co., Inc., 218

C

Campbell v. Metropolitan Prop. & Cas. Ins. Co., 69n5
Canal Barge Co. v. Commonwealth Edison Co., 76n5
Case story, 115–19
　importance of, used in closing arguments, 182
　medical malpractice case, example, 116–19
　Rules vs. story of your case, 115–16, 118, 151
　showing motivation and character in, 116
Causation defense, countering, 108–9
Clayton v. Hepp, 292
Closing arguments, 3, 175–84
　avoiding defense control of the case, 181–82
　damages instructions and Rules, 180–81
　displaying the weight of the evidence, 183
　instruction boards for, 176
　jury instructions and, 175–77
　"more likely than not" standard, 125

Closing arguments (continued)
　point to make, 183
　red-sticker technique, 183
　Rules portrayed as "for the protection of everyone," 184
　using boilerplate instructions to enforce Rules, 177–80, 178n1, 178n2, 179n3, 179n4
　using your own Rules, three alternatives, 181–84
Co-counsel, 186
Colby, Paul, 188
"Common sense" or "moral imperative" Rules, 26–28, 39n6
Comparative Closing Arguments on Damages (Masterworks video), 188
Complaint
　drafting, 3, 46–48
　example, reference to Rules source, 47–48
　number of Rules to disclose, 48
Complexity, confusion, and ambiguity
　avoiding defense control of the case and, 181–82
　as defense strategy, 1–2, 30
　expert witnesses and, 59
　in insurance bad faith cases, 5, 20
　judges and, 127, 128
　liability standards and, 7–12, *12*, 13, 15–16
　solving the ambiguity problem, 15–20, 28, 90, 142
Constantino v. David M. Herzog, M.D., 169n2
Cross-examination, 3, 163–74
　"blocking interrogatory" technique, 172–74

Cross-examination (continued)
 Cross-Examination of School Bus Company Manager, 273–85
 handling "learned treatises" at trial, 168–72, 169n2, 174
 intellectually dishonest witnesses, 168
 intellectually honest witnesses, 164–68
 "neutron bomb" against the defense, 174
 polarizing technique, 165
 principle used in, 53–54
 seeking favorable concessions first, 164
 using Fed. R. Evid. 803(18), 168–72, 168n1
Cross-Examination: Science and Technique (Pozner and Dodd), 187

D

Damages, 187, 124n3, 151n1
 closing arguments instructions and Rules, 180–81
Daubert motions, 44, 62, 63–70
 codified in Fed. R. Evid. 702, 64
 core concern, defensible methodology, 70
 "general causation" study and, 65
 Justice Breyer on trial court's gatekeeping, 64
 researching methodologies, 65, 65n3
 researching supporting literature, 67–68
 Rule 1: Find a Methodology Appropriate for the Expert's Field, 64–65

Daubert motions (continued)
 Rule 2: Find Literature Support for the Expert's Theory, 67–68
 Rule 3: Make the Expert Read the Relevant Literature, 68
 Rule 4: Go to the Top in Your Search for Experts, 69, 69n5
 Rule 5: Avoid Experts Who Won't Explain the Basis of Their Opinions, 69
 Rule 6: Enlist Help from the Other Side's Experts, 69–70
 Rule 7: Attack the Other Side's Experts, 70
 three requirements for allowing testimony, 64
Daubert v. Merrell Dow Pharmaceuticals Inc., 63n1
David Ball on Damages (Ball), 124n3, 151n1, 187
Deese v. State Farm Mutual Automobile Ins. Co., 135, 194, 195, 217, 220, 222
Defamation case, 137–40
Depositions, 3, 74–102
 asking "why?," 100–101
 avoiding defense witness ambiguity, 90
 expert and lay witnesses, 74, 82
 handling objections, 95–100, 96n14, 99n15
 "Mush-Mouthed Witness," 93–95
 noticing, examples, 76–77
 planning and conducting, 82–84
 polarizing the combative witness, 88–93, 88n13
 questions for the end of, 101–2
 Rules of the Road and, creating new rules, 93–95

Depositions (continued)
  Rules of the Road and, finding new sources for standards, 83–85, 83n10
  Rules of the Road and, finding out whether any rules were violated, 95–100, 99n15
  Rules of the Road and, securing agreement or disagreement, 85–93, 88n12
  semantic hide-and-seek, stopping, 91–93
  surgeon's testimony, 27
  "There is Nothing Authoritative" answer, how to counter, 84
  30(b)(6) witnesses, 3, 74, 75–82, 75n2, 75n3, 75n4, 76n5, 79n7, 80n8, 81n9
Direct examination, 3
  about Rules violations, 161–62
  Direct Examination of Plaintiff's Bus Stop Expert, 237–56
  Direct Examination of Plaintiff's Insurance Expert in a Bad Faith Case, 227–36
  expert witnesses, 157–62
  explaining reasons for the Rule, 157–59, 158n1
  explaining that the Rule is well recognized, 159–60
  objections, response to, 157
  setting up evidence from learned treatises, 160–61, 169, 169n2
  testimony about sources of Rules, 161
Disability case, 9, 116, 167, 196, 198, 199–200
  Proposed Jury Instructions in a Disability Bad Faith Case, 39, 211–25

Disability case (continued)
  Sample Insurance Bad Faith Rules of the Road, 202–3
Discovery, 3, 71–102, 186
  depositions, 3, 74–102
  Discovery Requests: Obtaining Rules of the Road and Impeachment Material, 256–60
  getting clear agreement or disagreement from defense witnesses on Rules, 71
  interrogatories and Requests for Admission, 73–74, 83n10, 256–58
  looking for new Rules in, 71, 93–95, 173
  looking for support for Rules, 71
  looking for violations of Rules, 71, 95
  requests for production of documents, 71–73, 258–60
Dodd, Roger, 187
Doyle v. New Jersey Fidelity & Plate Glass Ins. Co., 199

E
Egan v. Mutual of Omaha Ins. Co, 39, 39n6, 97, 98, 99, 134–35, 191, 193, 195, 212
Equitable Life Assur. Soc. of U.S. v. Watts, 199
Erickson v. Nationwide Mutual Ins. Co., 219
Evidence
  closing arguments, "preponderance of the evidence," 179–80
  coordinating with your Rules, 144
  Fed. R. Evid. 803(18) and, 174

Evidence (continued)
  on poster board, handling defense objections, 174
  "reliable authority," establishing, 169, 169n2, 170, 173
  Rules chart and, 155
  setting up from learned treatises, 160–61, 168–72, 169n2, 171n3, 174
Expert witnesses, 3, 59–62
  complexity, confusion, and ambiguity problem, 59
  Daubert motions, 62, 63–70
  defense experts, attacking, 70
  defense experts, cross-examining, 3
  defense experts, gaining concessions from, 69–70
  deposing, 74
  deposition of "Mush-Mouthed Witness," 93–95
  direct examination, 157–62
  Direct Examination of Plaintiff's Bus Stop Expert, 237–56
  Direct Examination of Plaintiff's Insurance Expert in a Bad Faith Case, 227–36
  Frye test of admissibility, 64
  "general causation," 65
  getting the best, 69, 69n5
  jury instructions as help for, 34
  methodology of, 65–66, 66n4
  preparation for, 3, 59–61, 68
  researching *caveat* and, 44–45, 67
  Rules and content of testimony, 62
  using words "reliable authority," 173
  who to avoid, 69

F
Farmers Ins. Exchange v. Young, 132
Farmers Ins. Group v. Stonik By and Through Stonik, 132
Farmland Mut. Ins. Cos. v. Chief Indus., Inc., 295
Farr v. Transamerica Occidental Life Ins. Co., 135, 194, 195, 220
Fed. R. Civ. P. 30(b)(6) witnesses (corporate designees), 74, 74n4, 75–82, 75n2, 75n3, 76n5
  know-nothing witness, 78–79, 79n6, 79n7
  noticing, examples, 76–77
  planning and conducting the deposition, 82–84
  proving a negative with a know-nothing witness, 79–82, 80n8, 81n9
  use of, 78
Fed. R. Evid. 803(18), 168–72, 168n1, 174
Ferrel v. Allstate Ins. Co., 219
Final Rule Declaring Dietary Supplements Containing Ephedrine Alkaloids Adulterated (FDA), 65n3
Fohl v. Metropolitan Life Ins. Co., 199
Freedom of Information requests, 45
Frye v. United States, 64n2

G
"General causation," 65
Generally Accepted Accounting Principles (GAAP), 66
Goldberg v. Boone, 54n3, 305n1
Grace v. Insurance Co. of North America, 219, 224

Groat v. Equity Am. Ins. Co., 79n7
Gruenberg v. Aetna Ins. Co., 195

H
Hangarter v. Provident Life and Acc. Ins. Co, 66n4
Harrison, Fred, 50n1
Hart v. Prudential Property & Casualty Ins. Co., 42n8
Harvard v. University of Medicine and Dentistry of New Jersey, 54n3
High School Football, Sample Rules and Principles, 311–12
Hohn v. Interstate Casualty Co., 199
Honeysucker v. Bowen, 199

I
Industrial Indemnity Co. of the Northwest, Inc. v. Kallevig, 135, 194, 195, 220
In limine motions, 145–46
  Response to Motion *In Limine*, 287–301
"Inoculation" strategy, 188
Insurance bad faith cases, 1, 7–13. *See also* disability case
  Annotated Rules of the Road: Master List, 191–200
  Arizona jury instructions, 7–8, 7n1, 8n2, 8n3, 8n4
  Bad Faith Case Opening Statement, 261–66
  closing arguments, 176–77
  creating a Rule the defense cannot dispute, 25
  depositions, handling objections, 95–100, 99n14, 99n15
  depositions, questions for end of, 101–2
  Direct Examination of Plaintiff's Insurance Expert in a Bad Faith Case, 227–36

Insurance bad faith cases (continued)
  direct examination of your expert, 157–59
  expert witnesses, 60
  first Rule, 29
  Friedman's anecdote, 4–5
  fundamental principle, 56
  making regulations easy to understand, 23–24
  motion to compel, 131–33
  pattern jury instructions for, 36–40
  property case, 10
  Proposed Jury Instructions in a Disability Bad Faith Case, 211–25
  providing principles and standards for the jury, 16–17, 20
  Requests for Admission examples, 73–74
  Rule list, 24, 24n2
  Rule, based on a state law requirement, 81, 81n9
  Rules chart, 5
  Rules source, administrative code provisions, 40–44, 42n8
  Rules source, contract provisions, 45n10
  Rules source, jury instructions, 39, 39n6
  Rules vs. story of your case, 116
  Sample Insurance Bad Faith Rules of the Road, 201–3
  sample Rules for failure to disclose benefits, 306
  summary-judgment brief, example, 133–36, 134n1
  30(b)(6) witnesses, deposition of no-nothing witness, 79–82, 80n8, 81n9
  30(b)(6) witnesses, noticing, 76

Insurance bad faith cases (continued)
  30(b)(6) witnesses, securing agreement or disagreement with your Rules, 85–88, 88n12, 88n13, 91–93
  uninsured-motorist claim, 9
Interrogatories, 3
  blocking defense "reliable authority" literature not identified in discovery, 73
  "blocking interrogatory" technique, 172–74
  Discovery Requests: Obtaining Rules of the Road and Impeachment Material, 256–60
  list of specific documents from defendant's home office, 72
  looking for new Rules in, 71, 173

J
Jet Ski/Personal Watercraft Case, sample Rules, 308–11
John Hancock Mut. Life Ins. Co. v. Cooper, 199–200
Johnson v. Kokemoor, 54n3
Joyce v. United Ins. Co. of America, 199
Judge
  administrative code provisions and, 43
  assumptions about, to avoid, 127
  complexity, confusion, and ambiguity, problem of, 127, 128
  endorsement of Rule by, 44
  impact of jury instructions, 34
  influences leading to unfair decisions, 129–30
  jury instructions and, 175–77

Judge (continued)
  motion against use of Rules board and, 155
  motions, what to state upfront, 130
  providing with legal standards, 133
  Rules of the Road list for, 143, 151
  who needs to be spoon-fed, 128–29
  your job with, 130
Julien, Alfred, 188
Jury
  automobile accident cases, plaintiff special problems, 121–25
  educating on authority of sources, 171n3
  investing in the case as safety guardians, 56
  "pain and suffering" damages, 180–81
  providing character and motive, 117–18
  questions on the minds of jurors, 115
  Rules of the Road list for, 142, 143, 151
  Rules paradigm for, 57
Jury instructions
  administrative code provisions as basis for, 40–44
  all-purpose negligence instruction, 35–36
  ambiguous liability standards, 2, 10
  complexity, confusion, and ambiguity used in, 1–2
  core concept of negligence law, 36, 36n2
  damages instructions and Rules, 180–81

Jury instructions (continued)
    drafting at the start of every case, 32–35, 137, 175
    finalizing the Rules and, 137
    as help for your expert witnesses, 34
    impact on judge, 34
    incorporating into your Rules, 35–40
    insurance bad faith cases, 7–10, 7n1, 8n2, 8n3
    as the judge's Rules, 175–77
    medical malpractice cases, 7
    pattern instructions for insurance bad faith case, 36–40, 36n3
    on poster boards, 176
    product liability cases, 7
    Proposed Jury Instructions in a Disability Bad Faith Case, 211–25
    "prudent insurer" standard, 10
    "reasonable" used in, 7
    as Rules source, 32–40
    using boilerplate instructions to enforce Rules, 177–80, 178n1, 178n2, 179n3, 179n4

K
Keenan, Don, 188, 29n4
Klonoff, Robert, 188
Kumo Tire Co., Ltd. v Carmichael, 64

L
Landowner's Duty for His Animals, sample Rules, 308, 308n3
Lapenna v. Upjohn Co., 75n4
Lasser v. Reliance Standard Life Insurance Co., 199
Levine, Moe, 124, 187–88
Lewis, Marvin E., 188

Linscott v. Rainier National Life Ins. Co., 223

M
MacFarland v. United States Fidelity & Guarantee Co., 42n8
Mariscal v. Old Republic Life Ins. Co., 135, 194, 220, 221
Marker v. Union Fidelity Life Ins. Co., 79n6
Massachusetts Casualty Ins. Co. v. Rief, 199
McCormick v. Sentinel Life Ins. Co., 221, 223
McNeil Pharmaceuticals v. Hawkins, 42n9
Medical malpractice cases, 1, 7
    case story, example, 116–19
    causation defense, countering, 108
    core concept, negligence law, 36, 36n2
    creating a Rule the defense cannot dispute, 25
    deposition of "Mush-Mouthed Witness," 93–95
    depositions, questions for the end of, 102
    expert witnesses, 60
    failure to diagnose case, 12–13, 18–20, 24–25
    informed consent, principle, 54–55, 54n3
    making your Rules specific, 104–7
    opening statements, first words, 153
    principles about medical records, 51
    Response to Motion *In Limine*, 287–301
    Rules about medical records, 51–52

Medical malpractice cases (continued)
  Rules in a Surgical Malpractice Case, 313–21
  sample Rules for an unnecessary surgery case, 304–5, 305n1
  sample Rules for poor handoff from generalist to specialist, 307–8, 307n2
  30(b)(6) witnesses, 78
  using boilerplate jury instructions to enforce Rules, 178–79
  voir dire, Rules portion, 148–49
Melville v. Southward, 291, 292
Meschino v. North American Drager, Inc., 169n2
Metropolitan Life Ins. Co. v. Lambert, 199
Mitsui & Co. v. Puerto Rico Water Res. Auth., 76n5
Mobile-home class action suit, 110–13
Moe Levine on Advocacy (Levine), 187–88
Moore v. American United Life Ins. Co., 225
Moss v. Mid-American Fire & Marine Ins. Co., 224
Motions, 127–36
  avoiding assumptions about the judge, 127
  citations to authorities, example, 133–36, 134n1
  defense *in limine* motions, 145–46
  influences leading to unfair decisions, 129–30
  law clerks and, spoon-feeding, 128, 129
  motion to compel, 131–33

Motions (continued)
  Response to Motion *In Limine*, 287–301
  summary-judgment motions, 80, 120, 133–36, 134n1
  what to state up-front, 120
  which judges to spoon-feed, 128–29
"Mush-Mouthed Witness," 93–95
Mutual Life Ins. Co. of New York v. Dowdle, 199

N
National Union Fire. Ins. Co. of State of Pa., Inc. v. Reno's Executive Air, Inc., 132
Negligence law
  core concept, 36, 36n2
  general principle of injury prevention, 55–56

O
Opening statements, 3, 151–56
  Bad Faith Case Opening Statement, 261–66
  Bus Stop Case Opening Statement, 266–71
  concluding thoughts on, 156
  first words, 153
  format for liability portion, 151–53, 151n1
  handling defense objections, 153–55, 154n2, 154n3
  plaintiff's, addressing ambiguous liability standard, 15–16
Opening Statements (Julien), 188
Oppenheim v. Finch, 199
Overkill, avoiding, 163

P
Pannu v. Jacobson, 36
Park Nelson HOA v. Franklin Group, Inc., 192

Paul Revere Life Insurance Company v. Jafari, 76n5
Paulson v. State Farm Mutual Automobile Ins. Co., 218
Pels, Jon, 110–13
Pemberton v. Farmers Ins. Exch., 131
People v. Shreck, 294
Polarizing the case
  automobile accident cases, 124–25, 124n2, 124n3
  combative witness and, 88–93, 88n13
  during cross-examination, 165
Polarizing the Case (Friedman), 88n13, 124n2, 125
Pozner, Larry, 187
Pretrial conference: list of stipulations, 154n3
Principles
  annotating, 52
  Bus Stop Safety Principles, 205–6
  Bus Stop Safety Principles Annotated, 207–10
  cross-examination using, 53–54
  definition, 49
  direct examination using word, 158n1
  formulating Rules from, 51–52
  general principle of injury prevention, 55–56
  High School Football, Sample, 311–12
  of informed consent, 54–55, 54n3
  of insurance bad faith cases, 56
  Jet Ski/Personal Products Case, Sample, 309
  labeling the Rules board and, 141, 141n2
  Medical Malpractice, Sample, 307

Principles (continued)
  of medical records, 51
  principle/Rule hybrids, 53–55
  rail safety example, 49–50, 50n1
  Rules vs., 23, 23n1, 49–57, 111, 112
  Travel Insurance Failure to Disclose Benefits, Sample, 306
  uncovering, during deposition, 93–95
Production of documents, 71–73
Product liability cases
  jury instructions, 7
  sample Rules for Jet Ski/Personal Watercraft Case, 308–11
  30(b)(6) witnesses, noticing, 77
Prudential Ins. Co. of America v. Girton, 200

R
Rail safety case, 49–50, 50n1
  depositions, asking "why?," 100–101
Rainey v. American Forest & Paper Ass'n, 75n3
Rawlings v. Apodaca, 135, 194, 195, 217, 219, 220, 222
Reasonable/reasonable man problem, 2
  failure to diagnose cases, 18–20
  insurance bad faith cases, 7–9
  solving the problem, 15–20
  traffic cases, 5
Recovering for Psychological Injuries (Barton), 188
Red-sticker technique, 144, 183
Reference Manual on Scientific Evidence, 65

Reptile: The 2009 Manual of the Plaintiff's Revolution (Keenan and Ball), 29n4, 188
Requests for Admission
  insurance bad faith cases, examples, 73–74
  school bus stop case, examples, 74, 74n1
Requests for Production, 72
Research, 112. *See also* sources for Rules
  common errors, 44–45, 67
  of expert's methodologies, 65–67
  of supporting literature for expert's theory, 67–68
Resolution Trust Corp. v. S. Union Co., 79n6
Rezendes v. Prudential Ins. Co. of America, 200
Rick Friedman on Becoming a Trial Lawyer 123 (Friedman), 125, 125n4, 179
"Rule fade-out," 103
Rules board, 139–40
  guidelines, 140–43
  handling defense objections, 153–55, 154n2, 154n3, 174
  labeling the chart, 140–41
  number of Rules on, 142
  proposing in pretrial conference, 154n3
  red-sticker each Rule violation, 144
Rules of the Road, 22–30
  1: Must Prescribe Conduct, 22–23, 23n1, 28–29, 106
  2: Easy to Understand, 23–25, 104
  3: Defense Cannot Credibly Dispute It, 25–28, 104
  4: The Defendant Has Violated It, 28–29, 104

Rules of the Road (continued)
  5: The Rule Is Important, 29–30, 107
  as active voice statements, 53
  archetype for a general Rule, 29n4
  attributes, 22–30, 61, 139–40
  for automobile cases, 121–25, 121n1, 124n3
  board for trial, 139
  in closing arguments, 175–84
  for cross-examination, 163–74
  for *Daubert* motions, 63–70
  defense objections to, 145–46, 143n3
  defined, 2, 50, 294
  depositions, four areas to develop, 82–84
  developing, 31–48, 52
  for direct examination of experts, 157–62
  discovery, four things to look for, 71
  establishing pedigree of, 160–61
  judge's list, 143, 151
  jury list, 142, 143, 151
  Keeping It Simple, 30, 142
  moral force of, 56
  motions and, 127–36
  as paradigm for the jury, 57
  principle/Rule hybrids, 53–55
  principles vs., 23, 23n1, 49–57
  purpose of, 21
  Rules in a Surgical Malpractice Case, 313–21
  Sample Insurance Bad Faith Rules of the Road, 201–3
  Samples of Rules in Different Types of Cases, 303–12
  solving the "reasonable" problem, 15–20
  source material, 3, 22, 23, 31–48

Rules of the Road (continued)
   story of your case and, 115–19
   troubleshooting, 103–13
   using when in mid-case, 185–86
   using with co-counsel, 186
   using with other advocacy advice, 187–88
   voir dire and, 147–49
Rules of the Road, annotated list
   Bus Stop Safety Principles Annotated, 207–10
   coordinating the evidence, 144
   for cross-examination, 164
   in depositions, securing agreement or disagreement with, 85–93
   developing a working list, 31–48, 52
   editing and massaging list of, 30
   finalizing, 137–44
   Master List, 191–200
   principles used in, 52
   running, during litigation, 30
   selecting to put on a board, 139–40
   your own version, 143, 151

S

School bus stop case, 11–12, *12*, 45–48, 53–54, 53n2, 185
   Bus Stop Case Opening Statement, 266–71
   Bus Stop Safety Principles, 205–6
   Bus Stop Safety Principles Annotated, 207–10
   Cross-Examination of School Bus Company Manager, 273–85
   Direct Examination of Plaintiff's Bus Stop Expert, 237–56

School bus stop case (continued)
   Requests for Admission, 74, 74n1
   using the Rules in midstream and, 185
Scott v. Matlack, Inc., 295
Shields v. Hiram C. Gardner, Inc., 224
Smith v. Hoffman, 293
Sources for Rules, 3, 22, 23, 31–48
   administrative regulations, 40–44, 41n7, 42n8, 42n9
   admissions in the answer to the complaint, 46–48
   "common sense" or "moral imperative" Rules, 26–28, 39n6
   common sources (list), 31–32
   contract provisions, 45–46, 45n10
   ethics codes, 307n2
   jury instructions, 32–40
   making easy to understand, 23–25
   setting up evidence from learned treatises, 160–61
   testimony about, 161
   textbooks, articles, and industry guidelines, 44–45
Sparks v. Republic National Life Ins. Co., 219
Spears Free Clinic & Hosp. for Poor Children v. Maier, 298
Spence, Gerry, 187
Spoor v. Serota, 292
Spray, Gould & Bowers v. Associated International Ins. Co., 42n8
Stark v. Weinberger, 199
State Bd. of Med. Exam'rs v. McCroskey, 292
State Farm & Casualty Co. v. Nicholson, 191, 212, 216

State Farm Fire and Casualty Co. v. Balmer, 218
State Farm Fire and Casualty Co. v. Bongen, 219, 224
State Farm Mutual Automobile Ins. Co. v. Weiford, 213, 214, 215, 216, 222
Stillwell v. Sullivan, 199
Summary-judgment motions
    citations to authorities, example, 133–36, 134n1
    plaintiff response, using no-nothing witness deposition, 80
    what to state up-front, 120

T
Trial, 3
    closing arguments, 3, 175–84
    cross-examination of defense witnesses, 3, 163–74, 273–85
    direct examination of your expert, 3, 157–62, 237–56
    document boards, 144, 174
    instruction boards, 176
    jury instructions, 1–2, 7–10, 7n1, 8n2, 8n3, 32–44, 36n2, 36n3, 137, 175–81, 178n1, 178n2, 179n3, 179n4, 211–25
    opening statements, 151–56, 261–71
    questions to answer during, 115
    red-stickering Rule violation, 144, 183
    Rules board, 138–43, 144
    Rules vs. case story, 115–19, 182
    showing motivation and character, 116
    using Fed. R. Evid. 803(18), 168–72, 168n1, 174

Troubleshooting, 103–13
    causation defense, countering, 108–9
    common mistakes, 109–10
    improving your rules, 110–13
    making your Rules specific, 104–7
    not quibbling, 107

U
Uninsured-motorist claim, 9
United Blood Services v. Quintana, 292
United Fire Ins. Co. v. McClelland, 134, 196
United States v. Taylor, 79n6
U.S. v. Hankey, 66n4

V
Voir dire, 3, 147–49

W
Wailua Associates v. Aetna Casualty & Surety Co., 134n1
Wallbank v. Sothenberg, 292
Weiford v. State Farm Mutual Automobile Ins. Co., 42n8
White v. Unigard Mutual Ins. Co., 191, 217
Wiener v. Mutual Life Ins. Co. of New York, 199
Winning Jury Trials: Trial Tactics and Sponsorship Strategies (Klonoff and Colby), 188
Wright v. Prudential Insurance Co. of America, 199

Y
Young v. Travelers' Ins. Co., 199

Z
Zhou v. Jennifer Mall Restaurant, Inc., 41n7